THE NAKED TRUTH

ABOUT YOUR MONEY

Bill DeShurko, CFP®

ALPHA

A member of Penguin Group (USA) Inc.

ALPHA BOOKS

Published by the Penguin Group

Penguin Group (USA) Inc., 375 Hudson Street, New York, New York 10014, USA

Penguin Group (Canada), 90 Eglinton Avenue East, Suite 700, Toronto, Ontario M4P 2Y3, Canada (a division of Pearson Penguin Canada Inc.)

Penguin Books Ltd., 80 Strand, London WC2R 0RL, England

Penguin Ireland, 25 St. Stephen's Green, Dublin 2, Ireland (a division of Penguin Books Ltd.)

Penguin Group (Australia), 250 Camberwell Road, Camberwell, Victoria 3124, Australia (a division of Pearson Australia Group Pty. Ltd.)

Penguin Books India Pvt. Ltd., 11 Community Centre, Panchsheel Park, New Delhi—110 017, India

Penguin Group (NZ), 67 Apollo Drive, Rosedale, North Shore, Auckland 1311, New Zealand (a division of Pearson New Zealand Ltd.)

Penguin Books (South Africa) (Pty.) Ltd., 24 Sturdee Avenue, Rosebank, Johannesburg 2196, South Africa

Penguin Books Ltd., Registered Offices: 80 Strand, London WC2R 0RL, England

International Standard Book Number: 978-1-59257-650-0
Library of Congress Catalog Card Number: 2007922827

09 08 07   8 7 6 5 4 3 2 1

Interpretation of the printing code: The rightmost number of the first series of numbers is the year of the book's printing; the rightmost number of the second series of numbers is the number of the book's printing. For example, a printing code of 07-1 shows that the first printing occurred in 2007.

Printed in the United States of America

Most Alpha books are available at special quantity discounts for bulk purchases for sales promotions, premiums, fund-raising, or educational use. Special books, or book excerpts, can also be created to fit specific needs.

For details, write: Special Markets, Alpha Books, 375 Hudson Street, New York, NY 10014.

Publisher: **Marie Butler-Knight**
Editorial Director: **Mike Sanders**
Managing Editor: **Billy Fields**
Acquisitions Editor/Development Editor: **Michele Wells**
Production Editor: **Megan Douglass**

Copy Editor: **Ross Patty**
Cover/Book Designer: **William Thomas**
Indexer: **Heather McNeill**
Proofreader: **John Etchison**

Contents

Foreword

A few years ago I taught a class at my daughter's high school that I called Reality 101. Each week we would go over what they would be facing in the real world upon graduation, with a healthy dose of how important it is to get your finances started right. Bill DeShurko has written a book which offers his readers a way to successfully navigate their personal investment ships through the hard realities of life.

Everyone wants to be able to retire "rich." But that is a hard-to-define goal. You need to narrow your pursuit of wealth down to reality. Let's start with a definition of rich. You are rich when you have enough assets to live off the income (return) from the principal in the style you want to, taking into account inflation.

For some people that is not a lot of money, as they have modest lifestyles and goals. I remember counseling one couple a few years ago who had built a sizeable nest egg over the years by living a very frugal lifestyle on what were very good dual incomes. They had no children and were planning on leaving their assets to a favorite charity. The husband had come to me to ask for investment advice, as he was worried about having enough income to last them for their probable lives.

He was looking for investments that had mid- to high-teen-plus returns. His current portfolio had a ton of risky investments, and fluctuated greatly. They had taken a great hit in the last tech wreck. When we went over their circumstances I just smiled. I told him he was taking way too much risk. He simply had to become an income investor and spend twice as much money as they were currently spending, saving the rest to see his portfolio grow well beyond inflation expectations.

Noting that he was an adrenaline investment junky, I told him to take a small portion and use it for the riskier investments, but to take his wife and travel more and spend more. His wife just sat there with a huge smile on her face. As we went over the numbers, he began to realize what I was saying.

"You have run the retirement race and won. Stop running." Now, there is nothing wrong with being a prudent manager of assets, and in working to maximize risk-adjusted returns, but they were close to their 70s and really had all they needed to live in a far grander lifestyle than they ever had.

That is not the normal experience. Most people do not save enough. Saving money and investing with reasonable risk parameters is the best way to watch your nest egg grow over time. Start sooner rather than later.

Yes, there are a few investment all-stars. But over the long haul, the average investor is going to be lucky to make more than 8-10% a year. That means 50% will do worse. Yes, you can have some good years, and after the 1990s investors seemed to think that 15% was reasonable. The '90s were an aberration. If you have managed to do 15% compound a year since 1999 on your entire portfolio, you have done very well. Very well, indeed. (Or you have had real estate in California. Hope you sold last year.) You have also probably taken a lot of risk, or had excellent timing.

The second way to build wealth is through building a business. Look at the various lists of wealthy people. All of them had at their roots a business. You might have to go back a few generations to find it, but a business was in there somewhere.

I should note there are a lot of people who have recently gotten rich through stock options. That is not investment. I consider that building a business. Maybe the secretaries at Microsoft got lucky when they decided to work for a young Bill Gates, but it was still a business that was the source of their wealth.

Some will argue that there are investors in real estate who have made large sums. Those who have done so would argue that buying and renting real estate is a business, even if it is part-time. Dealing with tenants is not easy.

Too many people spend their lives waiting for their "ship to come in." The reality is that it probably never will. You have to go out and get it. A ship that is in the harbor is not taking much risk. Ships are not built to stay in the harbor. But setting out on the investment seas can be a very risky venture if you do not have proper guides and a seasoned captain at the helm.

This book is a good start to do just that. Follow Bill's advice and you are unlikely to drown or be lost at sea. And with a little luck, and lots of discipline and hard work, you will be able to get your ship into a safe harbor when it is time to enjoy the fruits of your success.

John Mauldin
Two-time New York bestselling author of *Bull's Eye Investing* and *Just One Thing* and editor of *Thoughts from the Frontline,* which goes to over 1,000,000 readers.

Introduction

Talkin' About Your Generation

"9/11 without question is the defining moment for this 18–34 generation, and it will forever continue to be …. Because there's so much uncertainty from day to day, from year to year, you need to indulge yourself more than ever before," David Morrison [president and founder of TWENTYSOMETHING, Inc.], says. That's quite a statement, considering their predecessors, the Baby Boomers, are no slouches at consumer self-gratification. If you were to give 18–34s their own moniker, perhaps it would be the Bling Generation."—*Advertising Age*, January 2, 2006.

For all that has been written about my generation, we Baby Boomers will certainly be leaving our mark on this planet. I'll let history interpret that mark. But what evidence we have suggests a couple of things: first, that we were the forefathers of the golden age of consumption. From nearly day one, Madison Avenue saw us as one big dollar sign. By marketing directly to us they introduced new products and gadgets, one after another. And with a newfound way to spend, the credit card, we complied. In the United States, we Boomers account for approximately two thirds of our economy. If the Boomers sneeze, the world that manufactures for us catches a cold. But now it's your turn. Sure, you have catchy names of your own—Gen Xers and Gen Yers—and you even have sports competitions named after you (well, some people call skateboarding a sport, I guess), but your real legacy is that you are the offspring of the Baby Boomer generation. That legacy is also your curse.

For hundreds of years each succeeding generation counted on advancing the family's financial status a little bit further, on climbing up another rung on the social ladder. Early in the twentieth century, the youth movement came off the farm to the city and fueled the industrial revolution. Later generations were molded by the two great world wars. The latter, coming home on the heels of the GI Bill, was the first generation to go on en masse to get college degrees and define the term "middle class" for decades to follow. And then the Boomers hit. For any of the negatives, you have to give credit where credit is due. You, Gen X and Gen Y, were raised during a time when "poor in America" meant only two color TVs and a car or truck in the driveway. According to the U.S. Census Bureau, half own their own homes, two thirds have a microwave oven and cable TV. Even the "poor" in America can spend more than what many middle-class households could just a generation ago!

For many Boomers, it was easy to surpass our humble middle-class roots. As jobs moved from the factory floor to the corner office, wages rose as well. With higher paychecks came an unending supply of new toys to spend them on, and we complied. And for the past quarter-century we have driven this economy to new heights. Since 1980 the size of the U.S. economy has more than tripled. In 2006 the total value of goods and services was over $12.5 trillion dollars, two-thirds (or approximately $8 trillion dollars) of which was a direct result of our collective personal purchases. Today, middle class means a four-bedroom home, two cars (one of which is new every two years), four TVs, two family vacations a year, and a PC, cell phone, and iPod for every member of the family. Washers and dryers, microwaves, electric garage door openers, and cable TV are all considered standard equipment. Mall trips are officially designated as a "recreational activity." Yup, we Boomers have raised the conspicuous consumption bar pretty high.

So where does this leave you, the next generations, the Gen Xers and Gen Yers? You may be the first generation in U.S. history that doesn't spend your way en masse into a more lavish lifestyle than the generation before you. Not that you're not trying. According to Twentysomething, Inc., "51 percent of 18- to 29-year-olds said they would like to own an expensive car (13 points higher than the overall population), while 66 percent said clothes and jewelry define their personal identity (6 points higher than the overall population)." We didn't make it easy for you to match the lifestyle you're leaving behind as you move out on your own. As we've seen, minimum wage has fallen way behind inflation—meaning that it's harder to work your way through school on your own and graduate without substantial debt that needs to be repaid.

Strategy for Success

Although much has been made of the growing gap between the wealthiest and poorest segments of our population, the fact is that the middle class is doing better as well. As David R. Henderson, a Hoover Institution economist, says in *The Washington Post*, "... the middle class is thriving .... As a group they're earning more money than they have before, and their ranks have swollen with members who can afford the DVDs, SUVs, and MP3s now seen by many families as part of the essential backdrop to modern life. Whereas Census numbers show the median household earned $33,338 in 1967 when adjusted for inflation, that number was up by $10,000 in 2003. But when compared with those at the top, the middle has lost much ground. And many in the middle have dropped well behind their peers."

But that's the problem. We are a nation of "keeping up with the Joneses." And as the income gap has widened amongst the Joneses, keeping up has become harder and harder.

It also makes it harder to write a book on personal finance when the audience can be so disparate. On the one hand, as we'll see, living on typical liberal arts grad entry-level wages can be tough, especially if trying to keep up with your former engineering classmates. So one of our first steps will be defining "success," because now more than ever, the broad brush stroke of financial advice just will not work. And by the way, if you don't have a college degree, don't despair. Although it can be much tougher to move into a high-wage position, there are still ways in which the ambitious can get ahead—especially well ahead of their overspending neighbors. The one advantage you may have is that if your job has not yet been outsourced, your employment, albeit at a lower wage, may be safer than many of your college grad peers. But the one thing it seems that we all have in common is that, whatever the paycheck, it's never enough. Even among the income elite with legitimate multi-million dollar salaries, the news has been full of business scandals, accounting "irregularities," and stock options fraud. All illegal tactics that serve no other purpose than to further enrich those who, to most of us, are already about as rich as anyone needs to be.

So what's the game plan? On the one hand, it's pretty simple: we have to learn to live within our means. The problem is that with so much temptation surrounding us, most of us don't really know what "our means" really are. And that then becomes the first step—what does our career, our paycheck, really mean in terms of the lifestyle we can afford?

A Lifetime Game Plan to Create Wealth

That's what I want you to have by the end of this book. If you can first understand where your income dictates you are and what you can and can't do based on that income, you can then make decisions for your future. For example, are you too much in debt because you are bad at budgeting, or do you just not have enough income for the lifestyle you're trying to live? There's a big difference. I've seen couples with well over $100,000 of income who are in debt, with no savings and little hope of righting their financial ship. On the other hand, I have a client who makes $30,000 a year, is in his 30s, and has more than $100,000 in his retirement account. One thing is certain—success is not just about income; it has much more to do with our definition of it.

Hopefully, financial success for you is just about making smarter financial decisions. But if you find yourself in an income bracket that isn't going to meet your needs, then now is the time to do something about it. And throughout this book, I'll give you the knowledge to take those steps. Because after spending 20 years meeting, talking, and planning with hundreds of people just like you, I can say one thing for certain: life is just too tough and too short to spend it waiting for the next paycheck.

One final thought before we move on. When I originally read the opening excerpt from *Advertising Age* magazine, I was struck by what I thought was a contradiction: that as a generation "defined by 9/11," a rational reaction to life's uncertainty would be to spend your money. Now, I have no idea how accurate that statement is for you, but let me strongly suggest that a far more rational reaction to uncertainty would be to save your money and create wealth, instead of spending what you have now. Safety, protection, and peace of mind come from wealth, not from MP3 players, cell phones, or even a great car. So let's not start thinking that "budgeting" is synonymous with deprivation; it's not. It's a great way to create peace of mind, security, and certainty—the really valuable things in life.

And yeah, once you've created some wealth, it's okay to spring for a new MP3 player.

Acknowledgments

First and foremost I need to thank my friend, client, and writer Joris Heise for thinking enough of my work to introduce me to his contacts at Penguin Group. Without his support, I'm sure this book would have made it to the shelves with a different author.

I want to take a moment to acknowledge the good financial advisors out there who really do care about our profession and their clients' best interests. In an industry full of conflicts of interest, misinformation, and poor products that entice planners and advisors with high commissions, "doing the right thing" is not always the easiest decision. While good advisors can be found everywhere, I want to make mention of my fellow members of the National Association of Active Investment Managers (NAAIM), for their support of real research and dialogue on real investment strategies. I have never met such a group of really intelligent and dedicated individuals. They act as a true support group in a world of "buy-and-hold" misinformation.

Thanks to my family for putting up with me during the writing process—there wasn't time for much of anything else. And of course a big thanks to my office staff and advisors for keeping things rolling smoothly so I could spend my days trying to meet my deadlines.

And finally, thanks to Penguin Group, especially Michele, for the opportunity. I know I learned a lot from the process, and just hope I have met your expectations in sharing that knowledge with your readers.

Prologue

A Dollar Just Isn't What It Used to Be

Money has been around nearly as long as civilization has. And for most of history, money itself has had value. Ancient coins, dating all the way back to say 1965, were made with real silver and gold. The coin itself had value. Even paper money originally had value. From 1878 through 1957, the United States issued Silver Certificates, which were backed by silver. Gold Certificates were issued from 1863 to 1922 and were backed by gold. Gold and silver, things of value all on their own. All that changed in 1971.

More and more dollars were being printed in Washington to pay for the Vietnam War. In response, on August 15, 1971, President Nixon unilaterally imposed 90-day wage and price controls, a 10 percent import surcharge, and most importantly "closed the gold window," making the dollar inconvertible to gold directly, except on the open market. Unusually, this decision was made without consulting anyone, including his own State Department, and was soon dubbed the "Nixon Shock." In effect U.S. currency no longer had any value, other than what someone would give, or "trade," you for your coins. In other words, instead of our currency being backed by gold or silver, it was instead backed by the "full faith and credit of the United States." This is important, because it gave our government, and even-tually all world governments that followed our lead, the incentive to have as much money printed as they wanted, whenever they wanted. Now, granted, at the time of the "Nixon Shock," each dollar was only backed by about $.22 of gold. But since the Federal Reserve was charged with maintaining the value of our currency in 1973, it would now take $4.40 to buy what a buck would have bought then. And they get paid for doing such a fine job! And now there is nothing to stop the government from printing money at any pace they desire. Of course economists will tell you that there is a consequence of overrunning the presses … and that consequence is called inflation.

Money Facts

Inflation. We all hear the term, but what does it mean? Typically inflation is defined as "too much money chasing too few goods." For example, when the Spanish Conquistadors brought back shiploads of gold from the new world, there was a sudden spike in money that showed up as inflation throughout much of Europe at the time. An example of "too few goods" would be during major wars. The governments involved soak up the country's natural resources to build the war machinery, leaving shortages on the domestic front. The resulting shortages have typically resulted in a spike in inflation. But what does inflation mean to you? It's this, and this is why this book is so important: a dollar no longer has value on its own. Its value is simply the amount of stuff that you can buy. And if you have a pile of dollars today, and tomorrow you have a bigger pile of dollars, but you can't buy as much stuff tomorrow as you can today, then you have really lost money. The terms are *nominal* dollars versus *real* dollars.

> The cost of tuition and fees for a four-year public university in 1970 was approximately $480 for the entire year. Today, that year of tuition and fees will run you $5,491—an increase of 1041 percent.

In this case, the $5,491 is your larger pile of dollars, or "nominal" dollars. But in "real" 1970 dollars the cost of tuition and fees today would be $480 "real" 1970 dollars. "Nominal" means how many physical dollars it takes to buy something today. "Real" means how many 1970 dollars it would take to buy something today. So in 1971, when Nixon moved us off of the gold standard, meaning that gold could fluctuate in value, *to protect our currency*, one "nominal dollar" today (that's the dollar in your pocket), would only buy about 20 cents worth of real stuff in 1971. That's the *real* value, or how much stuff you can buy today versus yesterday—a dollar today versus 20 cents yesterday.

As you can see from Figure 1, inflation has had its ups and downs throughout history. In the 1800s you can see spikes around 1814 and 1865. But in both cases the spikes were followed by declines, which left the overall value of a dollar fairly constant until the 1920s. The constant upturn in inflation, the elimination of cycles, is credited to three historic events: the creation of the Federal Reserve in 1913, which allowed a private company to control our money supply; President Franklin Roosevelt outlawing private ownership of gold and fixing a government purchase price at $35 an ounce; and Nixon's ill-fated move in 1971. So with the apparent repeal of any type of inflationary cycle—periods of low or declining prices as well as periods of rising prices—the only rational reaction is to behave financially as if inflation is in fact here to stay.

Consumer Price Index Since 1800

Note: consumer prices near stable first 150 years then *wow!!*

1913 Birth of the Federal Reserve

Gold Standard Eliminated

Price Index: 1967 = 100

U.S. INFLATION

Minimum wage was $1.60 per hour in 1970. That has risen to $5.15 today, an increase of 221.9 percent. Sounds good—a 200+ percent increase, right? Well, to have kept pace with inflation, minimum wage in 2006 would have needed to be $8 an hour.

And that is the point—throughout history you had three things you could do with your money: spend it, hold on to it, or invest it to try to make more. Today we're down to two: you can either spend your money today, or invest it for the future. Because if you try to just "hold on" to your money, put it under the mattress or even put it in the bank for safekeeping, you are really losing money. Your pile may not change in size, but based on history, you won't be able to buy as much tomorrow as you can today.

If your parents had put $480 under their mattress in 1970 for their grandchildren's college tuition, today that money would barely pay for a semester's worth of books!

What You Need to Know Today

Inflation has become endemic in our economy. Despite the Federal Reserve's mandate to protect the U.S. currency (which would mean eliminating inflation entirely), prices of U.S. goods and services have risen every single year since 1954. If you currently earn $40,000 a year, based on inflation, in 40 years you will need to earn $250,000 a year just to maintain your current lifestyle when you retire. If you have your heart set on a new $30,000 car and hope to save enough for it over the next 16 years, you will need to save not $30,000, but over $46,000, based on inflation since 1990. Hoping to start stashing away a little money for a $10,000 wedding in 10 years? Based on inflation from 1970 to 1980, you'll actually need to save over $21,000 to pay for your $10,000 plans today.

> *"In the absence of the gold standard, there is* no way to protect savings from confiscation through inflation. *There is no safe store of value."*
>
> —*Alan Greenspan, 1966*

Inflation presents a double-edged sword in financial planning. While inflation provides incentive to buy now before prices go up, it also makes saving and proper investing even more important. Spend or invest, the consumer conundrum. Whichever you decide to do, you need to be informed to make the right choices. And in the following pages I hope to provide you with that information—because the choices we make today can have far-reaching consequences into our futures.

Part 1

Spend Where You Must, Save Where You Can

Moneynomics:
The Basics of Banking and Budgeting

What You Will Learn

- Seemingly small steps that can have dramatic results in the future

- How to get financially fit—and stay that way

- How to track expenses and make a (realistic) budget

The Butterfly Effect—A Hollywood Lesson in Economics

Chaos theory has been hot in Hollywood for several years now. First was a reference in *Jurassic Park*, where Jeff Goldblum mentions an esoteric math theory and turns it into a common phrase. He uses as an example a butterfly flapping its wings on one side of the world and causing a tornado on the other. A butterfly flapping its wings in Tokyo causes a tornado in Texas. More recently, Ashton Kutcher picked up on the idea in his starring role in the appropriately titled *The Butterfly Effect*. Kutcher's character finds that he has the ability to go back in time and "correct" the past, but he soon realizes that changing one small event in his past results in multiple changes later in his life and the lives of others.

In personal finance, as in the movies, an outwardly insignificant action now, especially while you're young, can cause important reactions later in life. This concept is known as *moneynomics*.

> **Moneynomics** is the understanding of how the seemingly small financial decisions you make today can have large effects your future.

What the Future Could Hold

I know, youth is supposed to be carefree, and here I am telling you that your entire financial future depends on what you do those first four or five years out of college. But it's important to understand that the financial decisions you make in your 20s and 30s will likely have as-yet unforeseen consequences in your future. A sort of butterfly effect, if you will.

Your 20s in particular really are a dichotomy. Fiscally sound steps you take now will undoubtedly pay off big down the road, but on the other hand, there is no question that you can make up for a few financial transgressions now over the next 30 years of a working career. So what's the best thing to do? Let's look at some numbers.

Table 1.1 was commonly used in the mutual fund industry as a way to sell IRAs, particularly to young people in their 20s, when the investment limit was $2,000. (The current investment limit is $4,000 if under age 50; I'll be discussing IRAs and other investments in Chapter 7.) The first column shows the age of a hypothetical individual investor. In this example, at age 25 she begins to invest $2,000 a year at the beginning of each year for 10 years. Her total lifetime contributions by age 65 are $20,000. Assuming a 10 percent rate of return, our investor has done quite well, accumulating $672,999 by the time she is 65.

Table 1.1: Contribution growth of an annual savings of $2,000, starting at age 25.

Age	Investment Year	Beginning Balance	Annual Contribution	10% Investment Return	Ending Balance
25	1	$0	$2,000	$200	$2,200
26	2	$2,200	$2,000	$420	$4,620
27	3	$4,620	$2,000	$662	$7,282
28	4	$7,282	$2,000	$928	$10,210
29	5	$10,210	$2,000	$1,221	$13,431
30	6	$13,431	$2,000	$1,543	$16,974
31	7	$16,974	$2,000	$1,897	$20,872
32	8	$20,872	$2,000	$2,287	$25,159
33	9	$25,159	$2,000	$2,716	$29,875
34	10	$29,875	$2,000	$3,187	$35,062
35	11	$35,062	$0	$3,506	$38,569
36	12	$38,569	$0	$3,857	$42,425
37	13	$42,425	$0	$4,243	$46,668
38	14	$46,668	$0	$4,667	$51,335
39	15	$51,335	$0	$5,133	$56,468
40	16	$56,468	$0	$5,647	$62,115
41	17	$62,115	$0	$6,212	$68,327
42	18	$68,327	$0	$6,833	$75,159
43	19	$75,159	$0	$7,516	$82,675
44	20	$82,675	$0	$8,268	$90,943
45	21	$90,943	$0	$9,094	$100,037
46	22	$100,037	$0	$10,004	$110,041
47	23	$110,041	$0	$11,004	$121,045
48	24	$121,045	$0	$12,104	$133,149
49	25	$133,149	$0	$13,315	$146,464
50	26	$146,464	$0	$14,646	$161,110
51	27	$161,110	$0	$16,111	$177,222

continues...

(Table 1.1 continued)

Age	Investment Year	Beginning Balance	Annual Contribution	10% Investment Return	Ending Balance
52	28	$17,222	$0	$17,722	$194,944
53	29	$194,944	$0	$19,494	$214,438
54	30	$214,438	$0	$21,444	$235,882
55	31	$235,882	$0	$23,588	$259,470
56	32	$259,470	$0	$25,947	$285,417
57	33	$285,417	$0	$28,542	$313,959
58	34	$313,959	$0	$31,396	$345,355
59	35	$345,355	$0	$34,536	$379,891
60	36	$379,891	$0	$37,989	$417,880
61	37	$417,880	$0	$41,788	$459,668
62	38	$459,668	$0	$45,967	$505,634
63	39	$505,634	$0	$50,563	$556,198
64	40	$556,198	$0	$55,620	$611,817
65	41	$611,817	$0	$61,182	$672,999
Total Contribution			**$20,000**		

In Table 1.2 we have a similar set of circumstances, but in this case our saver didn't start investing $2,000 until she was 35 years old, just 10 years later. But due to the late start she contributes $2,000 continuously for 31 years until she turns 65. By age 65 she has contributed $62,000 and has accumulated $400,275 (assuming the same 10 percent return). This is the power of starting early with any amount, no matter how small. Our second investor had to invest more than three times as much over her working career to have over a quarter-million dollars *less* at retirement!

Table 1.2: Contribution growth of an annual savings of $2,000, starting at age 35.

Age	Investment Year	Beginning Balance	Annual Contribution	10% Investment Return	Ending Balance
25	1	$0	$0	$0	$0
26	2	$0	$0	$0	$0
27	3	$0	$0	$0	$0
28	4	$0	$0	$0	$0
29	5	$0	$0	$0	$0
30	6	$0	$0	$0	$0
31	7	$0	$0	$0	$0

Age	Investment Year	Beginning Balance	Annual Contribution	10% Investment Return	Ending Balance
32	8	$0	$0	$0	$0
33	9	$0	$0	$0	$0
34	10	$0	$0	$0	$0
35	11	$0	$2,000	$200	$2,200
36	12	$2,200	$2,000	$420	$4,620
37	13	$4,620	$2,000	$662	$7,282
38	14	$7,282	$2,000	$928	$10,210
39	15	$10,210	$2,000	$1,221	$13,431
40	16	$13,431	$2,000	$1,543	$16,974
41	17	$16,974	$2,000	$1,897	$20,872
42	18	$20,872	$2,000	$2,287	$25,159
43	19	$25,159	$2,000	$2,716	$29,875
44	20	$29.875	$2,000	$3,187	$35,062
45	21	$35,062	$2,000	$3,706	$40,769
46	22	$40,769	$2,000	$4,277	$47,045
47	23	$47,045	$2,000	$4,905	$53,950
48	24	$53,950	$2,000	$5,595	$61,545
49	25	$61,545	$2,000	$6,354	$69,899
50	26	$69,899	$2,000	$7,190	$79,089
51	27	$79,089	$2,000	$8,109	$89,198
52	28	$89,198	$2,000	$9,120	$100,318
53	29	$100,318	$2,000	$10,232	$112,550
54	30	$112,550	$2,000	$11,455	$126,005
55	31	$126,005	$2,000	$12,800	$140,805
56	32	$140,805	$2,000	$14,281	$157,086
57	33	$157,086	$2,000	$15,909	$174,995
58	34	$174,995	$2,000	$17,699	$194,694
59	35	$194,694	$2,000	$19,669	$216,363
60	36	$216,363	$2,000	$21,836	$240,200
61	37	$240,200	$2,000	$24,220	$266,420
62	38	$266,420	$2,000	$26,842	$295,262
63	39	$295,262	$2,000	$29,726	$326,988
64	40	$326,988	$2,000	$32,899	$361,887
65	41	$361,887	$2,000	$36,389	$400,275
Total Contribution			**$62,000**		

Now go back to Table 1.1 and look at how much the first investor has in just 10 years. By saving $166 a month for 10 years, her total investment of $20,000 is now over $35,000. What could you do at 35 with $35,000? Yeah, I know what you're thinking, but the answer is not a sports car. Instead, how about a down payment on a home? Or better yet, a down payment on an investment property—one that you could turn into another $35,000 in another 10 years, and all with someone else's money! Now, that's exciting.

If you're upwardly mobile, maybe you leave the money in a retirement plan, but instead of just continuing with the $2,000 a year you double it to $4,000. Too much? Well, a good rule of thumb is that you should be saving about 10 percent of your pay. So is a $40,000 a year income too big of a stretch for you to reach by the time you're 35? Probably not. And if you can keep it up you'll have over a million dollars by age 65. All from having the foresight to save 166 bucks a month when you were 25.

Now you're saying, "But I don't have $2,000!" If you're just out of school, I understand where you're coming from. But let's look at a "typical" scenario. Check out Table 1.3.

Table 1.3: A 10-percent contribution growth from the age of 30 on.						
Age	**Year**	**Beginning Balance**	**Annual Contribution**	**10% Return**	**Ending Balance**	**Annual Salary**
30	1	$0	$2,227	$223	$2,450	$29,692
31	2	$2,450	$2,287	$474	$5,211	$30,731
32	3	$5,211	$2,349	$756	$8,315	$31,807
33	4	$8,315	$2,412	$1,073	$11,800	$32,920
34	5	$11,800	$2,477	$1,428	$15,706	$34,072
35	6	$15,706	$2,544	$1,825	$20,075	$35,265
36	7	$20,075	$2,613	$2,269	$24,957	$36,499
37	8	$24,957	$2,684	$2,764	$30,404	$37,777
38	9	$30,404	$2,756	$3,316	$36,476	$39,099
39	10	$36,476	$2,830	$3,931	$43,238	$40,467
40	11	$43,238	$2,907	$4,614	$50,759	$41,884
41	12	$50,759	$2,985	$5,374	$59,119	$43,350
42	13	$59,119	$3,066	$6,218	$68,403	$44,867
43	14	$68,403	$3,149	$7,155	$78,707	$46,437
44	15	$78,707	$3,234	$8,194	$90,135	$48,063

Age	Year	Beginning Balance	Annual Contribution	10% Return	Ending Balance	Annual Salary
45	16	$90,135	$3,321	$9,346	$102,801	$49,745
46	17	$102,801	$3,411	$10,621	$116,833	$51,486
47	18	$116,833	$3,503	$12,034	$132,370	$53,288
48	19	$132,370	$3,597	$13,597	$149,564	$55,153
49	20	$149,564	$3,695	$15,326	$168,584	$57,083
50	21	$168,584	$3,794	$17,238	$189,616	$59,081
51	22	$189,616	$3,897	$19,351	$212,864	$61,149
52	23	$212,864	$4,002	$21,687	$238,553	$63,289
53	24	$238,553	$4,110	$24,266	$266,929	$65,504
54	25	$266,929	$4,221	$27,115	$298,265	$67,797
55	26	$298,265	$4,335	$30,260	$332,860	$70,170
56	27	$332,860	$4,452	$33,731	$371,043	$72,626
57	28	$371,043	$4,572	$37,562	$413,177	$75,168
58	29	$413,177	$12,000	$42,518	$467,695	$77,799
59	30	$467,695	$12,324	$48,002	$528,021	$77,799
60	31	$528,021	$12,657	$54,068	$594,745	$80,522
61	32	$594,745	$12,998	$60,774	$668,518	$83,340
62	33	$668,518	$13,349	$68,187	$750,054	$86,257
63	34	$750,054	$13,710	$76,376	$840,140	$89,276
64	35	$840,140	$14,080	$85,422	$939,642	$92,401
65	36	$939,642	$14,460	$95,410	$1,049,513	$95,635
Total			**$197,004**			

Table 1.3 is similar to the first two, but in this case our young investor can't get started until age 30. She starts investing $2,227, which is approximately 7.5 percent of her pay, at the beginning of each year. If this is an example of a 401(k) plan, then part of the $2,227 could be made up from an employer contribution (more on this in Chapter 8).

For instance, let's say that she elects to contribute 5 percent of her pay and her employer matches 50 percent of what she puts in, or another 2.5 percent. And let's say that she has elected to contribute a percentage of her pay instead of a flat dollar amount. By selecting this choice, each time she gets a raise her contribution will go up as well. In this example the annual income is based on a 25-year-old starting at $25,000 per year. By age 30 she is making $29,692. Assuming an annual 3.5 percent raise each year, by the time she is 65 she will be earning over $95,000 a year. At age 58, I assume that she can increase her investment to $12,000 per year. Again, remember that this could realistically include a company matching plan if using a 401(k).

Although investments have a much greater value earlier on, the reality is that no matter how much sense it makes, sometimes we just can't do it. This is typical in real life, as incomes will generally rise rapidly in the last 10 to 15 years of a career. And at the same time your income is rising, usually in your mid-to-late 50s, your expenses can drop dramatically.

I frequently see clients who have a paid-off mortgage. They tend to buy less stuff simply because they already own a lot of stuff, and the biggest cost—children—have grown up, gone through school, and hopefully moved on. They're at both their peak earning years and at a time when their expenses are lower than they have been for decades. So by the mid-to-late 50s most people can take the money they've been spending on the kids, mortgages, and the rest of their stuff and start packing it away into a 401(k) or other retirement plan.

But back to our example. In this case, about 40 percent of the investor's contributions come in her last seven working years. All totaled, she ends up with over a million dollars at retirement with a fairly modest annual investment and very modest lifetime income that started at $25,000.

> ## Unsolicited Advice
>
> As much as I hate to say it, your only loyalty in your career is to *you*. With smaller firms, you may feel a loyalty factor—maybe a particular boss went overboard in mentoring you or gave you that big break. But even then, don't sell yourself short. Employment is a two-way street. By and large, a business isn't going to keep you if it doesn't make financial sense, and you're not expected to do anything different.

Remember our discussion on inflation from the Prologue? The $95,635 income at age 65 is the bigger pile of money I was talking about. If our hypothetical worker were only getting a 3.5 percent raise each year because inflation averaged 3.5 percent, then she really isn't any better off than she was at 25 when she made $25,000 per year. However, the average worker will change employers 7 to 10 times in a career. (This doesn't include job changes for the same employer.) Presumably, most of those job changes are for higher pay. So in constant dollars, a starting salary at any level can be irrelevant to what your final pay could be. Even government workers and teachers, who generally receive modest pay (but enjoy better benefits), will move into higher salary bands based on tenure and education levels. So the older you get, the easier it should become to roll those raises into savings. The key is just to stay prepared and remain flexible.

Developing a Smart Financial Lifestyle

When it comes to budgeting, everyone seems to have an opinion. Some think that there is some miraculous trick that will uncover hundreds of dollars of extra cash flow every month. For example, let's take a young man we'll call Tom, who came to see me several years ago. Tom was an ex-jock in his late 20s, married with kids. Both he and his wife had good jobs. Tom said that his purpose in meeting with me was to find extra cash so he could start investing. I asked, "Why do you want to invest?" His answer was that what he really wanted to do was find some partners and open a sports-themed bar/restaurant. (Like what 20-something ex-jock doesn't want to open a sports-themed bar/restaurant?)

Anyway, Tom seemed convinced that this was his future and had a surprising amount of details worked out in his head. However, when I asked if he had any experience in or knowledge of the food service industry, he said that he did not—at least, not from the business side of the bar. However, he did mention that he and his wife usually ate out every night after work, as well as on weekends. So I worked up some ideas and spreadsheets, similar to those you've seen here so far, showing what he could save and what the savings would grow to. When I showed him the numbers, his question was, "But where do I get the money?"

My response was that instead of eating out every night, he and his wife could take some free cooking classes together and eat in during the week. This would easily save them $100—if not $200—a week. And in addition to creating the capital to start his business, he would gain some knowledge of food preparation, which I thought would be useful in owning a restaurant.

I guess I was wrong. Tom reacted as though I had suggested that he cut off his right arm. "What a stupid idea!" he said. "How in the world could you expect us to cook dinner after a hard day's work? I thought this financial planning was supposed to find me money!" He flew out the door, and I didn't see him again.

Let's look closely at this less-than-successful example, because I think it illustrates a few points. The world is full of people with ideas (a sports restaurant/bar), far fewer people able to act (lack of _capital_), and even fewer people willing to invest the _human capital_ (save money by not eating out, learn about food preparation) to attain their goals. Tom came to me with an idea but no money and no experience, so I gave him a plan that would move him toward having a little of both. All he had to do was invest a little effort on his own.

> Assets available for use in the startup of a business or the production of further assets are known as **capital.**
>
> **Human capital** is people and their ability to be financially productive through investing time and energy. Education and training contribute to increase human capital.

The lesson? Budgeting isn't about "finding money" by moving numbers around on a piece of paper. It's about creating a better way to live. And that takes some effort.

Tom's experience teaches us that budgeting does not just create cash flow from thin air. To be able to "get ahead," accelerate debt payment, save for a wedding, or invest for retirement, you will need some decision-making skills. If you're not doing those things now, you're probably spending money on something else. Only you can decide what your priorities are. In Tom's case, being a partner in a sports bar/restaurant was obviously not the priority he thought it was, since he wasn't willing to put in the time to do it right. But you can do these things, no matter what your salary level is today, because budgeting—and, by extension, financial success—has more to do with your mind-set than it does your paycheck.

As I said in the Introduction, I've had "wealthy" clients who make $30,000 a year and "poor" clients who make well into six figures. A recent survey in the _Wall Street Journal_ supported the idea that it's all a question of mind-set—they found that for current retirees, the amount of money they had saved was irrelevant to how financially secure they felt. Instead, across all savings levels, those who felt the most financially secure were those who lived within their incomes. Believe it or not, fewer people who had between $750,000 and $1 million saved felt secure about their finances than did those with $250,000 to $500,000 saved.

> "You can have it all. You just can't have it all at once."
>
> —Oprah Winfrey

Defining Wealth for Yourself

Wealth, however you choose to define it, is created over time. And the only way to create wealth is to choose to save and invest instead of spending. Now for some people, like Tom, that's tough. Others relish saving a buck; while their friends are bragging about their new cell phones or iPods or other gadgets, the financially successful are thinking how much smarter they are, knowing that they can buy the exact same thing for a fraction of the overall cost if they just wait six months. While the spender is driving around showing off his new (leased) car, the saver is thinking about how he or she can buy the same car for half the price by just waiting a few months or shopping for a "lightly driven" used version. (For more on buying and paying for a car, see Chapter 3.) But whether you're a saver or a spender, together we can work out the plan that best fits your lifestyle.

But first, you need to recognize that the global corporate Powers-That-Be are waging a war for your money. Instead of fighting with bullets, they use advertising and marketing. And to the victor goes ... what else? The money in your pocket, your paycheck, your future earnings, your potential wealth. They want it all. No one cares if you have trouble making ends meet or if you didn't realize what a hindrance those charge card payments would be to your lifestyle. They won, you lost. The more debt you have, the less money in the bank or in your 401(k), the greater their victory.

If you want to be successful at winning the budget war, you have to learn to do one very difficult thing. You have to learn to enjoy saying "no" to the newest gadget, fanciest sports car, or latest outfit, and get satisfaction from being a winner instead of the latest victim of advertising. Now, you are probably thinking smugly that this doesn't apply to you. You're too smart to be swayed by advertising hype. Well, sorry to say, but according to Twentysomething, Inc., Gen Xers and Gen Yers are more likely than any other generation to be swayed by corporate branding and the media when it comes to buying decisions.

The Budget War: Winning the First Battle

If you've taken any basic marketing class, you've probably read about a case study similar to this one: a company comes out with product "A" and markets it as the low-priced leader. The product flops, so the company pulls the product, repackages it, raises the price—without changing the actual product. They then remarket it as the premium-quality leader in its category. The product goes on to become a huge success.

Packaging and high price do not translate to quality. Prices are more often set by focus groups that indicate how much they'd be willing to spend for a product than by any calculation of cost plus a "fair" profit margin. Certain products, especially in the tech gadget category, are priced based on the highest amount such groups say they would pay for a product. They even have a term for these consumers: "early adopters." They're the ones who run out and buy the latest toy, no matter what the cost. Now don't get me wrong, I love gadgets; but I also understand that when I buy something as soon as it comes out, I'm not just an early adopter, but to the ad execs, I'm also a sucker. With that understanding I've become a bit of an expert at shopping at places such as www.ecost.com and www.overstock.com. You can, too—it's all about attitude.

Affording the Lifestyle You Want

So let's understand the concept of budgeting. A few really smart and a whole lot of sorta smart (and really well-paid) people are trying to separate you from the cash in your pocket. They work for advertising agencies. They work in marketing departments. They come at you over the Internet, on TV, and even through your phone. Pick up a magazine or newspaper—which gets more space, the ads or the actual stories? They pitch everything to you: booze, bras, cars, computers, and the ever-popular George Foreman Grill. They make you think that you need these things—I mean really *need*—or else you will be left out, dateless, ugly, fat, depressed … But buy, buy, buy and you will be incredibly popular, beautiful, brilliant, and cool!

The reality is, as the old saying goes, "You can't live like a prince on a pauper's budget." In other words, to get a grasp on exactly what type of lifestyle you can afford, you need to know how much it costs. Then you can develop a lifestyle around it, instead of just hoping you can afford the lifestyle you want. And the only way to do that is to track what you spend now.

Paycheck Survival: Ending the Month with Money Left Over

So if you're ready to start taking control of your finances, let's get going. We'll start at the beginning—with your paycheck.

I've already said that your biggest asset is your income. The trick is to turn it into even greater assets, and not just spend your life paying bills. People in general, but young people in particular, tend to mistake high income for wealth. Wealth comes from owning assets. Ask someone who is truly wealthy and they will usually describe wealth as the ability to lose your income entirely, and have it not affect your lifestyle. Think about all these athletes who sign big professional sports contracts. How many of them end up poor and filing for bankruptcy? Quite a few—simply because they mistake a large, temporary paycheck for wealth. The ones we admire are the ones who have gone on and parlayed their income into real wealth that lasts long after their careers are over.

Yet budgeting can be tricky. Take, for example, some friends I'll call Bob and Sue. They make a budget and decide that they will spend $200 a month on eating out. By the third week of the month they have spent their $200 eating-out allocation. But now Doug and Mary call and ask them if they'd like to join them for dinner at the new restaurant that just opened up. "It is Saturday night, after all," they say. And Bob has had a particularly hard week, so he deserves a treat. So they decide to go out and bust the budget. Dumb idea. Didn't work. They decide that budgeting is a failure because it didn't work for them, so they just throw out the whole idea and spend even more time worrying about how to get by. This is why it's so important to track your cash to see what you're actually spending *before* trying to make a budget. That way, you can make sure that your budget fits your spending priorities.

Tracking Your Spending

So the first thing you need to do is track your actual spending to identify areas where you may be leaking some cash flow. If you just take a few minutes each day to write down what you spend, freeing up money can often be pretty easy. It'll be a simple question of looking at your expenses to realize how much money you're actually spending on some really unnecessary things—and adjusting your spending accordingly.

There are many budgeting software programs out there, but paper and pencil or a simple Excel spreadsheet work just fine. All you need is an idea of your _gross income_, your _take-home pay_, and your _net pay_. So grab your last paycheck or statement and write down the following information.

> **Gross income** is what you start with, your pay before any deductions. **Take-home pay** is just that—what you actually get as a check from your employer. (This is your gross pay after subtracting taxes and benefit deductions.) Your **net pay** is what you have left after paying your bills and other living expenses. This is the number that matters the most.

The first thing you need to do is identify what you have to work with. The easiest way to start, for now, is to convert to monthly numbers. Since there are approximately 4.33 weeks in a month, you need to do a little math. (Don't put down the book. You can do it, I swear.)

> ### Unsolicited Advice
>
> It's true that you could make this simpler by just converting your net income from your paycheck to a monthly number. But I want you to go through the procedure of converting all your pay stub numbers, so that you can see—and more fully understand—the cost of your deductions and the effect of taxes.

If you get paid weekly, multiply your paycheck numbers by 52 and divide by 12. If your payday is every two weeks, multiply by 26 and divide by 12. If you're paid twice a month, just double the single paycheck numbers. From here you can get to your net (take-home) pay. Although the deductions shown in the following table are mandatory, we do have a little bit of control over them. (We'll talk about your 401(k) deduction in Chapter 7 and taxes in Chapter 11.) The point of this process is to always subtract expenses immediately from your last net income balance. This will show you how much you can spend for the rest of the month. So first you will subtract out the stuff that has to go, such as taxes, health insurance, and other payroll deductions, as in Table 1.4.

Table 1.4: Monthly Budget Planner.	
Gross Income	**$2,500.00**
Deductions	
Social Security	$155.00
Medicare	$36.25
Federal	$275.00
State	$77.44
City	$18.86
Health	$40.00
401(k)	$150.00
Employer Match	$75.00
Take-Home Pay	**$1,747.20**

Okay, the next step, which really is easy and will only take a few minutes, is to write down all the "bills"—the things you have to pay every month or something bad happens. (Like your car is no longer in the driveway when you get up for work, or really nasty people start calling you at all hours of the day and night … you know, that sort of thing.) When you're done writing this information, you should have something that looks like Table 1.5.

Table 1.5: Net income for the previous example after bills are factored in.	
Take-Home Pay	**$1,747.20**
Rent	$700.00
Utilities	$75.00
Renter's Insurance	$20.00
Net Income, After Housing	**$952.20**
Student Loans	$227.00
Car Loan	$134.00

continues…

(Table 1.5 continued)

Insurance, Gas, and Maintenance	$120.00
Credit Cards	$200.00
Net Income	**$271.00**

So let's pause here and see what we have. We started with $2,500 a month in gross pay, which is $30,000 a year. (Just as a side note, I picked $2,500 a month because that seems like a realistic low-end starting salary for a college grad and a very realistic salary for a high school–only grad. The point to take away is that $30,000 a year is a livable salary, but only if not saddled with college loans or charge card payments.) After some "guesstimated" bills, we ended up with $271.00 a month to spend. Sounds okay, right? But wait, we haven't even subtracted things like groceries yet.

Where we go from here really depends on your situation. I would put most of you in one of three categories: low income/low prospects; low income/good prospects; high income/life should be good. Let me explain. The low income/low prospects group consists of people with net incomes not too different from what I'm showing here. (You could actually have much higher gross incomes, but also have higher car costs, rent, or mortgage payments plus higher student loans and whatever else.) In other words, whatever your gross income may be, you could still fall into this category because you don't have much net income to spend. Low prospects means that, for whatever reason, you don't expect to see your income rise much in the near future.

What Do These Numbers Mean?

It doesn't really matter what the numbers are on your budget so far. Big incomes with big debts are no different from small incomes with modest debts. So no matter where you started, if the net income looks too low, then the rest of this book is vitally important—because without action, you will be stuck in the proverbial rat race for the rest of your working career. Typically you rationalize that things will get better as soon as the student loans are paid, credit cards are paid down, whatever. But what I know from experience is that once the debts get paid down, new ones always appear to take their place. So what you need is more net income, and following the steps in the rest of this book is imperative. If you can get by without increasing your debt, pay your bills on time, and maybe tuck away a little in savings, I'll show you how to turn things around … permanently.

Unsolicited Advice

If, after payroll deductions and the must-pay bills, you have a net income that is truly too low to get by, then the best thing you could possibly do is find a second job. If you are really living this close to the edge, suck it up and spend a few weekends doing something to pay off the debts as soon as possible before new expenses hit, so you can give yourself some breathing room.

If you're in the low income/good prospects group, then we can look at things a little differently. The good prospects part means that although you may be on a shoestring budget now, you expect that fairly soon things will start to look much brighter. These are the typical "corporate" positions. In other words, although you're temporarily stuck in the "entry level" of corporate life, you expect your career position and income to start rising soon. Again, though, "low income" is a relative term, and the reference is to net income, not gross. So you could also be well into a career, but possibly due to additional training or education you expect to see your income rise significantly over the next few years—a common stage for young doctors who have high incomes and are starting to see the end of medical school bills on the horizon and others in a similar position.

This is probably the most difficult place to be in. On the one hand you want—and may truly need—to project a certain lifestyle but don't yet have the income. In this situation you will really need to understand the following steps on tracking your expenses. You need to cut out what isn't necessary to avoid increasing your debt too much. Notice I said "too much" instead of "at all." That is because this is typically the stage where you have too much house, too much in car payments, and too much lifestyle—all in anticipation of the future. For you, the next chapter will be very important. You will want to understand the ramifications of taking on too much debt too soon. The last thing you want is to see that income actually shoot up, but not be able to enjoy it because you are saddled with too much *lifestyle debt*. It is also important to focus on the later chapters on saving, investing, and insuring yourself. You'll need to be armed with this info before making decisions to take on *investment debt* and *prudent debt*.

For those of you lucky enough to be in the last group, high income/life should be good, the key is *should*. No matter what your gross income is, it can be easy to spend and borrow your way into a low net income position. Through my involvement in the mortgage business I've seen numerous occasions when a couple with an income well over $100,000 couldn't come up with just a couple thousand dollars of closing costs on a new mortgage. This is a sad state to be in when your gross income presents so much opportunity.

> There are three types of debt I'll discuss in this book: **investment debt, prudent debt,** and **lifestyle debt.**
>
> Investment debt is debt related to an appreciating asset that you expect to increase in value. (One example is real estate.) This is the only true good debt. Prudent debt is incurred to purchase something that you will own at least as long as the debt remains. (One example is a car.) While prudent debt may not be *good* debt, it is often necessary in today's world. Lifestyle debt, the one that gets most people in trouble, is borrowing for something that is done or consumed well before the final payment is made. (One example is a vacation.) Although many consider items in this category *necessary*, ideally they should be avoided if you have to borrow for them. If they can't be avoided, check out the next chapter where I discuss the decision-making process of taking on lifestyle debt.

If you're in this group and don't have enough net income, then pay close attention to the next few chapters. You need to put yourself in a position to be investing and saving, creating real wealth. If you don't start now, you will far too soon find yourself wondering how you don't have more to show for a lifetime of work. If you're in a position now to begin saving and investing, then I'll show you the right way to get started.

Spending Wisely

The first budgeting step is to track your actual spending. Once the bills are paid, you need to develop an understanding of what you can and can't afford. The rule, at the start, is for you to only track your *expenses*. I don't want you to modify your spending habits … yet. It is very important at first to understand what you're comfortable spending every month. What level of spending makes you feel good? You will be working for at least 30, if not

40 or more, years of your life. If you get nothing else from this book, take the understanding that life is meant to be more than living paycheck to paycheck for 40 years. And that true peace of mind comes from the knowledge that your wealth, not your paycheck, can sustain you no matter what circumstances may change.

Tracking Your Expenses

So how do you start tracking your expenses? The simple answer is, "Just write them down!" The trouble is, we are creatures of habit, and until something does become a habit it is too easy to forget. So here's what I want you to do. Take a piece of paper and at the top write down your net income (after the real bills are paid), and put that paper up on your refrigerator door. Think about it, where do you go most often after you walk in the door? If you've been out grocery shopping, then obviously you'll go to the refrigerator to put things away. If coming in from work, you'll eventually go to the fridge for dinner. And several times a day you will probably open the fridge for a snack or beverage. The fridge is convenient … and remember, the first goal is to make this as easy as possible.

Now, there are two steps to this process. The first is that every time you walk in the door, you go to the fridge and write down whatever you've spent money on while you were out. And you must write down *absolutely everything*. Every bottle of water, candy bar, newspaper … absolutely everything, no matter if you paid for it with cash, check, or debit card. (For now, don't add anything purchased on credit; that will show up in the next step when your purchase increases your credit card bill. If you use credit cards but pay off the balance each month, it would be better to write down the expense now, but a simpler plan is to just forego the charge cards for a month or two until you've worked through this step initially.)

Effective Expense Management

While you're tracking your expenses, there are a couple of tips you should follow. First, avoid the ATM as much as possible. Carrying around a lot of cash tends to add to "miscellaneous expenditures," money that just sort of "evaporates" and you're just not sure where it went. Remember, the goal of this exercise is to know exactly what you're spending your money on. But if you do use the ATM, remember to write down any ATM transaction fees you incur. If you stick with your checkbook and debit card only, you can audit, or double-check, your refrigerator list at the end of the month.

The second thing to remember is that at this stage, there should be absolutely no guilt or judgment passed on what is reported on the refrigerator list. If you're married, don't criticize each other's expenditures. If you feel guilty for writing something down, you are less likely to do it, right? We're after accuracy here.

Now to be really effective about this, every time you write something down, you should subtract the expenses from your net income figure. By doing this you will see how much money you have left until the end of the month. By simply being aware of this number you will start making smarter financial decisions. For example, if at the end of the month you really want to have an extra $100 to put toward the credit cards, and by the 25th of the month you're getting pretty close, maybe you'll pack your work lunch for a couple days, avoid the ATM, and fix dinner at home instead of getting carryout. And this is ultimately what I hope to accomplish with you in this book. I can't tell you what you can and can't buy, or how much to spend, but if I can get you to think about what you spend, when you spend, and how you spend, then you are about two thirds of the way to financial success. And there's another bonus here, as well: if this is done properly, you can probably skip the next step—making the actual budget.

A friend of mine is getting close to retirement and his wife is worried about whether they can afford it. Their income will be about $90,000 in retirement and his wife asked me whether that is enough to retire on. My honest answer was that I had no idea. Her response was, "Well, you should know, you're a financial planner!" Sorry, but it's just not that simple. Only you can determine what is enough. And the place to start, whether you're just starting out or getting ready to retire, is by tracking your expenses with the fridge list. My answer to her was to start a fridge list to determine what she needed in income and then decide how much more she wanted in income. Lifestyles vary so much that there can be no rules of thumb.

Budgeting—The Right Way

Many times just following the previous tracking steps accomplishes all you need to accomplish. If your refrigerator tracking list gives you enough motivation to leave money at the end of the month for mundane things like saving and investing, then that may be all you need to do. Still, the best thing to do is to come up with a comfortable budget. And here the key word is *comfortable*. If a budget is so stringent that it allows for no leeway, no fun stuff, then you know as well as I do that it is doomed from the start. So after a couple of months, I want you to take down the fridge sheets and sit down (with the roommate or significant other if applicable) and make out a budget everyone can live with.

> **Unsolicited Advice**
>
> Remember that your goal here should be "happiness," however you define it, not just how much stuff you can accumulate. There are plenty of studies out there that conclude that more stuff (even if that stuff is money!) does not buy happiness. Do what works for you to make you happy.

Step-by-Step Guide to Making a Budget

Step 1. Evaluate yourself. The first step in making a budget is to see how you did in tracking your expenses. Did you end up with money left over? Are you going further in the hole each month? Or are you breaking even, but not too happy about it? Whatever the case, I'm sure you've gone through this process because you want more, either to pay down bills faster or to start saving or investing for something important. And that is the first step. Just like with Tom, the prospective bar/restaurant owner, I need you to think about this: if we can find a way to come up with some more money every month, what exactly is it that you want to do with it? There must be some things that you're spending money on now that are less important to you than what you would do with that extra cash. And those are the expenditures we want to start looking for first.

Step 2. Add it up. As you add up what you've spent, start lumping things together. Don't be too general. It's better to have a budget with 100 items listed than one with 10 separated into big generic categories like "shopping." Your goal here is to go through every expense you recorded and decide, "Was it really necessary?" Now since the real bills were subtracted out, an argument can be made that very few items on the fridge list were necessary. But again, we're talking about your lifestyle, which is incredibly personal and subjective. So start off by including the things you really want to be able to spend on. If you really feel that you need your $5 Starbucks mocha-java-vanilla-bean-latte-thing before work, then go ahead and include it—at least for the first run-through.

Step 3. Decide what's important. The key here is to see what you're really spending on stuff, so you can realistically determine what stuff is most important to you. What can't you live without? What's more important right now than your financial goals? It's all about give-and-take. Throughout this book I'll be suggesting ways that you can not only have some of the things you *want*, not just *need*, but also how to do it a little more cost-effectively. But first we need a budget.

Making a budget is no different than tracking your expenses; you just write down what you're going to spend *before* you do it instead of after. Write down everything (and I mean *everything*) you plan to buy this month and how much you're willing to spend. That's it; making a budget is that simple. The hard part comes next—making sure you stick to it.

Sticking to Your Budget

After you come up with your budget I want you to do two things. First, at the very bottom, I want you to write down how much money you want to have left over at the end of the month. Up until now I've referred to this as money that you want for investing, or maybe accelerating your debt payments (I'll talk about the right way to do that in the next chapter), but it could also be that you just want more money to spend now. If you're in the low income/low prospects category, this is probably the case. Even so, I want you to come up with a budget that has *a set amount of money left over at the end of the month*. And I want you to write that number down at the bottom of your fridge list. When you're done, you should have something that looks like Table 1.6.

Table 1.6: Sample "fridge list" with end-of-the-month balance goal.	
Take-Home Pay	**$1,747.20**
Rent	$700.00
Utilities	$75.00
Renter's Insurance	$20.00
Net Income, After Housing	**$952.20**

Student Loans	$227.00
Car Loan	$134.00
Insurance, Gas, and Maintenance	$120.00
Credit Cards	$200.00
Net Income	$271.00
End-of-Month Balance	**$35.00**

Studies show that people will work harder for a prize bonus than they will for cash. Now, if given the choice between a three-day paid vacation or a $1,000 reward, most people will choose the $1,000. But if you take two separate groups and offer one group the $1,000 reward and the other the vacation, the vacation group will work harder to accomplish the same goal. The rationale is that although most of us could use the $1,000 more than the vacation, we get emotionally involved with the idea of going on vacation. There is little emotion in the money—especially if it would just be used for something mundane, such as paying off a credit card. The interesting part is that the dollar reward can be significantly higher than the value of the reward and we will still work harder for the nonmonetary reward. The point of all this is to use this same concept for your budget.

Reward Yourself!

No matter how frugal you may already be or how much you want to pay off your bills, start saving, whatever, if in any month you spend less than the budget allows, I want 100 percent of that extra savings to go toward buying something. Period. No arguments. The more frivolous the expenditure the better. For example, if you planned on saving $200 a month and end up with $201, go buy yourself a candy bar. If you save more, then go out to eat, get a massage, do something that you didn't have in the budget because you didn't think you could afford it. You worked hard on your budget, you stuck with it, you did better than you thought you could, so you deserve a bonus. Take it and enjoy it.

Now with the money you budgeted for savings, do with it what you said you would, and don't be tempted to do otherwise. If your goal was just to have some extra money to spend, then go spend it. But wait until the end of the month. Don't ever "pre-spend" thinking that you will reach your goal by the end of the month. Inevitably that will be the month that the unexpected happens, and instead of having a surplus at the end of the month, you end up with a big deficit. In order to have a successful month, whatever your saving goal is, it has to be reached at the *end* of the month. Pre-spending the surplus is strictly forbidden. Track, plan, and reward—all it takes is three simple steps to create and stick with a livable budget!

The Bottom Line

- Starting to save early can make a big difference. You never know what kind of "butterfly effect" saving today may have on your future.

- Budgeting and spending habits are more about your attitude than how much money you make. Taking an "us" against "them" attitude against the marketing execs may help motivate you to win the budget war and keep spending in check.

- Life is too short to not enjoy it. Even with mundane tasks like budgeting, establishing rewards can make the task more fun and thus more successful. Make sure to reward yourself for staying on track!

The Things We Need
and How to Get Them

What You Will Learn

- How to decide on your essentials in life

- Why good credit is crucial to maintaining your lifestyle

- How to find out, improve, and maintain your credit score

- How to regain control if your spending starts to get the best of you

In the last chapter you learned how to track your expenses. By doing so you have come to a better understanding of where your money goes, right? Right. So now let's get down to making some decisions.

We have control over how we get around (I'll tackle auto buying in Chapter 3) and where we live (the renting versus buying decision in Chapter 4). These are two decisions that are essential for almost everyone. The only variable is how much we choose to spend. Which neighborhood should we live in? New car or used car? For now, though, we're going to go over some very different buying decisions—the things that you need to be you. Not the things that I or any other financial guru, or even your friends and relatives, tell you that you need, but the things you know you have to have to get through the day. This is the point where you get to decide what your life requires, and ultimately redesign your lifestyle. So let's take a look at Table 2.1, which shows where we are with our sample budget.

Table 2.1: The current status of the sample budget.	
Take-Home Pay	$1,747.20
Rent	$700.00
Utilities	$75.00
Renter's Insurance	$20.00
Net Income, After Housing	**$952.20**
Student Loans	$227.00
Car Loan	$134.00
Insurance, Gas, and Maintenance	$120.00
Credit Cards	$200.00
Net Income	**$271.00**

"Nondiscretionary Expenditures"— More than Food, Water, and Shelter

After your withholding expenses from work have been figured in and you've paid the bills, it's time to allow for nondiscretionary expenses. To most people this means things like housing costs, utilities, insurance … the things we lump together and call "our bills." I agree with this definition, but I'd also like to include basic lifestyle expenses. And this can take some thought.

What are the things you need to make going to work eight hours a day, five or six days a week, better? For some people cable TV and a couch is all that's required. For others work is an end unto itself because their jobs provide the mental stimulation and social atmosphere that defines their lives. For still others work is just a paycheck that enables them to do everything else in life that they enjoy. From the mall to travel in Europe, fine wine and art, a paycheck is just a way to acquire the things in life we really want. But for most of us, the definition will evolve with our careers. If after going through your budget you find out that you're just in the wrong career or that you're never going to be able to afford what is really important to you, you'll need to make some major changes. And that is really important to know, now, while you're young and can do something about it.

> ### If You're Still in College …
>
> In college your biggest financial goal should be to graduate with the least amount of debt possible. Table 2.1 shows that even the "average" amount of student debt can inhibit your post-graduation lifestyle. For now, you should start deciding on your future lifestyle based on your starting salary. Table 2.2 is a listing of estimated starting salaries for undergraduates found at CNN.com. Using this information, you can see what type of discretionary income you'll likely have after graduation.

The biggest reason you need to start budgeting early is so you really know what it costs to live your lifestyle. The objective is not to adjust a lifestyle to your income; the real goal is to learn to generate the income necessary for the lifestyle you want. You may need to start re-evaluating your career decision as soon as you have your first job, and that's okay. At this point, you still have time to add qualifications and make plans to get where you really want to be financially. That realization may mean making room in the current budget for additional education or training, or it may mean building job skills for a career change. And it also means knowing approximately what you should be making, and what salaries are like in other fields. Take a look at Table 2.2.

Table 2.2: Average starting salaries for college graduates as of 2005.	
Major	**Starting Salary**
Chemical engineering	$54,256
Electrical engineering	$52,009
Computer engineering	$51,496
Computer science	$51,292
Mechanical engineering	$51,046
Aerospace engineering*	$50,701
Industrial engineering	$49,541
Accounting	$43,809
Information science	$43,732
Civil engineering	$43,462
Economics/finance	$42,802
Business administration	$39,448
Marketing	$37,832
Liberal arts	$30,337

SOURCE: National Association of Colleges and Employers

Also aeronautical and astronautical engineering degrees

One thing is certain—we Americans are defined by how we spend. So let's get a handle on it early to make all those long hours on the job worthwhile. The official definition of *non-discretionary expenses* would be things that we have no control, or choice, over buying. But in this section we're going to redefine non-discretionary expenditures to include the things that, technically speaking, we don't have to buy, but that you as an individual need. This includes the Starbucks Grande Double Mocha French Café Latte thing for $5.00 before work every day, if that's what you really need to get going. You can have it, and you don't have to feel guilty … you just need to find a way to afford it.

The Essentials Are Different for Everybody

If you went through the budget-tracking exercise from the last chapter, you are then in one of two camps: you either have money left over at the end of the month, or you don't. Let's tackle the last, and obviously more difficult, situation first.

This is decision-making time. You need to go through every item on the fridge list, think about it, and decide how important that spending decision is for you to continue making in the future. (If you found that you still had a little discretionary cash at the end of the month, this may not be necessary, but it's still prudent.) So let's jump right in and start with some examples of typical lifestyle expenditures that are also common budget-busters. Remember that one person's discretionary budget-buster is another person's necessity, so don't feel singled out or limited by these examples. This exercise is intended to show you how to view and question your expenses to make sure that they are really necessary to you, and whether they are worth the overall cost.

Eating out. For many of us, eating out is entertainment. For others, eating out is a time- and energy-saving necessity. But we do pay a price financially. (And in nonmonetary terms, dieticians will correlate eating out to obesity, diabetes, high blood pressure, and high cholesterol levels.)

Probably the simplest budgeting solution for most is to "brown bag" lunch. Restaurant—especially fast-food—lunches are notoriously high in fat and calories, and, more important to our discussion, expensive. If you habitually eat out at work, it's easy to save $5 to $10 a day by packing a healthier lunch. For dinner, try to make a point of eating in one night a week. Your budget, and your health, will be better off.

> **Unsolicited Advice**
>
> If you're single, make a social night out of staying in by having a rotating group dinner at someone's house. In the Midwest we are known for our love of backyard grilling. For me, a glass of wine and a hot grill makes for a great way to unwind after a long day. And even a turkey burger tastes pretty good with the right wine—without breaking the budget.

Bottled Water. In 2002 Americans paid $7.7 billion for bottled water, and sales continue to increase. The image is that bottled water is safer, healthier, and more environmentally sound than tap water. Is this image fact or fantasy? Consider that companies such as Nestle, Coke, and Pepsi are making a fortune from bottled water sales. What do you think? (Consider our marketing discussion in the last chapter.)

I'll admit that I'm guilty of succumbing to this one. And to the extent that a bottle of water replaces pop or soda, the bottled water craze isn't such a bad thing. But my personal issue is with people who complain about the cost of a gallon of gas while sucking down a bottle of store-bought water. At $1.00 for a 16 oz. bottle, that would be $8.00 for a gallon of bottled water. Comparing the work involved in creating a gallon of gasoline versus a gallon of bottled water, we should be happy we're not paying $20.00 or more for a gallon of gas!

Unsolicited Advice

If you make a habit of buying bottled water, consider buying a water bottle and filling it at home before you leave each day. If you're still worried about the water quality or taste, you can add a high-quality water filter to your faucet. Even after the price of the filter you're only paying about $.13 a gallon for your water—which quickly adds up to significant savings.

Shopping. In one of those notorious e-mail forwards was the following: "A woman will spend $10 on a $20 item she doesn't need, and a man will spend $20 on a $10 item he does need." I think the lesson is that we can learn from each other's habits. Whether you're guilty of impulsive buying (which can lead to overpaying) or live for the thrill of a bargain (which can lead to overbuying), it is best to decide *why* you're shopping and *what* you're shopping for before leaving the house. And every time you leave the house you should look at the fridge list to see what's left in the monthly budget. No matter how good the deal is, if it doesn't fit into the monthly budget, don't buy it. There will always be deals, discounts, and sales. Products are marked up just so they can later be marked down to capitalize on impulsive buyers' buying habits. Don't fall for it!

Cable TV. As a Gen Xer or Gen Yer, you probably watch less TV than the rest of us, but make up for it on the Internet. Evaluate the cable bill for the channels you really use. Shop around for satellite, if available. And, if you're signing up for a temporary pricing offer, don't just let it renew at full price at the end of the offering period. That is what they're counting on—the eventual bill for multiple channels you never watch anyway. (This holds true for Internet and cell phone service, as well.) Keep an eye on your actual usage and don't give in to paying more.

Making It Work for You

When all is said and done, does this attention to detail really matter? What's the difference in a couple bucks a day on water, a couple extra pairs of shoes in the closet, or a couple extra lunches at work? What you need to know is how you can buy the things you really want, like an HD TV, a nicer car, season tickets to the games or the Philharmonic, and a down payment for a house, right? Well, let's see what those few extra dollars each month can do with a little bit of budgeting.

Let's say you pack a lunch for work three times a week. That's a $15 to $30 savings right there. You eat in for dinner just once a week and save another $10 or $20. Cut the cable bill by $20 a month, skip one shopping trip that would have cost $30 or $40, and buy eight fewer bottles of water. That's over $260 a month in savings! Now, if you're living on the edge with your bills, $260 a month can go a long way. And if you're in the low income/low prospects group, then this extra money will make a huge difference.

In the sample budget in Table 2.1, I listed a $200 monthly payment for credit card debt. A typical minimum monthly payment on credit cards is now 2 percent of the balance. With this payment, a $10,000 balance, and a 16 percent interest rate, you would have your credit cards paid off in about seven years. By adding the $260 a month in budget savings, you could have the cards paid off in just about three years. By that time you would not only have that $260, but also the original $200 a month from the credit card payment to add to cash flow. If you can't get it from your employer, this is a great way to get a $460 a month "raise" in your net income in just a three-year period.

For those of you in the other two lifestyle categories, who anticipate higher wages in the near future, increasing debt at this stage is really not that awful. Take a look at your fridge list and you'll see that I entered $134 a month for a car loan. That is calculated from using www.car.com's estimate of the value of a three-year-old Ford Focus, financed for four years at a 7 percent interest rate. By simply following budget steps such as the ones in the example above, you could step up to a $14,000 car instead of a $6,600 one. Or you could finance $8,000 worth of furniture, or an additional $25,000 on a mortgage for a new home. Trading off a few daily conveniences might be worth some of the really big things we can get with proper budgeting … right?

The Payoff

The key to budgeting is to first track your spending and understand your own spending habits. Then make decisions on what is really important to you and what is less so. Writing it down and checking your fridge list daily will help in your awareness of where your monthly spending is relative to your monthly income. But the biggest success factor in budgeting is to build in a reward system. If you save money somewhere, you have been doing without something. So if you can stick with it for a full month, make sure you build in some type of reward to make it worthwhile. The real pay-off here is financial stability, but I'm sure you'll enjoy that extra treat now and then, too.

> If your budgeting goal is to save or invest more, then once you've tracked your expenses and determined how much you can afford to save, use an automatic investment plan to start saving. If your employer is willing to add a direct deposit, the investment will come directly from your paycheck. Otherwise, you can have an ACH (electronic withdrawal) made from your checking account.

Credit and Credit Repair

No matter how strictly you budget or even how quickly your income rises, there will always be a need to take on some debt. That means you'll need to borrow, and in order to borrow you'll need credit. The better your credit score, the lower your interest rate—and the kinder borrowing will be on your budget. So if (and when) you need to borrow, here is what you need to know.

What Is Your Credit Score (and Why Should You Care)?

The best way to prepare to apply for a loan is to build your credit score. With a good credit score you will qualify for loans in your name alone and qualify for the lowest interest rate—without a parent as a co-signer.

What is a co-signer? When an applicant for a loan doesn't meet the lender's guidelines, he or she may be asked to provide a co-signer. This is someone, typically a relative, who signs for the loan with the borrower and assumes responsibility for the loan if the debt is not repaid. So if you take out a loan that you can't pay, the co-signer must make the payments instead—or both of your credit scores will be severely damaged. Before asking someone to act as a co-signer, it's a good idea to seriously evaluate your ability to pay back the loan. Preparing a budget beforehand is a smart way to prevent defaulting and forcing your co-signer to make your payments.

If You're Still in College …

If you build your own credit record in college you can avoid relying on a co-signer later. Take out small loans, such as a computer or student credit card which you pay in full at the end of each month, in your name. This helps build good credit, which you'll need in the future.

In 2005 Americans had a negative savings rate, which means that we spent more money than we made. So if your parents are typical you may not be able to count on them as co-signers anyway. If they've been helping you pay your way for four or more years and have borrowed to pay tuition bills, their ability to get a loan may be no better than yours. It's far better to build your own credit and not have to rely on others when you want to finance a purchase.

The Process of Credit Scoring

Unfortunately, it's pretty hard to make it through a career, especially the early years, without taking on some debt. Having owned and managed a mortgage company for several years, I can tell you that a bad credit score can do as much damage to your financial success as poor investments. So let me explain the process of credit scoring.

Your credit score, or FICO, is kept by three separate credit reporting agencies: Equifax (www.equifax.com or 800-685-1111), TransUnion (www. transunion.com or 877-322-8228), and Experian (www.experian.com or 888-397-3742). Each time you borrow money, whether on a credit card, through a finance company (leases included) for a car or home, or through a line of credit, the details of the loan are reported to the three credit agencies. On a monthly basis the lenders will report the status of your loan—the original balance, current balance, monthly payment, and whether the payment was on time. Reports will show if payments are 30 days, 90 days, or more than 120 days late. Your report will also show charge-offs (if you've been sent to a collection agency) and bankruptcies. Based on this information you will have a credit score at each agency.

> A FICO score is a credit score developed by Fair Isaac & Co. Credit scoring is a method of determining the likelihood that credit users will pay their bills. Scores range from 400 to 900, with the higher the score the better. Borrowers with higher scores will qualify for better borrowing terms than borrowers with lower scores.

You are entitled to a free credit report from each reporting company once a year. But the free reports do not give you your actual score; they provide only a detail of your credit history. So it's a good idea to request a report from each company every four months so that you can stay on top of your report. (Reports can be ordered online from annualcreditreport. com or at the links above for each company.) Once you receive your credit reports, it's important to review each one to make sure all the information is accurate as reported. This is the best way to head off potential problems that result from fraudulent or erroneous information. If you feel that any information is incorrect, you can click on the specific credit agency's link at annualcreditreport.com to dispute it.

> Sometimes contacting the original creditor and explaining that you did not receive a billing notice or any other correspondence for a bill is sufficient for having the collection removed from your report. (This works only if you truly haven't received anything, as it's the most common excuse for not paying a bill.) Tell the creditor that you are more than happy to pay the bill, but that you need a letter to have the collection removed from your credit report. Note: this solution takes a lot of talking, a great reason why the bill wasn't paid, and the money to pay it off.

Sound like a lot of work? Well, it's even more work to clean up the mess incorrect information can cause. I had clients come in to refinance their home a couple of years ago. During the process, the loan originator told me they had a problem. Apparently, there was a delinquency on their credit report from a phone bill in another state. When I asked my clients, they knew nothing about it—they had never lived out of state, let alone set up out-of-state phone service. Unfortunately, the phone company had been subsequently bought out, making it nearly impossible to get four-year-old phone records. Long story short, it took three months to get the error corrected and removed from their credit report. Now in this case, we were just refinancing—but since a lender won't give a mortgage to someone with an outstanding charge-off on his or her account, what would have happened if my clients had been trying to buy their dream home? Do you think that the sellers would have waited 90 days while my clients cleaned up their credit report, or would their dream home have become someone else's reality?

These types of issues are pretty common, and the only way to catch them is to keep an eye on what's being reported. Monitoring your credit report is also the best way to catch identity theft before it becomes a huge problem. Identity theft, which happens when someone obtains your personal or financial information and makes purchases in your name, can foul up your life for years if not caught early. It's sad that this has become necessary, but investing 20 minutes three times a year can save years' worth of misery.

> ### Unsolicited Advice
>
> Remember that there are two parts to opportunity. The first is to know an opportunity when you see one; the second is being able to take advantage of it. Don't risk missing out on an opportunity for the perfect home or investment property due to erroneous information on your credit report.

In addition to reviewing your credit reports, once a year you need to pay to actually get your credit score. Your score represents the risk you present to the lender; a higher score means that you're a better risk than someone with a lower score. It follows that the lower your score, the higher the interest rate you will be charged, and the more money you'll end up paying. So let's look at how big of an effect your credit score can have on your finances.

Table 2.3: Sample interest rates based on credit score. It is important to note that how a credit score is interpreted varies from lender to lender.					
Interest Rates					
	Score Range	Excellent 740+	Good 690–740	Average 620–690	Fair 580–620	Bad Below 580
Mortgage	$150,000	6.25%	6.25%	6.25%	6.75%	7.50%
Home Equity Loan (HELOC)	$20.000	8.25%	8.25%	9.50%	10.50%	N/A
Auto Loan	$20.000	5.85%	6.25%	8.00%	10%	14%
Credit Card	$10,000	10.50%	10.50%	16%	21+%	21+%
Monthly Payments					
30-Year Mortgage	$150,000	$924	$924	$924	$973	$1,049
HELOC 20 Years	$20,000	$170	$170	$186	$200	N/A
Auto Loan— 5 Years	$20,000	$385	$389	$406	$425	$465
Credit Card— 10 Year	$10,000	$135	$135	$168	$200	$200

In Table 2.3, I have laid out a grid of sample interest rates based on the type of loan and typical credit score ranges. In the bottom table I have corresponding payments based on the info in column 1 and in the top table. These are examples only. Interest rates and credit score ranges will vary, sometimes greatly, among lenders. Other factors, such as income, length of time on the job, and credit history, may also come into play.

You can see from the table what poor credit can do to a budget. If you total the payments under the excellent credit example you get a monthly payment of $1,614. For the same amount of credit, our fair credit example has a total monthly payment of $1,798, or $184 more that is just going to pay interest. Now, if you can't come up with something better to do with $184 a month, try this: add the $184 to your credit card payment from Table 2.1 and a borrower with excellent credit would have his cards paid off in just over 3 years instead of 10! No part-time job, no budgeting—all it would take is a little bit of time a few times a year checking your credit report coupled with some discipline in paying your bills on time. And if you invested $185 a month for 30 years in your 401(k).... (Okay, you've heard that one already. And I guess if you can maintain a 720 score or better you deserve to do whatever you want with a little extra cash flow!)

What Do I Do with My Credit Score?

Here are a couple of things you can do once you've established (and checked) your credit. If your score has gone up since you first took out a loan, refinance it! For example, say you took out a five-year car loan two years ago when your credit score was lower than it is today. By knowing your credit score you can get specific rates and terms by calling various lenders. If you can lower your rate, refinance. You can do the same thing with credit cards. Take out a new card with a lower interest rate and transfer the balance. In either case, whether a car loan or a credit card, before you refinance make sure you give your current lender the opportunity to come down and match the rate. This can be particularly effective with credit cards. Even though a new credit card may have come with a low rate, that interest rate will many times balloon with just one late payment. After resuming on-time payments for four to six months it may pay to try to negotiate your rate back to the original lower rate. If they don't give in, shop around for a better deal.

> One factor in your credit score is how old a credit line is … and the older the better. So it doesn't always pay to "roll over" your debt into new, lower-rate loans. If you plan to apply for new credit, hold off on any refinancing until your new loan has been finalized.

12 Steps: 12 Months to an Improved Credit Score

Whether you've let your credit slip or want to maintain a top score, here's a list of things to do. If you're thinking about applying for a loan (especially a mortgage loan) or deciding whether to refinance, you should start this process 12 months before you apply for credit.

Step 1. Pull your free annual credit reports. You have been given the right to know what's on your credit report. Know what is on it! And pay for your actual credit score once per year. Knowing your score helps with budgeting for major purchases.

Now that you have the report, dispute inaccurate reporting. Accounts not yours? Balance owed is wrong? Monthly payment is wrong? Duplicate reporting? Highest credit limit wrong or missing? Creditors reporting late payments when you have not been 30 days or more late? If you think there is an error, here's what you need to do to dispute it.

- Call the creditors to see if they will make the inaccuracies right with the credit reporting bureaus—and get *written documentation*.

- Write dispute letters to the repositories reporting inaccuracies on your credit report. You may need supporting documentation, and you may need to do this several times in order to get the inaccuracy corrected. Be persistent.

Step 2. Pay your bills on time, every time. Never, under any circumstances, should you be 30 or more days late!

> If you are going to be applying for a loan soon, *do not* pay off collections. Doing so may initially lower your credit score, because it makes the reporting newer—and it shows that you have admitted defaulting with a creditor. In most cases, after the lender has pulled your credit they may require the collection to be paid, but they already have your score and will not pull it again, so the initial score for your loan will be "locked in." At that time, it will be safe to pay off the remaining collections, if they are legitimate.

Step 3. Look at your balances and credit limits. Make sure that the balance owed is always less than 40 percent of your credit limit. For example, if you have a card with a credit limit of $5,000, your balance should always be under $2,000. If you are currently above 40 percent, work at paying down your balances. (You can also raise the limit on the account or take out additional lines of credit to spread the balances out, but be careful—too many open lines of credit can be bad, too.) Work on one credit line at a time to get below the 40 percent mark, and make sure that your balance doesn't get up over this amount again.

Step 4. Limit the number of inquires made to your credit file. An inquiry will be recorded each time you apply for credit. To creditors, multiple inquiries look as though you are overextended, and therefore lowers your score. Refrain from the store credit cards, which try to suck you in with

10-percent discounts for applying on your first purchase—but which also require an inquiry on your credit. It may ultimately cost you more than that 10 percent in the increased interest rate due to a lower credit score. A good rule of thumb is no more than three to four inquiries each year.

Unsolicited Advice

If you're a new grad getting your first job or further along in your career and getting a big raise, avoid the credit trap of applying for multiple new credit cards at once. Too many new inquiries appear to the reporting agencies as though you are overextended and trying to borrow your way back to solvency.

But don't worry, multiple inquiries in the same period of time (such as when applying for a car purchase or mortgage) will not affect your credit score. So don't let concern for your credit score stop you from shopping for the best financing deal—especially for large purchases.

Step 5. Give yourself credit! You've got to have credit to prove your creditworthiness. Most creditors look to see that you have three to four credit accounts (often referred to as trade lines) open and in good standing with a rating history of at least 12 to 24 months.

Unsolicited Advice

Having credit does not mean being in debt. Go ahead and use your credit card, just make sure it's paid off—entirely—every month.

Step 6. Don't constantly roll credit cards for lower interest rates. Closing credit accounts in good standing, especially those with a long history of good reporting, will actually lower your score. So unless you are paying an annual fee for the account, keep it open, even if you don't use it. It may also be a good idea to use it once in a while—by doing so you may improve your credit score. Activity on older credit lines has a higher impact than activity on newer lines.

Step 7. Know when to cut your losses. If you find yourself overextended and unable to make the minimum monthly payment, cut up the card, hide it from yourself … do whatever it takes to stop using it. Call your creditor(s) *immediately* to make payment arrangements. Do this before you are 30 days late, and make sure to get any agreements you make in writing.

Step 8. Discipline yourself to manage your money. Question yourself: do you really need that flat-screen plasma TV? One way to get your money management on the right track is to have your paycheck automatically deposited into your checking account.

> **The Rule of Cash:** Whatever cash you have in your pocket on Monday will be spent by Friday. And whatever cash you have in your pocket on Friday will be spent by Sunday night. Carry as little cash as possible!

Step 9. Pay it online. Use an online bill payment system to have your bills automatically debited out of your account. Caution: do this only if you know that the money will be there! (This may be more difficult for people on commission-based compensation to do.) Many creditors will allow you to set up your account to receive an e-mail notification that your bill is due. And most credit card companies will allow you to make two to four payments toward your balance each billing cycle. This is nice because it allows you the opportunity to take that extra money you found you had in between paychecks and apply it to your balance.

> Make a schedule for when you will pay certain bills that corresponds to your paydays. For example, if you get paid twice a month, decide which bills you need to pay in the first half of the month and which you will pay in the second half. You can then record in your checkbook how much you have to spend until the next check arrives.

Step 10. Know your debt-to-income ratios. What are debt-to-income ratios? These are key to managing your debt, and will help to keep you from getting in over your head. There are two ratios that creditors look at: total housing cost to gross income and total debt (including housing cost) to gross income. To calculate your ratio you simply add up all your monthly debt payments and divide by your gross (before tax) income. Housing expenses include mortgage payment or rent, homeowner's insurance, mortgage insurance, real estate taxes, and condo or homeowner association dues. When applying for a mortgage, a typical rule of thumb is that not more than 43 percent of your gross income should go to your creditors (with housing expenses); it's 29 percent for other expenses. The Federal National Mortgage Association suggests that a total debt-to-income ratio should be around 36 percent. But remember, just because you can qualify for a loan with ratios within these guidelines doesn't mean that you *should* borrow that much. In general, the lower your income, the more important it is to stay below these guidelines.

Step 11. Find other income. If you're having trouble making all your payments, then it might be time to get a part-time job. (Stop with the horrified looks.) If you have borrowed money from someone and are having trouble repaying that debt, a great way to fix the dilemma is to take a second job to pay your obligations. A year or two of weekend work sure beats a decade of worrying about how to pay bills! And listen, if that doesn't motivate you, just think about actually having spare money, once some of the loans are paid off. That would be nice, right?

> ## Unsolicited Advice
>
> If a second job working for someone else doesn't appeal to you, consider one of the many "home-based" business opportunities that are available. Benefits can include everything from tax deductions to getting your own products at wholesale cost. For example, if personal health is your thing, look into a nutrition company. Or combine a supplemental job with an outside interest—for example, if you work out, consider selling gym memberships; you'll probably end up with a free membership of your own. Be creative and use your skills and interests to your advantage.

Step 12. Shake it up. If all else fails, it may be time to consider a career change. If your lifestyle just doesn't fit into your budget, a new career may be a better alternative to lifestyle adjustment. Never stop networking. Don't be afraid to ask people who appear to be more successful about what they do for a living. And although a high-paying position won't just fall into your lap, the best way to get there is through hard work.

So now that we've made some headway into building, rebuilding, or maintaining good credit and have some money put aside from our successful expense-tracking and budgeting exercises, it's time to figure out what the next steps will be toward getting what we need.

Paying Down Your Debt

You're doing pretty good if you're still with me. If you are still reading, that means you really are motivated to improve your financial condition. And that's good because now is when we start taking positive steps toward improvement. You've freed up a little cash from your expense-tracking experience and have reduced the interest rates on any loans you have outstanding. Now you want to pay off, or at least pay down, your remaining debt. So how do you go about it?

Two Ways to "Roll Down" Your Debt

Most credit elimination strategies revolve around a concept termed "rolling down" your debt. Strategies may differ slightly, but they all use the same concept. First, you need to list your credit card information: monthly payments, balances owed, and interest rate. Then, using one of two methods, you'll put the payments in order of importance to be paid off.

In both scenarios, you make the minimum payment on all but one debt. You then apply all the extra cash that you have for accelerating your debt payoff to the debt at the top of your list until it is completely paid off. Then you take 100 percent of the payment you were making on the first credit card and add it to the minimum payment you've been making on the second card on your list. Continue the process as long as possible, or until all your credit cards are paid off. As I said, where the strategies differ is in their approach to ordering your debts.

In the first option, the recommendation is to order your debts from the *highest interest rate* down to the lowest. By getting rid of the highest interest rate first, you'll ultimately save the most in interest payments. This is definitely the best option if you don't think you can dedicate your extra cash flow to your debts for a long enough period to pay them all off. If that's the case, you'll definitely benefit by getting rid of the highest-interest-rate cards first.

Option 2 says to order your debts from the *smallest balance* to the largest. Don't pay attention to interest rates at all if you choose this strategy; the idea is that you will see progress sooner, since a credit card with a smaller balance can be paid off relatively quickly, which will help to motivate you to keep going.

So which strategy works best? Let's take a look at Table 2.4. In both cases, the total amount owed is $10,500 with a minimum monthly payment of $225. In each case, the tables reflect adding an additional $100 a month to the minimum payment.

Table 2.4: Two different strategies for rolling down debt payments.

Roll-Down Debt Summary—Highest Rate to Lowest Rate

	Amount Owed	Interest Rate	Monthly Payment
Credit Card 1	$5,000	18%	$10
Credit Card 2	$3,500	15%	$7
Credit Card 3	$1,500	12%	$3
Credit Card 4	$500	9%	$2

Roll-Down Payment Schedule

Year	Current Payment Schedule			Roll-Down Payment Schedule		
	Payments	Interest	Balance	Payments	Interest	Balance
			$10,500			$10,000
1	$2,700	$1,580	$9,380	$3,900	$1,476	$8,076
2	$2,644	$1,414	$8,150	$3,901	$1,054	$5,229
3	$2,400	$1,238	$6,988	$3,765	$552	$2,016
4	$2,400	$1,043	$5,630	$2,107	$90	$-
5	$2,400	$814	$4,045	$-	$-	$-
6	$2,330	$547	$2,262	$-	$-	$-
7	$1,667	$271	$846	$-	$-	$-
8	$911	$65	$-	$-	$-	$-
Totals	$17,472.00	$6,972		$13,673.00	$3,172	

Interest Saved: $3,800

Roll-Down Summary—Lowest Balance to Highest Balance

	Amount Owed	Interest Rate	Monthly Payment
Credit Card 1	$500	9%	$2
Credit Card 2	$1,500	12%	$3
Credit Card 3	$3,500	15%	$7
Credit Card 4	$5,000	18%	$10

continues...

(Table 2.4 continued)

Roll-Down Payment Schedule

Year	Current Payment Schedule			Roll-Down Payment Schedule		
	Payments	Interest	Balance	Payments	Interest	Balance
			$10,500			$10,500
1	$2,700	$1,580	$9,380	$3,785	$1,529	$8,244
2	$2,644	$1,414	$8,150	$3,851	$1,194	$5,588
3	$2,400	$1,238	$6,988	$3,687	$758	$2,659
4	$2,400	$1,043	$5,630	$2,858	$199	$-
5	$2,400	$814	$4,045	$-	$-	$-
6	$2,330	$547	$2,262	$-	$-	$-
7	$1,687	$271	$846	$-	$-	$-
8	$911	$65	$-	$-	$-	$-
Totals	**$17,472**	**$6,972**		**$14,181**	**$3,680**	
Interest Saved:		**$3,292**				

As you can see from the two examples, paying off the cards with the higher interest rates saves about $500 more in interest expense as compared to paying off the cards with the smaller debts first. But this strategy also depends on your specific debts. Just $100 a month extra cuts in half the time to be debt-free instead of paying minimum payments. I personally am a fan of the second strategy, paying down the smallest debt first, because I think the reward of completely paying off a debt is worth a slightly higher interest cost—but only if the difference is small and you are concerned about your own motivation to keep at it. There is a great calculator for comparing the two options at www.dinkytown.net.

If you're willing to do a little extra work, there is a variation. Pay down each card, in order of highest interest first, until you get to 60 percent of the initial credit limit. Then move on to the next card, and repeat the process. This way, if you need to apply for new credit during the process you'll see impact on increasing your credit score sooner. Having multiple credit lines with 40 percent credit remaining looks better than one card paid off but two or three others maxed out. After you get each card down to the 60 percent level, start over with the highest card and proceed with paying the cards off entirely, one by one.

Bankruptcy—The Final Solution?

I'm not going to spend much time on bankruptcy. I'm not a lawyer, and not only can laws vary from state to state, but interpretation of those laws can even vary from judge to judge in the same jurisdiction.

What I do know is this: a bankruptcy can be very expensive in terms of future borrowing costs. You probably know someone who has filled bankruptcy. There were about 1.5 million personal bankruptcy filings in 2005. If you assume that those filers either have jobs, or did have a job in 2005 (they wouldn't have qualified for loans without income), that means that about 1 out of 10 of your co-workers will file bankruptcy in the next year based on 2005 filings. One of those people may have actually bragged about their bankruptcy and how easy it was to get a loan afterwards. Yes, you can get a loan after a bankruptcy. Yes, you can rebuild your credit score, too, but the bankruptcy will stay on your credit report for seven years. And after you file for bankruptcy, your new loans will come at a significantly higher price. Auto loans for those who have filed bankruptcy can easily run into the 18 percent and higher range (as opposed to around 6.5 percent for someone with a good credit score). On a five-year loan for a $14,000 car, that would mean nearly $5,000 of additional interest payments due to the higher rate.

> A bankruptcy can affect more than just your credit score and ability to obtain credit. Auto insurers are now pulling credit reports, and statistically bad credit translates into a higher insurance risk and higher premiums. Employers are also pulling credit reports for new job applicants—not just in the banking, finance, and accounting fields, but many other industries as well. Bankruptcy calls into question reliability and personal discipline, and raises concerns regarding future job performance.

In most cases bankruptcy is just a temporary fix. Due to the higher rates, filers will often end up in trouble again, and in even less time, because the cost to finance their lifestyle has become so much more expensive.

There are truly legitimate reasons for getting into financial trouble. Take a look at Table 2.5. This is a list that breaks down the most common reasons people gave for filing bankruptcy. (Many gave more than one reason, so the total is well over 100 percent.) But two of the top three reasons do not reflect well on an individual's ability to manage their own finances. Would you want someone who can't manage his or her own finances to be involved with either handling your business or making recommendations for you? Although not an automatic disqualification, whether you have ever filed for bankruptcy is a question that you will be asked if applying for many types of jobs. Many companies, as well as banks and credit unions, will consider applicants who have filed for bankruptcy to be less desirable candidates.

Table 2.5: The seven most common reasons for filing bankruptcy (some respondents indicated more than one reason).	
63%	credit card debt
50%	job loss or pay cut
37%	bad financial management
28%	medical bills
15%	business troubles
13%	divorce
12%	lawsuit or legal bills

The bottom line is that personal financial responsibility goes beyond a budget. But a budget, and routinely tracking expenditures, can go a long way in keeping you on track for financial success.

The Bottom Line

- Once you know where your money is going it's easier to make decisions when trade-offs are required.

- You need to account for your bills first so that you can make your payments on time.

- It's a lot easier to afford the things you want with a good credit score. Monitoring your credit report and maintaining a top score means lower interest rates, so more money goes to what you purchase and less to the bank.

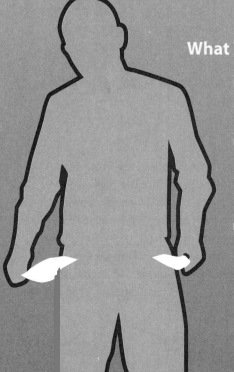

Let's Go Buy a Car

What You Will Learn

- How to do your homework before heading for the car lot

- Why you should look at the total cost of car ownership before you buy

- How to make the big decision: to lease or buy

Literature is full of stories about Americans and their cars. To many, a car instills a sense of freedom, power, and status. Even though recent research indicates that our love affairs with our cars may be cooling off, I somehow doubt if it will ever entirely end. But perhaps due to higher gas costs or to the higher costs of the cars themselves, more and more cars are being viewed for what they are: an expensive and environmentally unfriendly way to get around. Whichever represents your view (it's probably something in between), we can all agree on one thing—with the overall cost of owning a car today, no one wants to pay more for a set of wheels than they have to.

What to Buy and How to Buy It

One of the biggest, if not *the* biggest, budgeting decisions most people will make is what type of car to buy and how to pay for it. There are lots of options: should I get the car new or used? Should I lease or buy? How long should I finance it for: 48 months, 60 months, longer? Aside from these basic decisions, the trouble for many people is that buying a car is a very emotional process. And when emotions and finances mix, the outcome is seldom pretty.

In the first chapter I talked about the goal of marketing execs being to separate you from your cash. I doubt if you can find any purchase process that exemplifies this better than that of buying a car. Nowhere else does advertising, marketing, and salesmanship so conspire to separate you from your money as it does on the showroom floor. But don't worry. In this chapter, I'll provide all you need to know to have a fighting chance the next time you venture onto auto-dealer turf.

Come Up with a Budget

The absolute first thing that you must do is check your fridge list to see the status of your budget. (I say check the fridge list, not the bank account, because I'm going to assume that the availability of a down payment is highly unlikely. If, by chance, you do have cash burning a hole in your pocket, I'll tell you what to do toward the end of this chapter.) When checking your budget, remember that four things need to be factored into the payment you think you can afford: the price of the car (more specifically, the monthly payment), insurance premiums, gas consumption, and anticipated maintenance and upkeep costs.

You need to use the fridge list as a starting point to determine a monthly car payment that fits into your budget. Do not, under any circumstances, go out to a car lot "just to look around" without doing this first! I don't care if you're the ice queen or king, once on the lot and at the mercy of a good salesperson, it becomes very easy to rationalize how you can afford something that is way out of your budget range. And although anyone, even the most experienced salesperson, would have a hard time justifying that most luxury cars are really worth two and three times their economy counterparts, this is where the emotion comes in. You see that shiny new car. You need it. You want it. But you have to remember that it's just the "bling," and auto makers, dealers, advertisers, and especially salespeople know that bling sells. So if you head to the lot armed with the right information and with your budget firmly fixed in your mind, you'll find it a lot easier to stay on target instead of being swayed when the salespeople start talking.

So take a look at the budget list. After coming up with a monthly payment number that works comfortably within your budget, go to an Internet loan calculator, such as the one at www.dinkytown.net/java/SimpleLoan.html. (I like this calculator because it allows you to enter the payment, interest rate, and term, and it will tell you how much you can finance.)

> The **term** of a loan refers to the amount of time that is set for repayment. Auto loans are generally referred to in months (such as 48 or 60 months), rather than in years (such as 4 or 5 years).

Let's say that according to your budget on the fridge, you have determined that you can comfortably afford $250 a month for car payments. So let's fill in a payment of $250 for 60 months at 6.5 percent interest and find out that you can finance $12,777. Assuming that you have a 7 percent local sales tax rate (it varies from state to state—make sure to fill in the correct sales tax for the state in which you live), and that the dealer is going to tack on $500 of junk fees, you end up paying about $11,300 for the car itself. To come up with this, I multiplied $12,777 times .93 (1.00–7 percent) to get the amount that adds up to $12,777 after paying 7 percent sales tax, and then subtracted the $500 of junk fees. This is not 100 percent accurate but it does err on the conservative side—when estimating payments that you'll be stuck with for a while, it's better to be cautious.

> **Junk fees** are common in the auto and mortgage indus-
> tries. They are fees that do not represent direct costs to
> the seller, but instead are a way of increasing profit. For
> example, a fee for title and transfer may be a legitimate
> cost, but a fee for "dealer preparation" is not. When nego-
> tiating the cost of a car, make it clear that the price you
> are offering is the "out the door" fee, plus sales tax and
> titling fees.

How Long Should the Loan Be For?

I use a 60-month loan in the following examples, mainly because cars
have become so expensive that it is hard to afford them on a shorter loan.
I know that some places will now go out a full six years, or 72 months, on
new car financing, but my recommendation is to plan on owning your car
at least until the loan is paid off. For example, if you finance a car for two or
three years but keep it for four or five years, you'll have several years without a car payment. This strategy builds in time to re-budget the former car
payment into saving for a down payment on the next car. By doing this,
you would grow into a more upscale car every four or five years.

Hanging on to a car that has been paid off for a year or two also provides
plenty of cash flow to help get the rest of your financial house in order.
That's why I caution against long-term car loans just to make the payment
affordable. Let's say that you buy a $15,000 car, setting a term of 72 months
to make it affordable on your budget. After three years, you get a new job
and a raise, and decide that you want a new car. On a 72-month, $15,000
loan at 7 percent (interest rates will typically be higher the longer term you
borrow for), you would still owe $9,400 on your loan. So you try to sell the
car, but all you can get for it is $8,500. You would then have to pay $900
just to trade in your old car! In other words, you would be _upside down_ on
your loan.

> Being **upside down** on a loan means that you owe more on
> the loan than what you bought is worth.

So now that you know what you can afford, let's sit down and go shopping.
That's right—sit down, because before you go anywhere else you're going
to get on the Internet and do some surfing.

The Actual Cost

The first thing you need to do is get a realistic grip on what a car will cost. Although a nice new car may be tempting, if you think you might be in over your head with it, you probably will be. Is a car worth jeopardizing the rest of your lifestyle? You need to realize that cars are not assets—they are major expenses. So your goal here should be how you can manage to get around while spending as little as possible. To get an idea of some of the other things you need to consider, let's take a look at a car's real cost.

In the following tables I calculated the monthly payment for our $12,777 automobile purchase, based on three different interest rates. Table 3.1 shows a good rate for someone with good credit; Table 3.2 represents a decent credit score, but definitely one with a few "issues"; and Table 3.3 shows a representative rate for poor credit.

Table 3.1: The total loan and interest payment that someone with good credit would pay for a $12,777 car.	
Purchase Price	$12,777
Down Payment	
Term of Loan in Years	5
Annual Interest Rate	6.50%
Monthly Payment	$250
Total Loan Amount	$12,777
Total Loan Payment	$15,000
Total Interest	**$2,223**

Table 3.2: The total loan and interest payment that someone with fair credit would pay for a $12,777 car.	
Purchase Price	$12,777
Down Payment	
Term of Loan in Years	5
Annual Interest Rate	9.00%
Monthly Payment	$265
Total Loan Amount	$12,777
Total Loan Payment	$15,914
Total Interest	**$3,137**

Table 3.3: The total loan and interest payment that someone with poor credit would pay for a $12,777 car.	
Purchase Price	$12,777
Down Payment	
Term of Loan in Years	5
Annual Interest Rate	14.00%
Monthly Payment	$297
Total Loan Amount	$12,777
Total Loan Payment	$17,838
Total Interest	**$5,061**

Table 3.1 and Table 3.2 don't show a huge difference in monthly payment. But that $15 a month adds up to more than $900 in payments over the life of the loan. If you walked into a car showroom and picked out a car with a sticker price of $12,000, would you offer the dealer $12,900? Of course not! So if you wouldn't pay the car dealer an extra $900 for the car, don't pay it to the bank.

In Table 3.3, an example of an interest rate and payment for someone with poor credit, the monthly payment jumps pretty significantly, up to $297.00. Total interest costs are more than twice that of a borrower with good credit. With nearly $50 extra a month going out the door for the exact same car, you can see why it is so hard to recover once you let your credit score get too low. If you stay within your initial $250-a-month budget with this interest rate, you have pretty much priced yourself out of any new car on the market today. (This rate would probably not reflect a bankruptcy or collection, but you would have to have a lot of maxed-out credit cards and numerous late payments that were at least 30 and maybe 60 days late to come up with a credit score like this one.)

By knowing your credit score in advance, you can call around to local banks and credit unions to find out exactly what your rate will be. This will allow you to calculate how much car you can buy based on the best interest rate you can find. Even if you have a low credit score (maybe *especially* if you have a low credit score), be sure to shop around. Car loans are treated a little differently by some lenders because typically these are the last loans that someone will default on. We need a car to get around, to get to work, and even to move our stuff out if we lose our lease. Knowing this, some lenders will offer pretty good rates on a car loan even to a borrower with a low credit score. This is why you need to know your FICO score and have a general idea of the interest rate you will qualify for. This information will prove to be invaluable later on in the buying process.

The New vs. Used Decision

Now that you know what you can afford, let's find out what you can buy and whether it should be new or used. Looking at cars.com for a point of reference, I found both a new 2007 Saturn Ion and a 2003 Pontiac Grand Am with 36,000 miles, which is about average for a three-year-old car, for about $12,200. Of course, it's also possible to go for an even older vehicle, but a more upscale model, for the same price.

Like so many financial decisions, it depends on where you fall in terms of your finances. Here are a couple of examples. In Table 3.4, I've listed three different cars from different manufacturers and in different price ranges. Using various Internet sources, I've listed a 2006 price for a new car and averaged a couple of prices to come up with used car prices for a 2003 and a 2001 model. (Prices vary dramatically around the country, so this information is *not* a substitute for doing your own research. It is essential to find out actual car costs in your area.) To me, buying a car means always looking for the value.

		Value	
Year	**2006**	**2003**	**2001**
Honda Civic	$15,900	$11,150	$7,000
Mitsubishi Eclipse	$27,000	$15,900	$11,000
Saab Convertible SE	$47,000	$22,000	$17,000

Table 3.4: Depreciation Comparison.

In this table, we can see that the Honda Civic loses about 30 percent of its value over the first three years and 37 percent in the next two years. By comparison, the Mitsubishi loses 41 percent of its value in the first three years and 31 percent over the next two. The Saab loses 53 percent and 23 percent, respectively. Based on these numbers, you would be better off buying a new Honda Civic, because it actually loses less per year in the first three years than it does the next two. In other words, it holds its value very well. Compare that to the Saab. The new Saab owner loses over half the value of the vehicle over the first three years, but it *depreciates* even less then the Honda over the next two. So in this case, a buyer of the Saab would be better off buying a used Saab, letting the original owner eat the heavy depreciation over the first three years.

> ## Unsolicited Advice
>
> I'd recommend being cautious with cars with over 50,000 or 60,000 miles. That used BMW or Volvo may seem like a good deal, but remember that cars often start to break when they go over 50,000 miles. Remember that one key to budgeting is to not have budget "surprises," like car repairs, that end up on a credit card. So if you do opt for an older used car or one that has high mileage, have a mechanic look it over.

The Actual Value

Look at it this way. If you were to finance a new Saab convertible that costs $47,000 for five years, your payment would be $920 a month (that's more than some mortgage payments!), and over 36 months your total payments would be $33,120. The car is now worth $22,000, based on current prices for a three-year-old Saab convertible. But you still owe $20,664, for net equity, or net value of $1,334. So it would cost you $33,120 to have an asset that is worth $1,334! You shouldn't need me to tell you that's not a very good investment.

> When a car loses value, it is said to **depreciate.** By contrast, items that increase in value or worth are said to appreciate.
>
> **Net equity** means the total asset minus the total liability, or the amount the car is worth minus the amount you still owe on your loan. This can sometimes be a negative number, so be careful to consider your payments and the depreciation value of the car!

On the other hand, if you were to buy the 2003 Saab, you'd have a monthly payment of $430 a month, still owe $14,045 at the end of two years, and have a car that's worth $17,000. So you would have paid $5,160 (24 payments × $430) to have an asset worth $2,955 ($17,000 value – $14,104 loan balance) still owed. So which would you rather do, pay $33,120 to have $1,334 or $5,160 to have $2,955? That's a pretty obvious financial decision. And if the body style hasn't changed, no one will even know whether your "new" car is really new, or just new to you

In general the numbers in these examples will be consistent among brands. Lower-priced cars will hold their value better than high-priced luxury brands. So if your option is to buy a new $22,000 car or a three-year-old Saab, the Saab is a great deal. If you're patient and have an idea of what you want, you can usually find a good deal on a recent model used car with low mileage.

More Research

Don't get up from the computer yet. You're not just doing research for price and cost; you're looking to find out how likely you will be to be happy with your purchase. You're going to spend a lot of hard-earned money on your car (remember the fridge list!), and you're also going to spend a lot of time driving it.

So if you go for a model that has been out on the market for at least three years, you can Google the car (www.google.com) to see if there's a consumer website or blog dedicated to that vehicle somewhere out there. These websites are good ways to find out if other buyers were happy with this car two or three years after purchase. Some websites also list any repair surprises that are associated with a particular make and model.

Another great site to check out is www.kbb.com. This is the website for the Kelley Blue Book, which is one of the original and most respected resources for auto pricing. For any used cars on your list, you can use Kelley Blue Book to get a price that a "typical" car of the same make, model, and year should sell for in your area. For new cars, kbb.com will give you the retail price and dealer's price for that make and model. You can then expect to pay something in that range for the vehicle.

> Car dealers love to sell used cars because they don't have an official sticker price. If you go to a dealer already knowing what you should pay for the used car on their lot, you'll come out on top.

A Note on Used Cars

Some people will tell you not to buy a used car because "you don't want to buy someone else's problems." This is a great testament to the perception of the U.S. auto market. Back in the 1970s the auto manufacturers adopted a great manufacturing concept called _planned obsolescence_.

> **Planned obsolescence** is a manufacturing technique that came about with the advent of mass production. The technique involves manufacturing products, or parts of products, to become obsolete or nonfunctional in a certain period of time. The idea is to force consumers to make new purchases as their existing product wears out.

As I remember it, in the 1970s a legal hurdle was cleared that allowed the auto manufacturers to own their own replacement-part supply companies. This led to the wholesale adoption of planned obsolescence in the auto parts industry, and forced consumers to continually buy new parts to keep their cars going, which in turn kept a constant flow of cash going to the auto manufacturers through their parts companies. When the car owners finally got sick and tired of repairing their cars, or the cars just rusted out from underneath them, the owners would eventually acquiesce and buy new ones.

Think of it this way—today's computer printer manufacturers practically give away printers so that they can capture the recurring revenue that comes from purchases of new ink cartridges. Lots of frequent small purchases for ink provide more consistent revenue than the purchase of a new printer every two or three years. Similarly, automakers were just trying to capture a revenue stream in between the time that a consumer purchased a car and the subsequent purchase.

This idea of manufacturing cars just to break is what contributed to the American car as being seen as, well, a piece of junk. And it may well have been, but the point is that it was intentionally manufactured to be a piece of junk. Manufacturers of Japanese cars, on the other hand, proved that people would pour more money into vehicles made by a manufacturer with a reputation for making a quality reliable car over one that had a reputation for constantly breaking down. The end result was exactly what it should have been from a little friendly capitalistic competition: the Japanese manufacturers made larger, more luxurious cars that

Americans actually liked, and the American manufacturers started making cars that didn't fall apart as soon as you drove off the lot. According to consumeraffairs.com, General Motors actually topped a quality survey conducted by Strategic Vision Inc., a San Diego-based marketing research firm, in 2005.

Not all repairs are due to planned obsolescence; there are parts that do wear out as part of normal operation. Tires and brakes, for example, will need to be replaced within the first 50,000 miles. As you approach the 100,000-mile mark you may start seeing major repairs for things like transmission, clutch (if manual transmission), and suspension.

The result of this quality push is that buying a used car is not the dicey proposition that it once was. While a decade or two ago 100,000 miles was a milestone for a car, today's cars should be very serviceable way beyond that mark. However, the 100,000 mile mark is still a mental top for many buyers, and almost any model will only sell for a nominal value as the mileage approaches 100,000. So if you're looking at a car with, say, 60,000 miles and hope to be able to sell it and step up in three years, make sure that you are buying it cheap enough now to justify having very little trade-in value in three years.

Unsolicited Advice

With today's cars not being exactly home-mechanic friendly, it doesn't make sense to save on the price of a car just to "buy" repair bills. Make sure that you carefully consider the condition, age, and mileage of the car in addition to the make, model, and color!

Review of Points to Consider

It's almost time to head out to the car lot, but before you do, take a look at this list. If you've considered each of these points, you're ready to go.

Make sure that you've come up with a reasonable monthly payment. Use the budget on your fridge list; don't stretch to get into a slightly better or newer model—there will always be additional unplanned costs. Always.

Know your credit score.

Call around for auto loan rates. Check both your local banks and credit unions. If you're leaning toward a used car, find a lender who will give you the same interest rate for a used car as they do for new cars. Especially for a late model (more than three or four years old), you should not have to accept a higher loan interest rate.

> Get a pre-approval letter from the lender with the best rates. This is a letter that states that the lender will lend you money, up to a limit, to buy a car. Typically, a pre-approval letter will be provided only for a new car, on the assumption that you know better than to pay more than the sticker price for it. For a used car, they may not be willing to actually give you a letter until they know what you're buying. That way they know they're not financing a car for more than it is worth.

Make a list of new and used cars in your price range. Check listings in the newspaper and on the Internet. A sweet spot in used car buying is the three- and four-year range. Usually, there is a good supply of vehicles in this range being turned in from leases, and leased cars often have low mileage.

Do your research. Use Kelley Blue Book online, Google, and other sources to research the value of the cars on your list, as well as to check into the satisfaction of previous owners, if this information is available.

Look up prices online. Compare older models of the same makes and models you are considering to get a feel for which models will hold their value best. The easiest way to step up to a nicer car is to have substantial value remaining in your car at trade-in time, and use that value as a down payment.

Call your insurance agent. Make sure you find out how much the different cars on your list will cost to insure.

Check the gas mileage and estimate fuel costs for the car based on your monthly driving. Your current driving costs could change if you're stepping up to a bigger car, so do a little research to estimate out how much your monthly gas costs will be with the new car.

Don't forget the trade. If you're trading in your car, look up its value as well, so you know what to expect when the dealer gives you an offer. Use the "good" condition price even if you think it's in excellent shape—used cars never look as good to anyone else as they do to the owner!

Unsolicited Advice

If you're a male, under 29, and single, you're in the highest risk category for insurance companies. If you have your heart set on a new sports car, your insurance company will see it not a matter of *if* you will have an accident, but *when*—and your premiums, or insurance payments, will reflect the higher risk. (Your premium represents the anticipated damage to the other vehicle, in addition to repairs to your vehicle.) The least expensive car for someone in this demographic, insurance-wise, is an older-model sedan.

Often-Overlooked Expenses

Remember to budget in all the costs of car ownership. It's important that in addition to the payment, you figure in your insurance premium, gas, and maintenance. When you did your research, you should have weighed the insurance increase on a new car, the anticipated maintenance cost, any known maintenance issues reported by previous owners of the same make and model car, and the average gas mileage. If any of these expenses seem trivial, think again! These seemingly small increases can add up when you least expect it and bust that budget you've been working so hard to maintain.

Okay, by now you should have a pretty good idea of what you'd like to buy. Grab your list of new and used cars that fit your budget and lifestyle, and head for the door!

Off to the Dealer

I know that for a used car you obviously don't have to go to a car lot. But my experience has been that individuals who are selling a car themselves are doing so because they owe more money than the dealer will give them on a trade-in. This means that you're really not going to get such a good deal anyway.

I also appreciate the fact that time is money. After spending so much time doing research, you don't need to be running all over town checking out used cars from the classified ads. So when looking for a car, go where the cars are!

If this is one of your first car purchases, take a little time and do it right. Test-drive as many cars as you can, and compare features and comfort as well as looks. I always suggest shopping with a friend or spouse, just to have some support if your emotions start getting the best of you and you start wandering out of your budget range.

On the other hand, this may be an easy thing for you, because by going through the steps listed previously you should know exactly what you want and what you should pay for it. With this knowledge, you should be able to buy a car quickly and at the right price. But you might just want to bring someone else along because, well … this is the fun part!

The Moment of Truth: Making the Offer

Other than Saturn dealerships, which have fixed pricing for their vehicles, car buying is almost always a haggling process. Even at Saturn, if you have a trade-in it may be in your best interest to shop at a couple different dealers to see which will give you the highest value for your car.

There's really no way to go through a buying checklist at this point. There will be so much variance based on whether you have a trade-in or not, whether you're buying new or used, and whether the car you decide on was even on your original list or not. If you're looking at a new car, that's not a huge problem since the price is clearly marked on the window sticker. (Not that you want to pay full sticker price for the car, but it will serve to tell you if the car you're looking at is in the right price range or not.) If you find a used car that you really want I would strongly suggest going home and doing you research before making an offer. Remember, your goal is to buy the car for the lowest price, but their job is to get the most from you that they can.

Tricks of the Trade

Below are a few of the "tricks of the trade" that should act as warning signs that the salesperson is trying to take advantage of you. You're making a major purchase here—you deserve to be treated with respect. And knowing the following information is a great way to ensure that you get it.

The switch. If you've done your homework and know that you can afford a particular vehicle but the salesperson keeps trying to push you into buying a different one, it's probably because he or she can make more money if you switch. Don't listen; remember that you have made an informed decision ahead of time.

Sexist or condescending talk. The car business is notorious for this type of thing. If the salesperson is talking down to you, or better yet, if you're buying the car but the salesperson directs the conversation to your spouse or the friend you brought along, you can do one of two things: go somewhere else, or make it a point to negotiate the car down to the lowest price possible!

Appraisal issues. If you're trading in a car and after the sales manager drives it for an appraisal he or she comes back commenting on something wrong with it that you know to be untrue, then you are just being set up for a low offer on your trade. Stand your ground.

Dealer add-ons. Dealers will still try to sell things like rust-proofing, paint protection, and upholstery stain protection to an unsuspecting buyer. These services have huge markups and really aren't necessary. You can always buy a can of upholstery protectant for 10 bucks, and spray it on yourself. Don't fall for it.

Extended warranties. Extended warranties are often expensive, and usually not worth it. And if you are buying a new (or newer used) car, it will probably still be covered by the manufacturer's warranty. That's all you'll need.

Unfortunately, I've either experienced these tactics myself or know someone who has. That said, I've also had some very pleasant experiences with straightforward salespeople, and have really enjoyed buying a couple of my cars. The best thing to do is be informed and give the salesperson the opportunity to respond appropriately. And if the salesperson does, make it a point to recommend him or her to others.

Auto Finance 101

At this point you should have an agreed-upon price for the car that is about to be yours. But understand that this is not the time to let your guard down! With so much auto pricing information available on the Internet, dealers count more and more on the financing to add to their profits when selling a car. Car dealers will get paid for placing loans with certain banks. They will also get paid more the higher the interest rate is. This is why I suggested that you shop for rates before you go to the dealership.

So How Do You Do It?

After agreeing on the price, you can ask the salesperson what the monthly payment would be. If he or she comes back with a payment higher than you expected, ask for the interest rate that is being used. If it's higher than you found on your own, simply say that that is too high and if that's the best they can do you'll finance it elsewhere. If it is during a regular business day, the dealer can actually check your credit and give you an accurate rate right then and there. If it's after hours or over the weekend, just have them call you with the best deal they can come up with. Tell them that you can get your own financing, and make arrangements for when you will pick up your new car.

At this point, you have not told them that you know your credit score, nor that you have already found a better deal. Remember, they not only want to sell you the car, they want to secure the financing, too. By securing the financing at the dealership, not only do they profit, they avoid the possibility that you will back out of the deal by saying that you couldn't get a loan.

Many times if you are buying a new car, the manufacturer's own finance company will offer very good rates to help sell vehicles. Remember, your goal is simply to get the best rate possible; you don't really care who it's from. Knowing your credit score, interest rate, and payment before walking into the dealership simply prevents you from being taken advantage of. I've been told that my rate was high because I didn't qualify for the best rate. Since I already knew my score, I knew better and went elsewhere for my car and financing.

Leasing

Normally I wouldn't suggest *leasing* a car, but I think it makes sense under some circumstances. For example, if you really need a nicer car for work, you can save on cash flow by leasing. But don't give up on buying used. Remember that luxury cars will lose close to half of their value in three years. Many will be low-mileage lease returns.

> **Leasing** a car is similar to renting. You pay a fixed pay-
> ment for a fixed period of time, and at the end of the lease
> you simply turn your car back in.

The logistics of a lease are a bit complicated, and you need to understand a lease to avoid common traps. In a lease, you are basically paying for the car's depreciation over the life of the lease. So if you lease a $16,000 car, at purchase the leasing company will calculate what they anticipate the vehicle to be worth at the end of the lease. This is called a *residual value*. In the example of the $16,000 car, let's say the residual value is calculated to be $9,000. Your lease payment will then be the principal and interest on $7,000 (purchase price–residual value) over the term of the lease, plus interest on the residual value. (Remember that you pay sales tax on each payment as well!)

Leasing can make sense in several situations. Here are a few to consider.

Reasons to Lease

Think about how long you plan on owning your car. Some people take great pride in how long they can drive the same car. Others are looking for their next car as soon as they drive off the lot. As I said earlier, a great way to get ahead financially is to drive a paid-off car and use what would be the car payment to get the rest of your finances in order. However, if you know that you will always want a new car, and realistically will probably have a car payment all the time, then leasing a car makes sense.

In addition, between higher gas prices and global instability, there appears to finally be a movement toward alternative fuel vehicles and hybrid fuel vehicles. If the momentum continues in this direction, anything you buy today may become obsolete as new and better *hybrids* or *E85 fuel* become readily available. If so, you may be better off leasing today and just turning in your car at the end of the lease instead of trying to sell or trade in what has become a car running on obsolete technology.

The residual value can also affect you at both the beginning and end of a lease. If a car manufacturer is anxious to sell cars, they can make leasing very attractive by raising the residual value. Since you are only paying prin-cipal on the difference between the purchase price and the residual value, a high residual value means a lower lease payment. At the end of the lease, you have the option of buying the vehicle from the leasing company for the residual value, or just turning it in.

> A **hybrid vehicle** is technically any engine that runs on two different types of fuel. Today's hybrids are a combination of traditional gas and electricity. **E85** refers to fuel that is 85 percent ethanol (which can be produced from renewable resources, such as corn and sugar cane) and 15 percent gasoline. Today's car engines run normally on 85 percent gasoline, and need to be adapted to run on E85.

But remember, the purchase price can be negotiated. If the leasing company doesn't want to deal with reselling your car, they may be willing to sell it back to you for below market price. In this case you have a low lease payment for say four years, and at the end of four years you have the opportunity to buy it back at a good price. If they don't sell it at a price you're happy with, or you just don't want to keep the car, you can just turn it back in to the dealership or leasing company.

So How Do You Do It?

The best way to use a lease is to follow the steps earlier on buying a car. After agreeing to a purchase price, ask for a lease payment based on that price. Ask for the residual value that they are using. (Remember that this is the estimated value of what the car will be worth at the end of either a lease or purchase over the same time period.) If the difference in payments adds up to a value close to the residual value, take the lease.

Ideally you can save the difference between the lease and purchase payment so you have a down payment at the end of the lease. But if you're having a hard time making ends meet, or have high balances on your credit cards, you'll be better off using the savings to accelerate your debt payments.

Lease Drawbacks

Unfortunately, as they say, nothing that is worthwhile in life is easy. And buying a car certainly falls in that category. So, in the interest of equal time, here are a few drawbacks, or things to watch out for when leasing.

Make the comparison. Always compare a purchase payment to the lease payment for the same time period, especially if the manufacturers are offering special financing. A "0 percent" purchase loan may offer a payment that isn't too different from a lease payment at a normal, or what we call "market," interest rate.

Read the fine print. Advertised lease rates will be based on a mileage limit during the term of the lease. The lower the miles, the lower the lease payment. To get buyers in the door, many times dealers will advertise very low payments with a low mileage limit, such as 10,000 miles per year. The average car is driven between 12,000 and 15,000 miles per year. If you're thinking of leasing, get a realistic estimate of your annual mileage beforehand. Typically, you will be penalized $.15 a mile for every mile over the preset limit. So if you average 12,000 miles a year on a four-year lease based on 10,000 miles, you'll owe your car plus $1,200 at the end of the lease.

Read the fine print *again*. Leases are often advertised based on a dollar amount due at signing. You may have been planning on putting a down payment on your purchase anyway, so this might not look so bad. But do the math. A $3,600 down payment for a three-year lease is the equivalent of adding $100 a month to the payment.

Don't pay more. Since in a lease you are paying interest only on a portion of the value of the car, the loan amortizes, or is paid down, slowly. And since a new car loses its value quickly in the first few years, it is likely that up until the very end of your lease you will actually owe more money than you car is worth. This can make it very expensive if you want to trade out of your car before the end of the lease.

Cars really are a unique American experience. They have come to symbolize not only the person, but the American Dream as well. Don't let your dream become a nightmare by letting a poorly planned purchase ruin the rest of your lifestyle. Budget, decide, and stick to it! This way you can ensure that you're always driving your new vehicle with a smile on your face.

The Bottom Line

▫ Your car shopping should begin where you start all purchases—with your budget.

▫ The auto industry appeals to our emotions to sell their cars. To get the best deal, leave your emotions at home.

▫ The whole process can be complicated, but by following the right steps and doing a little homework, you can find the right car for you, and stay within your budget.

▫ There's no mystery to the lease or buy question. Once you understand the ups and downs of both purchase options, you can drive your new car off the lot with confidence.

Gimme Shelter

What You Will Learn

- How to make an educated decision on where to live

- The pros and cons of living at home or with friends

- The pros and cons of renting

- The pros and cons of home ownership

- How to choose the situation that makes the best financial sense for you

For most of us, making a decision on where to live is as much about lifestyle as it is about finances. It's always been common to want to live near work, family, or social destinations. But more and more, where we live has become a significant factor affecting our finances.

According to 2005 U.S. census data reported in *USA Today*, 35 percent of homeowners and 46 percent of renters are spending 30 percent or more of their monthly income on housing. For those making less than $20,000 a year, 95 percent of homeowners spend more than 30 percent of their income on housing. For reference, mortgage lenders have historically considered the 30 percent mark as the maximum affordable percentage of income that should be put toward a mortgage when approving an application. Yet despite the cost, property ownership—specifically home ownership—is consistently linked to the ability to create wealth.

So how do you decide what to do? The first step is to differentiate between two concepts in finance: cash flow versus balance sheet. In business, especially a new business, cash flow is king—you can't create assets without cash flow. So although there is little doubt about the long-term advantages of home ownership (an asset), the question du jour is one of cash flow creation, not necessarily wealth creation. And while a home is an asset, it is also an expense.

> **Cash flow** is the ability to generate income after all expenses have been paid.
>
> A **balance sheet**, also called a statement of financial condition, is a document that shows a company's financial situation (assets minus liabilities).

Failure to Launch

In the movie *Failure to Launch*, a 30-something slacker, Tripp (played by Matthew McConaughey), chooses to live with his parents, where he has a nice, big house, a doting mother (Kathy Bates) who cooks him pancakes for breakfast and does his laundry, and very little financial responsibility. Tripp's lack of expenses allows for a great lifestyle highlighted by a very nice set of wheels. Despite Tripp's complacency, however, Bates and her husband (Terry Bradshaw) launch a plan to "encourage" him to finally move out on his own.

With nationwide rents averaging from $479 in North Dakota to more than $1,000 a month in major urban centers and mortgage payments averaging even higher, living at home as long as possible can certainly be attractive financially. In fact, that same census report shows that a growing number of people (more than 25 percent) in their 20s and 30s have "failed to launch," instead opting to live at home with their parents. The problem begins when that extra money is put toward financing a "fun" lifestyle, rather than paying off debt and saving for the future.

Consider an average rent cost of $700 a month and apply it to our budget from Chapter 1 (Table 4.1). If that $700 were applied to debt payments, $20,000 of student loans and $10,000 of credit cards could be wiped out in about three years. Once those debts have been eliminated, the additional cash flow could then be used to start accumulating a down payment for your first home (based on a typical "starter" home cost of approximately $100,000). In addition, you could also start saving for all the extras that go with home ownership—but more on that later.

Making Your Wealth Take Off

Let's take a look. In Table 4.1, the $700 rent cost we used in our Chapter 1 & 2 budgets was used along with $400 of the savings from living at home to accelerate payments on charge cards and student loans. For the student loan, an extra $250 was applied, which shortened the payoff time from 120 months to 48. The credit cards went from a 7-year payoff to a mere 37 months.

Table 4.1: Debt Acceleration.			
Total Saved in Housing Costs: $700			
Student Loans		**Loan Summary**	
Loan Amount	$20,000	Scheduled payment	$232.22
Annual interest rate	0.07%	Scheduled number of payments	120
Loan period in years	10	Actual number of payments	48
Number of payments per year	12	Total early payments	$11,816.51
Optional extra payments	250	Total interest	$2,964.66

continues...

(Table 4.1 continued)

Credit Cards		Loan Summary	
Loan Amount	$10,000	Scheduled payment	$198.62
Annual interest rate	0.16%	Scheduled number of payments	84
Loan period in years	7	Actual number of payments	37
Number of payments per year	12	Total early payments	$5,400.00
Optional extra payments	150	Total interest	$2,687.31

At the same time, the remainder of the $700, or $300, was put into an account that pays an interest rate of 5 percent. When the credit cards were paid off, the extra $150 per month was added to the regular payment in Table 4.1. At the end of 48 months, another $250 was added as well. The results are in Table 4.2.

Table 4.2: Savings fund balance, months 1 to 72.

Month	Contri- bution	Monthly rate 0.42%	Balance	Month	Contri- bution	Monthly rate 0.42%	Balance
1	$350.00	$1.46	$351.46	19	$350.00	$28.77	$6,934.13
2	$350.00	$2.92	$714.38	20	$350.00	$30.35	$7,314.49
3	$350.00	$4.39	$1,058.77	21	$350.00	$31.94	$7,696.42
4	$350.00	$5.87	$1,414.64	22	$350.00	$33.53	$8,079.95
5	$350.00	$7.35	$1,772.00	23	$350.00	$35.12	$8,465.07
6	$350.00	$8.84	$2,130.84	**24**	**$350.00**	**$36.73**	**$8,851.80**
7	$350.00	$10.34	$2,491.18	25	$350.00	$38.34	$9,240.14
8	$350.00	$11.84	$2,853.01	26	$350.00	$39.96	$9,630.10
9	$350.00	$13.35	$3,216.36	27	$350.00	$41.58	$10,021.69
10	$350.00	$14.86	$3,581.22	28	$350.00	$43.22	$10,414.90
11	$350.00	$16.38	$3,947.60	29	$350.00	$44.85	$10,809.75
12	**$350.00**	**$17.91**	**$4,315.51**	30	$350.00	$46.50	$11,206.25
13	$350.00	$19.44	$4,684.95	31	$350.00	$48.15	$11,604.40
14	$350.00	$20.98	$5,055.92	32	$350.00	$49.81	$12,004.21
15	$350.00	$22.52	$5,428.45	33	$350.00	$51.48	$12,405.69
16	$350.00	$24.08	$5,802.53	34	$350.00	$53.15	$12,808.84
17	$350.00	$25.64	$6,178.16	35	$350.00	$54.83	$13,213.67
18	$350.00	$27.20	$6,555.36	**36**	**$350.00**	**$56.52**	**$13,620.18**

Month	Contri-bution	Monthly rate 0.42%	Balance	Month	Contri-bution	Monthly rate 0.42%	Balance
37	$350.00	$58.21	$14,028.39	55	$700.00	$105.09	$25,326.36
38	$450.00	$60.33	$14,538.72	56	$700.00	$108.44	$26,134.80
39	$450.00	$62.45	$15,051.17	57	$700.00	$111.81	$26,946.61
40	$450.00	$64.59	$15,565.76	58	$700.00	$115.19	$27,761.81
41	$450.00	$66.73	$16,082.49	59	$700.00	$118.59	$28,580.40
42	$450.00	$68.89	$16,601.38	**60**	**$700.00**	**$122.00**	**$29,402.40**
43	$450.00	$71.05	$17,122.42	61	$700.00	$125.43	$30,227.83
44	$450.00	$73.22	$17,645.64	62	$700.00	$128.87	$31,056.69
45	$450.00	$75.40	$18,171.04	63	$700.00	$132.32	$31,889.01
46	$450.00	$77.59	$18,698.63	64	$700.00	$135.79	$32,724.80
47	$450.00	$79.79	$19,228.42	65	$700.00	$139.27	$33,564.07
48	**$450.00**	**$81.99**	**$19,760.41**	66	$700.00	$142.77	$34,406.84
49	$700.00	$85.25	$20,545.66	67	$700.00	$146.28	$35,253.12
50	$700.00	$88.52	$21,334.18	68	$700.00	$149.80	$36,102.92
51	$700.00	$91.81	$22,125.99	69	$700.00	$153.35	$36,956.27
52	$700.00	$95.11	$22,921.10	70	$700.00	$156.90	$37,813.17
53	$700.00	$98.42	$23,719.52	71	$700.00	$160.47	$38,673.64
54	$700.00	$101.75	$24,521.27	**72**	**$700.00**	**$164.06**	**$39,537.70**

In this case, the entire monthly schedule for six years was included. Although six years is a long time to "fail to launch," the savings are significant. But the same concept can be applied to savings from sharing an apartment with roommates, so if you can't commit to living at home that long, consider sharing an apartment with a friend.

Note that in 36 months, most of the debt is eliminated, and there is now $13,620 in the savings account! That $13,620 is enough for a 10 percent down payment on a $130,000 starter home. So there is no question that you can make a great start on your financial future by living with others—as long as you choose to use your savings wisely.

One caveat that I feel I must add, however, is that this is your parents' time to pack away some bucks and get their retirement on track. On average we Boomers, your parents, have done a horrible job of preparing for retirement—and our time is running out. According to a recent Fidelity survey, American workers are on track to replace approximately 57 percent of their income at retirement. In the glass-half-empty way of viewing the scenario, the average household will take more than a 40 percent pay cut in retirement.

Table 4.3 shows what it would take, at age 50, to save an extra $500,000 for retirement by age 65. (And that's not a lot. Most planners would calculate that $500,000 would generate only about $20,000 of annual income.)

Table 4.3: Retirement Savings at Age 50.					
Age	**Investment Year**	**Beginning Balance**	**Annual Contribution**	**10% Return**	**Year-End Balance**
50	1	$0	$14,355	$1,436	$15,791
51	2	$15,791	$14,355	$3,015	$33,161
52	3	$33,161	$14,355	$4,752	$52,268
53	4	$52,268	$14,355	$6,662	$73,286
54	5	$73,286	$14,355	$8,764	$96,406
55	6	$96,406	$14,355	$11,076	$121,837
56	7	$121,837	$14,355	$13,619	$149,812
57	8	$149.812	$14,355	$16,417	$180,584
58	9	$180.584	$14,355	$19,494	$214,433
59	10	$214.433	$14,355	$22,879	$251,668
60	11	$251,668	$14,355	$26,602	$292,626
61	12	$292,626	$14,355	$30,698	$337,679
62	13	$337,679	$14,355	$35,203	$387,238
63	14	$387,238	$14,355	$40,159	$441,753
64	15	$441,753	$14,355	$45,611	$501,719

I've seen plenty of cases where retirements are put on hold while parents are supporting adult live-in children. If you have moved back or are considering moving back in with the parents, be sure to have a frank financial discussion with them. Parents aren't likely to volunteer that they may not be adequately prepared for their own financial future, so you may have to think ahead.

Whatever you decide to do, remember that time is on your side. You have plenty of time to accumulate wealth and save for your future. Your parents may not be so lucky. If that's the case, you might want to consider one of these other options …

Renting

"Don't throw your money away on rent."

"Why rent when you can own?"

It seems as though the advice is stacked to one side: the side of home ownership. Well, not here! Remember that your early years are all about flexibility and cash flow—neither of which is consistent with buying a home. Let's look at a few things that renting has on its side, for a change.

- **Location.** Rental properties can be anywhere, not just in the best or worst neighborhoods. You may find that housing in your ideal neighborhood is more affordable if you rent.

- **Flexibility.** With the average worker changing jobs three to five times by age 30 and with relationships coming and going, isn't it best to be able to pick up and relocate without the hassle and risk of having a home to sell?

> **Unsolicited Advice**
>
> One solution may be to pay rent to your parents, whether they let you or not. If they insist on letting you stay rent-free, suggest paying them anyway—but ask that they save or invest the "rent" money on your behalf. They probably have more investment experience than you do, and they may even be working with a financial advisor already who can help make the most of your "rent."

- **Affordability.** Rent costs are fairly fixed. You don't have to worry about plumbing issues, a new roof, storm damage, new appliances, a new water heater …

Benefits of Renting

If you look at the rent versus buy argument from a cash flow standpoint, you'll see that it leans pretty heavily toward the rent option. But what about all the equity that you could be building up if you bought a house? Let's look at the numbers.

Let's say that you buy a house for $150,000 with 10 percent (or $15,000) down. At the end of the first year, assuming a 3.5 percent appreciation rate, your home is now worth $154,500—a gain of $5,250. A $5,250 gain on a $15,000 investment (your down payment) looks pretty good. Or does it? The costs don't stop after your down payment! Let's look at what happens when we add in the other cash flow costs: mortgage payment, insurance costs, taxes, and those inevitable upkeep costs (Table 4.4).

Table 4.4: An example of the return on a $15,000 down payment over the first year of home ownership.

Home Ownership Costs—First Year	
Enter values	
Loan amount	$135,000.00
Annual interest rate	0.066%
Loan period in years	30
Scheduled number of payments	360
Annual Costs	
Scheduled payment	$10,346.27
Insurance and PMI	$1,440.00
Taxes	$1,800.00
First year fix-up costs	$3,000.00
Down payment	$15,000.00
Total first year cost	$31,586.27
Home appreciation at 3%	$4,050.00
Gain on investment	12.82%

Home ownership doesn't look so good from a short-term standpoint, does it? Now, let's take a look at this same situation over a five-year period, again adding in cash flow costs.

Under the "Buy" side in Table 4.5, I've appreciated the property at 3.5 percent a year. The result is a net equity figure that comes from subtracting the mortgage balance (a 30-year mortgage at 6.6 percent) from the appreciated value, ending with a net equity of $51,633.72. On the cost side, by adding up five years of mortgage payments, taxes, insurance, "fix-up" costs, and the original down payment, I end up with $82,931.35 of investment costs. This leaves our home buyer soundly in the hole after five years of home ownership. By comparison, our renter comes out in pretty good shape.

Table 4.5: A five-year snapshot of buying a home vs. renting.

Home Ownership		Renting	
Mortgage Balance	$126,519.22	Rent ($850/mo.)	$51,000.00
Home Value Appreciation at 3.5%	$178,152.95	Investment Balance $500/mo. + $15,000 down payment at 8%	$60,055.50
Net equity	$51,633.35		
Five year cost (mortgage, taxes, and insurance)	$67,931.35		
Down payment	$15,000.00		
Total five year investment	$82,931.35		
Net Gain	($31,297.63)	Net Gain	$9,055.50

Assuming that in a community where a starter home runs about $150,000, a decent apartment can be rented for $800 a month (plus $50 for renter's insurance—more on that later), our renter has total costs of $51,000. If she were to astutely invest the difference between her rent and what would be her housing costs along with the $15,000 she didn't use as a down payment, she would have $60,055.50 in investments, for a net gain of $9,050.55.

Obviously, the rent-vs.-buy comparison will vary dramatically from city to city. And although $800 a month may be a reasonable monthly rental cost for an apartment, you may not be getting the same amount of square footage as you'd likely get from a $150,000 home. If your rent would equal your total housing cost, then the equation swings solidly to owning. On its own, the $15,000 used for the down payment would only grow to about $22,000 at an 8 percent return, without adding additional monthly investments. In this case your _breakeven rent_ would be about $1,100 a month. So if you can rent for less than $1,100, it makes more sense to rent; if the rent is over $1,100 a month, buying makes more sense.

> Your **breakeven rent** is the point where renting and buying are about equal over five years, from a cash flow point of view.

There are many calculators on the web that compare renting versus buying. However, the ones I found are provided by mortgage lenders and skew the calculation to buying. They don't suggest including an amount for higher monthly costs of home ownership, like utilities, or the up-front opportunity cost of tying up your funds in a down payment. And they exclude things like the higher cost of more household goods, furniture, lawn equipment, and utilities that typically come with home ownership. At a minimum, to get an accurate comparison, also use an investment calculator like the one at www.swlearning.com/finance/investment_calculator/starthere.htm. Click on <financial calculator> and then <basic future value>. Here you can input your down payment and other financing costs and an interest rate. The calculator will then tell you what your money will be worth at some date in the future that you choose.

With the current problems in the mortgage industry over defaults, getting a low-down-payment mortgage is becoming more difficult. The higher the down payment you are required to make, the more important it is to factor in the opportunity cost of what your down payment for a mortgage could grow to if you continue to rent instead.

It may not be an easy process to accurately compare the cost of renting to home ownership, but it is worth the time and effort. Remember that a home is typically the largest purchase you will make in your lifetime.

In Table 4.5, a couple thousand dollars per year was added for "home improvements." These are really the financial killers of home ownership. Too many times I see a couple put everything they have into the down payment for a house and the mortgage closing costs, and then have nothing left over. New homes come with plenty of new costs. Aside from actual home improvements such as paint, carpet, and maybe new appliances, there are all kinds of extras that go with owning a home. For example, if you're moving from a smaller apartment, there is the issue of additional furniture. If this is the first time you've had a yard, then you will need yard maintenance tools: a lawn mower, weed whacker, patio furniture, and perhaps even new landscaping. All these costs can add up. If your new house is sucking up all your cash flow and you're adding new debts (and new payments), you could find yourself in a financial hole very quickly.

Comparing the Options

So the rent-vs.-buy decision really comes down to comparing two specific options to see which one is right for you. It is much more involved than just comparing a potential mortgage payment to your current rent payment; knowing this will help you make the right decision. So, let's get specific. Using Table 4.5, plug in your numbers to analyze the true costs of renting versus owning. Make sure to account for flexibility—do not assume that a home will appreciate every year! After mortgage costs and realtor fees, a home needs to appreciate significantly to make home ownership worthwhile if you're planning to stay for only a short period of time (say, if you're thinking of buying a starter home while you wait for your dream man or woman to come along, or for your first child to make an appearance). When your cash flow is limited, take advantage of the fixed costs of renting while you continue to save for a home.

So When Do You Buy a House?

Ah, your new house, the American Dream. Just when do you take the plunge? Well, we just came up with the answer: when you can afford the house and all the expenses that come with it. So the next obvious question is this: "With all those expenses, is buying a house worth it?" Once again, the answer is, "It depends."

From an emotional standpoint, there is a lot to be said for owning (or paying the bank for) your own home. Financially, there are three things that home ownership has in its favor:

- ☐ The effect of income taxes on home ownership

- ☐ The equity that builds up in your home

- ☐ The potential to secure a home equity loan

Benefits of Owning

One of the few remaining tax deductions for us regular folk is the home interest tax deduction. I'll go into this more in Chapter 11, but for now what you need to understand is that 100 percent of the interest you pay on your mortgage is tax deductible. In the early years, the majority of your monthly mortgage payment is interest. And as time goes by, more of your payment is directed to principal.

The _equity_ that builds up in your home is the largest financial asset that you will have. While you're working you can tap the equity in your home by using a home equity loan. In this type of loan, the bank or lender will use your home as _collateral_ for the loan. In other words, if you don't make payments the lender can _foreclose_ on your home. Since most people don't want this to happen, they tend to make payments on their mortgages and home equity loans. With this added bit of security, lenders will typically offer some of their lowest lending rates on home equity loans.

> **Equity** is the difference between what your home is worth and the balance on your mortgage(s).
>
> **Collateral** is a type of property that is used to secure a loan. For example, with a car loan your car is collateral for the loan. If you don't make your car payments the lender can come and take your car away as repayment for the balance of your loan.
>
> **Foreclosure** is the process by which a lender forces the sale of property so that they can use the proceeds to repay themselves for an outstanding debt.

In addition, since a home equity loan is a form of mortgage, the interest may be tax deductible. So the combination of tax deductibility and a low interest rate makes home equity loans a very attractive way to borrow money. Home equity loans can be used for anything; typically, after running up other debts, consumers will consolidate or pay them off with a low-interest, tax-deductible home equity loan. This is one advantage of home ownership that can save thousands of dollars in interest payments over a working career.

Using equity in one's home and converting it to cash via a home equity loan has become so popular that this process has added nearly 1 percent to the annual economic growth for the United States over the last two or three years. As home values have increased, Americans have used this equity to buy, buy, and buy some more.

Home ownership is one of the few times that most everyone agrees that it is okay to borrow for. In fact, I'll go so far as to say that it is silly not to. Remember that the only good borrowing is borrowing to acquire an asset. And a home is an asset. But whenever I read articles on this subject, it seems to me that most advisors miss that point. Some will recommend a short-term mortgage, say 15 or 20 years, for a savings on interest payments. A new guy on one of my satellite radio stations recommends being completely debt-free, which means having no mortgage payments. And an old planning concept has always been to be mortgage-free at retirement.

But consider our discussion in the Introduction (you did read the Introduction, right?) on inflation. A basic assumption I will make is that inflation is endemic to our economic system. Considering that the Federal Reserve's main responsibility is to protect the purchasing power of U.S. currency, yet in the past 30 years the value of a dollar has dropped by nearly 75 percent, I see very little hope that they will do a better job in the future. Even though we're facing strong deflationary global forces (low foreign wages), we have still managed to average a 2- to 3-percent or better inflation number for the past decade. So how do we apply this to a mortgage? It's very simple: we borrow for as long as we can. Let's look at Table 4.6.

Table 4.6: Mortgage payment in real dollars over 30 years.

Age	Mortgage Year	Monthly Payment Real Dollars	Age	Mortgage Year	Monthly Payment Real Dollars
25	1	$1,000	40	16	$586
26	2	$965	41	17	$566
27	3	$931	42	18	$546
28	4	$899	43	19	$527
29	5	$867	44	20	$508
30	6	$837	45	21	$490
31	7	$808	46	22	$473
32	8	$779	47	23	$457
33	9	$752	48	24	$441
34	10	$726	49	25	$425
35	11	$700	50	26	$425
36	12	$676	51	27	$410
37	13	$652	52	28	$396
38	14	$629	53	29	$369
39	15	$607	54	30	$356

Table 4.6 shows the monthly cost (payment) for a 30-year mortgage, with a nominal payment of $1,000 a month, for a 25-year-old borrower. Each year, it can be assumed that the value of that buyer's money is depreciating by 3.5 percent due to inflation. So the third column shows the real cost of his or her payment at the end of each year.

In other words, by year 15 the buyer's initial nominal $1,000 payment will be the equivalent of $607 in real dollars. By the end of 30 years, the final payment will only be worth $356 in real dollars. This is the main reason to buy, and finance, real estate. With real estate you have a powerful financial force—inflation—working for you, instead of against you. Inflation can be your friend; it will cause the value of your home to appreciate over time. And although inflation is usually your enemy because it robs you of your purchasing power, it works for you when making monthly payments over time. Inflation allows you to exchange a depreciating asset (money) for one that appreciates (real estate). By the end of 30 years, you will be paying $356 a month in 2007 dollars for a home that is worth over $450,000 in 2037 dollars. Now that's a deal.

In this example I used a 30-year amortization to emphasize the long-term effects of inflation. Later, in Chapter 6, I'll discuss different financing options, and how to choose the best one for your situation.

In all my examples I have assumed that your real estate purchase will appreciate at the same rate as inflation, which I've been assuming to be 3.5 percent a year. However, as we've seen over the last five or six years, housing prices can rise much faster than inflation. And although housing prices are currently on their way back down, I'm sure that they will level out at a point that will still show an appreciated value since the year 2000. In other words, someone who bought a home in 2000 will likely still see appreciation in their property at the end of the housing price decline. If you're one of these people, be patient—real estate prices move much slower than the stock market. A decline may take two or three years to fully run its course.

Equity as a Cash Flow Tool

Because a house will generally appreciate even under marginal economic conditions if given enough time, and equity is created by paying down principal with your mortgage payment, a home can become a significant asset fairly rapidly. However, I strongly caution you about considering your home equity as a true asset. Think of it in terms of a cash flow tool. Depending on the economy, a home equity loan can be much cheaper to borrow with than credit cards or even traditional auto loans. But as an asset, it has little value.

Think about it—you need a place to live. Too many people think that when they retire they can "downsize" their home. This assumes that a smaller home comes with a smaller price tag. The trouble is, many of the new smaller homes designed for this market cost much more per square foot than an existing larger home! I'm starting to see clients and neighbors pay more to downsize from their existing home. So when I plan finances with clients, I just assume that their house is a wash at retirement. If it appreciates more than surrounding property and allows a client to downsize for less, then the resulting gain just gives us a cushion or provides a down payment on a vacation property.

No matter what, where you choose to live is one of the most important factors in your financial life. Make sure that you consider all the options before deciding whether your best bet is to live with parents, get a place with some friends for a few years, rent an apartment while saving for a house, or buy a home. The most important point to consider is whether renting or buying makes the most financial sense for you—not what other people are doing at the time.

The Bottom Line

- Where you live has a major impact on your finances.

- When you're young, it's better to let cash flow rule your decision-making.

- When your cash flow is limited, take advantage of the fixed costs of renting while you save to buy a home.

- Home ownership comes at a price, but trading depreciating property (money) for one that appreciates (real estate) is an example of moneynomics working twice for you.

Part 2
You Finally Have Money Left Over! Now What Do You Do?

Take It to the Bank!

What You Will Learn

- The ins and outs of banking

- How to choose the right bank for you

- Why a checking account is like a gallon of milk

- Why saving is not the same as investing

Okay, so we've been through four chapters of basic money stuff, and you think you've got a handle on it, right? Well, before reading any further, please take the following quiz.

A Simple Banking Quiz

Circle only one answer for each of the following four questions. (It's okay to write in the book. Really!)

1. What should you use a bank for?

   A. Everything! They are local and the tellers are really nice and I can trust them with anything I need!
   B. As much as I can so if I really need money sometime they will be more likely to give me a loan.
   C. All my long-term saving and investing.
   D. As little as possible, unless they have the best deal.

2. How do you balance your checkbook?

   A. Why bother?
   B. I look online and if I have money I spend it.
   C. I look at my ATM receipt and if I have money I spend it.
   D. I manually track my balance by adding all deposits and subtracting all withdrawals.

3. What are the similarities between a gallon of milk and a checking account?

   A. I wouldn't know—I'm lactose intolerant.
   B. My mom says I need both, but I don't know why.
   C. Milk comes from cows and I have a leather checkbook cover.
   D. Both are priced to sucker you in so you spend more money.

4. How would you describe the interest that the bank pays you on a savings account?

   A. It's the same everywhere so I don't pay attention.
   B. Way too little because the banker is ripping me off.
   C. I don't bother with a savings account; I invest in mutual funds where I can make real money.
   D. A fair rate for a guaranteed safe and liquid account based on current economic conditions.

The correct answer to all of these questions is D. If you had trouble figuring that out or understanding why, then this chapter is for you.

Banking Industry Basics

Imagine that you're a wealthy nobleman in, say, fourteenth-century England. Police are scarce and marauding bandits are everywhere. Wouldn't you be thrilled to have a place to put your money that was safe? And wouldn't it be even better to know that you could get your money back anytime you wanted it? How much would you pay for that kind of service?

Well, it's not the fourteenth century and the streets are a bit safer, so today we take that service for granted. But basically that is what banks do—they keep your money safe and give it back to you when you want it. And sometimes they even pay you a little for holding your money, too. In today's financial world, banks are major players in the global economy. But for your purposes, banks are simply money depositories that let you get your cash back when you want it.

The other side of banking involves lending. Banks don't always pay you interest when you give them your money, but they do always charge you interest when they lend money to you. Read this last sentence again, because it explains a lot about the banking industry.

Banks make money on the difference between what they pay to hold your money and what they charge you to borrow their money. They provide different accounts for you to choose from, and offer different fees and interest rates. The important thing to remember is that there are a lot of banks (and credit unions, which we'll talk about in a minute) out there, and they all want your money so they can lend it to some other sucker and make lots of money for themselves. And whenever there is more than one player, there is the option to shop around for the best deal. So before we talk about the different types of accounts, let's talk about how to pick the right bank for you.

Banks and Credit Unions

First, you need to understand the options, their differences, and what they mean to you. Banks and community banks (formerly called savings and loan associations, or S&Ls) are structured as corporations, meaning that they issue shares of stock. Most banks' stocks are traded on one of the major stock exchanges, although some smaller community banks may still be held privately by individuals.

Credit unions offer many of the same services as banks, but they are owned by their customers, who are called "members." Savings accounts in credit unions are called "share accounts," because by having an account there you own a "share" of the credit union. Unless otherwise stated, when I refer to "banks" and "banking" from here on out, I am also including credit unions because they serve the same functions for our purposes. "Banks" and "banking" just sound better than "credit unions" and "credit unioning."

So let's understand the ground rules. Banks and credit unions offer a place for you to put your money. They are safe because your money is insured against loss by federal government agencies, either by the Federal Deposit Insurance Corporation (FDIC) for banks or the National Credit Union Administration (NCUA) for credit unions. Each insurer creates rules that the banks and credit unions must follow to be able to be insured by them.

What does this mean to you? Well, the way banks operate does not always make sense, because the regulators, not the banks, make the rules. So go back to our quiz at the start of the chapter and take a look at Question 1. Many people assume that if they do business for a long time with a certain bank, or have numerous accounts, or deal with a credit union instead of a bank, they can get a better "deal." They may think that the bank will look favorably on them when it comes time to borrow money if they do these things. Some even think that the bank will be more lenient in granting loans if their credit is "less than perfect" as long as they've been with the bank for a while or have several accounts there. Frequently, business owners will tell me that they are afraid to move away from their bank, thinking that if the business ever hits a rough patch, the bank will bail them out due to past loyalty.

Not true.

Here's the deal. Banks follow _risk-based lending_. Most important in their decision to lend or not is the customer's credit score. For some loans, such as mortgages, they will ask for more info, but all the assets and income in the world won't get you a loan if your credit score is too low—and neither will your loyalty to the bank.

> **Risk-based lending** is when a bank uses a scale that bases interest rates on customers' credit scores, and automatically denies loans for customers with scores that are too low.

The credit score scale is used so that if a bank happens to run into a larger-than-usual number of defaults, they can point to their lending criteria and show the regulators that the bad loans fell within the proper guidelines.

Why Loyalty Is Not a Factor

Back in the "good old days," you could count on your friendly credit union or local bank to bend the rules a little when they wanted to. This is probably where the idea that customer loyalty would be rewarded came from. But this doesn't happen anymore because if a loan that falls outside the bank's guidelines is approved, the bank could be found at fault by the insurance auditors or find themselves facing a discrimination lawsuit.

Let's say that you really don't qualify for a certain loan, but your bank gives it to you anyway to reward your years of loyalty. Seems like a good business practice, right? But let's say that the next guy comes in with the exact same qualifications "on paper" as you have, but they deny the loan. Suddenly, the bank has a discrimination suit on its hands. That's why banks will rarely risk "bending the rules" for anyone.

But it's not like the bank would have cut you much slack anyway. Credit unions, at least historically, have had the reputation of lending to people who needed money when they needed it. Unfortunately, in many cases credit unions have been handcuffed when making their lending decisions as well. There may actually be some smaller credit unions left that actually lend based on relationships and need, but they're few and far between.

My point in all of this is twofold. First, it is absolutely imperative that you keep a good credit score. The fact that your daddy's daddy has been doing business with a particular institution for the last 100 years will have little bearing in the loan process unless your credit score justifies the loan on its own. Second, since banks are unable to reward loyalty, you needn't offer it either. There may be exceptions with some credit unions, and as you'll see in a moment, you should always give your credit union a shot, but many times they fall under the same or similar regulations as the banks. They just say no with a smile instead of a smirk.

Choosing the Bank That's Right for You

So what are the most important things to look for in a bank? There are a few factors you should consider: the features and fees of a checking account, the convenience of the locations, and the potential cost of services. Whichever bank does the best job of satisfying these criteria will become your bank.

Interest Rates

Don't spend much time comparing interest rates. Interest rates are so low on checking accounts that even a high rate makes very little difference unless you keep a high balance. And if you have a high minimum balance, say $2,000 or more, I'll be showing you better alternatives soon anyway.

From the basic services standpoint, checking accounts are like a gallon of milk at the grocery store. Have you ever noticed that milk is all the way at the back of the grocery store, and you have to go through the snack and candy aisle to get there? The reason for such placement is that grocery stores know that people (especially those with kids) are always running by the store to "pick up a gallon of milk." So stores will typically put milk on sale, or price it so low they may actually lose money selling it to you, because they know that people (parents in particular) will shop where milk is cheap because they buy so much. And while stopping in for a gallon of milk on the way home from work, people are likely to be tempted to pick up a few other high-profit-margin items—especially those snack foods they have to pass on their way back to the milk cooler. So grocery stores make up for their lack of profit on milk by selling you other, more profitable, items once they get you in the door.

That's the similarity between a checking account and a gallon of milk. Bank marketing has shown that where you keep your checking account is very important, because that will be the bank you consider as "your bank." By keeping basic checking account fees low and appearing competitive with mostly irrelevant interest rates, banks try to get you in the door so that you will become a customer of their higher-profit-margin services.

> **If You're Still in College …**
>
> This same thinking also applies to credit cards, which is why banks target college students with those special credit card offers you see all over campus. They hope that if you use their card in college, you will become a full-service customer after you graduate. And you thought they were just being nice!

Checking Account Cost and Convenience

The main thing most people need from a bank is a checking account. A checking account meets the basic definition of a banking service. This account holds your money, and gives it back to you whenever you want. Since you will be frequently making deposits and withdrawals from your account, the first thing to look for is convenience. Checking accounts generally pay little, if any, interest, so you need to find an account that is cheap.

Getting your money into the bank is pretty straightforward; practically every employer offers direct deposit of your paycheck. This means that your "check" will simply travel electronically from your employer's checking account to your checking account. So in looking for cost and convenience, we're mainly talking about accessing your money. To do that, you should look at three things: branch and ATM locations, check writing and debit cards, and online account access and bill payment services. You'll have to decide for yourself which services you'll use most frequently, and which are the top priorities, but here's a quick breakdown for you.

Branch and ATM Locations

Even in the electronic era we usually need some cash in our pockets, and the fastest and easiest way to get cash is at the closest ATM. And although it's true that you get money from your account at any ATM, there will usually be a fee to do so unless the ATM belongs to your bank. Since credit unions are much smaller and have fewer locations, many have entered into agreements that allow you to access your account for free from any credit union's ATM. Still, you may have trouble finding an ATM at a credit union in your area. This is what swings my primary checking account decision to a bank instead of a credit union.

In my area it costs around $2.00 each time I use an ATM that is not owned by my bank. I typically use an ATM twice a week. Let's say that once a week I use an ATM that is not one of my bank's. This would amount to $104 in ATM fees per year. Now, there are a number of things I'd like to do with $104, but not one of them involves giving it to the bank for the privilege of getting my own money! Think of it like this: $104 of ATM fees would negate all the interest you would earn if you maintained an average balance of $3,400 and your bank paid a 3 percent interest rate (which would be a pretty generous rate).

I'm a big fan of online banks (not just banks with online services, but banks with no brick and mortar offices at all), because online banks often reimburse you for a certain number of ATM fees per month. But be honest with yourself as to whether you'll actually save your ATM receipts and mail them to the bank for reimbursement. As much as I like to keep my business account at an online bank, I keep my personal accounts at a local brick-and-mortar bank because they have the most convenient ATM locations.

Check Writing and Debit Card Services

If you've been good about using the fridge list—your monthly expense tracking system—then you will want to choose a bank that offers the lowest fees for check writing and debit card services. While bill paying is more efficient with online services (I'll get to that in a minute), to keep track of day-to-day purchases there is nothing better than writing a check. And some banks charge a fee if you exceed a certain number of checks written, or debit card purchases made, per month.

For the fridge list to work, it has to be as accurate and detailed as possible. The easiest way to lose track of where your money goes is to use your debit card or cash for purchases. You'll forget to write things down and end up with incorrect accounting on your fridge list. So you might want to find a bank that allows you to write an unlimited amount of checks each month with no fee.

With all checking accounts you will have to pay for new checks as you need them, but many times the bank will offer you a pretty good supply when you initially open your account. When ordering checks for your account, be sure to get the kind that come with a copy. They'll cost a little bit more but are well worth it because even if you forget to write down your purchase, the copy will provide a record of who you paid and how much. But if you can get a quick handle on your budget, and are diligent about tracking your account online, a free first box of checks can go a long way.

> Banks will generally compete for your business by advertising special offers on checking accounts. But you still need to be aware of service fees—don't get suckered in with a great introductory offer only to get stuck paying high fees for services you may need further down the road.

For the most part, costs and fees are pretty straightforward with a debit card. Most banks now provide a free debit card with free transactions and no monthly fee.

This is not to say that checking accounts can't be extremely profitable for the bank if you veer off the basic services path—or don't keep your account _balanced_.

> To avoid potential problems and fees, you must keep your account **balanced.** This means you must keep a ledger in which you record all your deposits and subtract your withdrawals so that you know how much you have in your account on a daily balance. An accurate fridge list should help with this.

Online Account Access and Bill Payment

Don't assume that in the Internet age all banks are created equal when it comes to online features, or that the bigger the bank, the more sophisticated the website. Recently I was helping a client with some tax issues and we needed to know the interest expense on several loans. For his accounts at a major regional bank, he had to call a commercial lending representative (who didn't call him back) for the information we needed because it wasn't available on his bank's website. For his personal accounts at a mid-size credit union, all the information we were looking for was right there online.

The nicest thing about online banking is that it becomes so easy to balance your accounts. You can see what checks have cleared, what withdrawals and deposits are pending, and whether the bank has made a mistake (more on this in a minute). But don't just rely on the online account summary. You should still use the ledger that comes with your checkbook to keep your own balance. Remember that the bank only records transactions that have actually cleared, so it is important to note any discrepancies. I've had checks that were apparently "lost" clear my account more than six months after I wrote them. If I relied on the online account information for my balance and had let my balance get close to zero, a check clearing my account after six months could have easily bounced.

Online bill paying becomes more important the more bills you have to pay. It probably won't take much to convince you to stop writing paper checks, buying stamps, and addressing envelopes, but you should pay attention to fees and shop for the best deal. Some banks offer these services for free; some don't. But for $6 or $7 a month, online banking may offer a level of convenience that is worth the price. Basically, you can enter the information for bills you pay on a regular basis, such as cable TV, once online. Then each month when you receive the bill, you just log in, enter the dollar amount you are paying, and click. For recurring bills that are always the same, you can even select an autopay option so the bill is paid automatically each month. Just be sure there is enough money in your account to pay your auto pay bills. If not, you'll be slapped with a non-sufficient funds (NSF) fee from your bank, and probably from your vendor as well.

Many businesses also have their own online payment options on their websites, and it's usually free for payments made in advance. It may be a bit more work to go to the different credit card websites, but it might be worth it to you to do that rather than pay bank fees.

Miscellaneous Fees

We all hate the fine print in any document. However, when shopping for a bank, I strongly recommend that you request, read, and compare all the "miscellaneous" fees that your prospective bank may charge you. Table 5.1 is a partial list of fees, prepared from information found on a great site called BankRate.com, that banks may tack on to accounts. You may be thinking that this is irrelevant because you don't need these services (and of course you plan on keeping your account balanced). The way I look at it, though, is that by comparing them you can identify the bank that is trying to rip you off the least. What you are likely to find is that the fee-friendliest bank won't be a bank, but a credit union.

Table 5.1: List of miscellaneous fees that your bank may be charging you.

Account maintenance fee	Some accounts charge a monthly fee no matter what the balance.
Account research/ Reconciliation	A per-hour fee that's charged if there's a discrepancy between your records and the bank's; often the bank will charge a minimum of one hour.
ATM/debit card replacement	You may get one new card a year for free if your bank is nice, but you'll pay for any beyond that.
Counter checks	Forget your checkbook or run out of checks? The bank may give you a few for free but charge a fee beyond that.
Credit reference	If you need to rely on the bank for a credit reference, expect to pay.
Debit card	Purchases made with a debit card are deducted from your checking account. Unfortunately, a growing number of banks are charging a fee for every purchase.
Deposited item returned (DIR)	If you deposit a check in your account and the check doesn't clear, you'll be charged a fee.
Early-withdrawal fee for CDs	Imposed when you close a CD account before maturity.
Inactive account	This monthly or quarterly charge is assessed if you have no deposits or withdrawals over a specific period of time. Some banks charge if your account has been inactive for as few as 90 days.
Money orders/ cashier's check	A cashier's check will cost more than a money order.
Monthly service fee	Charged if a checking account balance falls below a certain amount.
Non-sufficient funds (NSF)	Bounce a check and you'll pay one of the highest per-item fees banks charge.
Notary fees	A notary public is someone who can certify or attest to documents. If you need something notarized, you'll pay a variety of fees depending on the document.
Overdraft	If you overdraw your account and the bank pays the check or debit, it will charge you a fee.

continues...

(Table 5.1 continued)

Return of checks	You used to be able to get your canceled checks returned for free; now many banks charge a monthly fee for that service.
Safe deposit box	An annual rental fee based on the size of the box.
Stop payment	Imposed when you use a check to pay for something and then change your mind.
Teller fee	Some accounts require you to do most trans- actions online, at the ATM, or by phone. These accounts usually limit the number of times you can visit a teller each month and charge a fee for additional visits.

You may have picked up on the fact that banks are not my favorite businesses. Although the reasons are many, a good start is Table 5.1. Here's a closer look.

- **Fees for debit card usage.** None of the banks in my area are doing this, but I'll certainly start using cash and checks a lot more if they do. Banks are already making a profit on the money you have on deposit, and they charge the merchant for every time you use a debit or credit card. It is unbelievable that they would start charging you a fee to access your money as well.

- **Credit reference fee.** I actually don't have a problem with this, depending on how high the fee is. I just want to point out that this is a service you may need to use. Some landlords require this, particularly from prospective tenants who don't have a long job or credit history.

- **Inactive account fee.** This is why you don't want to open more accounts than you need. Remember, having many accounts at a bank doesn't mean you'll get any special deals should you want a loan or credit card.

- **Teller fees.** This one is the last straw. I concede that with direct deposit, online banking, and ATMs there is little need to walk into a bank and see a teller. But these fees just punish people who can't afford home computers or Internet access.

Now that you've taken into consideration all the service fees, the account features you'll need, and the bank locations, you're ready to open an account.

But how do you manage your account and get the most out of your bank? Read on.

Basic Banking How-Tos

Now that you have a checking account, you need to learn the responsibilities that come along with it. The most important one is knowing that once you put your money in the bank, it is your responsibility to know how much you have remaining after making withdrawals. If you take out more than you put in, you will pay dearly. So I'll show you some how-tos for banking … some of which are good, and some of which are not. The first example is one that is most definitely not good.

A Guide to Messing Up Your Finances, Part I: Bouncing a Check

If you write a check for more than you have available in your account, your check will "bounce." This means that the check will be returned unpaid, and fees will be applied to your account by both your bank and the business to whom the check was written. (It is also possible to bounce an ATM withdrawal, an online bill payment, or a debit card point of sale purchase.) The most common reason for bouncing a check occurs because you've glanced at your balance online or on an ATM receipt, assumed that the balance shown was the actual amount of money in your account, and spent more money. There are several problems with doing this. See Table 5.2 for an example.

Table 5.2: How to bounce a check.	
November 10	Write a check for $65.00 to the grocery store.
November 12	Check balance online, shows $85.62. Go out and spend $30.00 using your debit card.
November 13	Debit payment clears account. Balance is $55.62. Check to grocery store for $65.00 tries to clear. Bank returns check unpaid.
November 14	Check balance on ATM. Shows balance of $55.62. Withdraw $20.00 cash. Grocery store resubmits check.
November 15	Check to grocery store tries to clear. Bank returns check unpaid.

In this example, a $65.00 grocery purchase will cost $175. How is that possible? Well, the person in the example paid $65.00 for the groceries. The bank charged an additional $30 in returned check fees the first time the check was submitted. The check was submitted again, and another $30 in returned check fees was applied. Then the grocery store charged another $50.00 fee for a returned check. $65 + $30 + $30 + $50 = $175.00 for $65.00 worth of groceries.

Moral of the story? Spend 10 minutes a week balancing your checkbook or it'll cost you!

A Guide to Messing Up Your Finances, Part II: Trusting the Bank

Those fees are pretty brutal. But the biggest reason to balance your checkbook is shown in Table 5.3.

Subtractions (continued)

Checks   * check missing from sequence

Check	Date	Amount	Check	Date	Amount	Check	Date	Amount
1131	7/17	72.90	*1168	7/31	107.89	13090	7/7	152.13
1132	7/5	125.00	*1170	7/27	300.85	13091	7/11	946.11
1133	7/6	179.78	1171	7/27	364.07	13092	7/7	370.41
1134	7/7	4,166.00	1172	7/28	27.18	*13094	7/10	278.34
1135	7/7	1,125.22	1173	7/28	75.15	13095	7/13	89.09
1136	7/11	313.69	1174	7/31	130.00	*13097	7/11	104.21
1137	7/18	875.29	*1176	7/31	250.00	*13103	7/7	97.20
1138	7/26	440.89	1177	7/31	635.00	*13106	7/25	163.32
1139	7/14	480.00	*1233	7/26	165.96	13107	7/28	64.15
1140	7/13	167.76	*3082	7/12	236.53	13108	7/26	241.17
1141	7/13	254.50	*13033	7/7	61.89	13109	7/27	94.73
*1143	7/17	1,853.22	*13044	7/7	47.05	13110	7/21	233.28
1144	7/17	103.00	*13049	7/3	3.27	13111	7/26	635.99
1145	7/18	352.57	*13053	7/13	285.22	13112	7/26	185.24
1146	7/13	250.00	*13059	7/10	26.26	13113	7/24	132.59
1147	7/18	629.30	*13064	7/11	54.32	13114	7/24	419.80
1148	7/17	480.00	*13070	7/6	34.98	13115	7/27	272.98
1149	7/13	2,500.00	*13074	7/5	53.75	*13117	7/21	243.86
1150	7/17	23.50	*13076	7/5	16.55	13118	7/21	149.27
1151	7/14	943.24	*13078	7/10	121.66	13119	7/27	679.15
1152	7/19	131.87	13079	7/12	60.91	13120	7/26	946.69
1153	7/17	250.00	13080	7/10	362.04	13121	7/26	321.06
1154	7/21	4,187.48	13081	7/14	148.84	13122	7/27	84.79
*1156	7/21	75.89	*13083	7/7	349.51	13123	7/25	82.73
1157	7/26	62.25	13084	7/10	357.91	*13125	7/26	76.13
1158	7/27	163.30	13085	7/10	316.55	*13130	7/26	111.15
1159	7/24	42.60	13086	7/10	511.84	*13132	7/26	70.25
1160	7/20	980.37	13086	7/11	511.84	*17101	7/10	97.74
*1162	7/20	223.68	13087	7/7	79.37	**Total Checks Paid**		**48,818.92**
1163	7/21	250.00	13088	7/17	88.36			
*1165	7/25	480.00	13089	7/11	209.45			

TABLE 5.3: Copy of a real bank statement showing what would have happened had the account owner trusted the bank to balance his statement properly.

This is a copy of a real bank statement that a CPA friend let me copy. Look down toward the bottom in the middle columns and you'll see two entries for check number 13086. The bank cleared the same check twice; first on July 10, and then again on July 11. If this person had trusted his bank to accurately balance his account, he would have lost $511.84.

Note that if you're just using your fridge list to "balance" your account, an error like this could cause you to start bouncing checks that were written on money that was erroneously withdrawn from your account. Sure, the bank would eventually reimburse your overdraft charges, but good luck in getting back the fees charged by businesses for your checks that were returned for non-sufficient funds.

> Be sure to ask what your bank's policy is for correcting errors. Don't assume that mistakes will be corrected no matter when they are discovered; credit cards, for example, only allow 60 days to catch mistakes. And never assume that the bank will catch its own mistake. Errors can sometimes slip through the cracks, leaving you responsible for the lost money.

Doing It Right: Balancing Your Checking Account

Now you know you should, but exactly how do you balance a checkbook? A checkbook ledger will basically mirror your fridge list. You just enter the starting balance of your account in the balance box and subtract each withdrawal as it's made.

Figure 5.1 shows a typical transaction register that comes along with your checks when you open a checking account. Simply enter the check number, date, description, and amount of the transaction. If you're making an ATM withdrawal or any other withdrawal that has a fee, be sure to include it in the fee column. I prefer to separate fees instead of adding them into the withdrawal. For example, if I withdraw $20.00 from an ATM and pay a $2.00 fee, I'll enter the $20.00 as an ATM withdrawal under the description column and make a second entry for the $2.00 fee. This way, I can quickly see how much I'm paying in fees. If you choose to separate out the fees, make sure you remember the lesson from the chapters on budgeting. You have to really learn to enjoy not paying fees more than you dislike balancing your account!

Record all charges or credits that affect your account

Number	Date	Transaction Description or Payee Name	Payee Code	Payment or Withdrawal	Fee or ✓	Deposit or Interest	Date Transaction Effective	Balance
				$		$		$

FIGURE 5.1: Sample checkbook ledger.

> If you are sure you won't run up the balance, you may choose to use a credit card with a rewards program as a debit card so that you'll get the benefits of the reward program on all your daily purchases. If you do this, make sure that the reward program actually saves you money. For example, while a discount on gas will save money, a discount on airfare may cost you a bundle when you pay for the rest of the trip. Also, make sure that you record your credit card purchases in a ledger just as you would with a debit card. That way you will be sure to have enough money each month to pay the credit card balance off in full, instead of getting hit with interest charges. (Paying interest negates the benefit of those rewards.)

Using Your Bank to Help Save

Sooner or later you'll arrive at a point in life where you are doing something besides just making ends meet and paying off debt. And this brings us to the second function of banks—saving money for the future.

The problem with today's consumption/debt-based society is that most people don't even consider saving. If we want something, well, that's what credit cards and home equity loans are for. Right? Well, not ideally. Let's take a look at what the true cost of borrowing versus saving really is.

Saving vs. Borrowing

Let's say you want $10,000 for a dream vacation. Table 5.4, shows a comparison of the cost of saving for seven years at 5 percent interest to accumulate that $10,000 versus borrowing the $10,000 at a 14 percent interest rate and paying it off for seven years.

Table 5.4: Saving vs. Borrowing		
Save Monthly	**Time**	**Savings Goal**
$100	7 Years	$10,000
5% annual rate	Total cost:	$8,400
	OR	
Borrow	**Time**	**Pay monthly**
$10,000	7 Years	$187.40
14% annual rate	Total Cost:	$15,750

Example of saving vs. borrowing for large purchases.

You only need to save $100 a month to reach $10,000, and your money earns $1,600 of interest, or 16 percent of your goal. If you borrow $10,000, you end up paying 87.5 percent more out of pocket for that same $10,000 vacation, or $187.40 per month instead of just $100! Another way to look at it is this: if you can afford the $187.40 a month payment, you could have $18,740 … and think how much nicer that vacation would be. (Or maybe you'd get a vacation plus a new car, or a down payment on a house, or …)

Unsolicited Advice

When you are young and in debt, you should save and accelerate debt simultaneously. If you focus all your resources toward eliminating debt, you are just likely to get back into debt every time you make a major purchase. By saving and accelerating debt simultaneously, you will eventually get to the point where you are taking on less and less debt every time you have a major purchase.

Hopefully this example is enough to convince you to save instead of borrowing for all of life's slightly larger joys of living. I know that it isn't always feasible to take a vacation only once every seven years, or put off a wedding for seven years (although statistically most people would be better off), or wait to buy a new car when yours spends more time at the mechanic's garage than in yours, but again this is not an all-or-nothing proposition. Anything you can save will simply reduce the cost of a purchase significantly from borrowing 100 percent of the cost.

CDs Aren't Just for Music: Ways to Save

Whenever you walk into a bank branch, you probably notice all sorts of posters for various accounts touting different interest rates. To fully understand your savings options, you'll need to understand two things about how banks determine interest rates on deposit accounts.

> A **deposit account** is a general term that refers to any one of a number of accounts in which you deposit your money with the bank. Savings accounts and certificates of deposit (CDs), for example, are deposit accounts that offer different interest rates depending on how long the bank requires you to keep your money in them.

Banks have reserve requirements, which are set by the Federal Reserve (the Fed). The reserve requirement is the percentage of all money deposited with the bank that the bank actually needs to have on hand at all times. Anything above the reserve requirement is then available to be loaned out to bank customers. Currently the reserve requirement is set at only 10 percent. In other words, if every single depositor of a bank asked for their money back at the same time, the bank would only be able to give you back $.10 for every dollar deposited. Your other $.90 has probably been loaned out to other customers at a higher interest rate than they pay you. These loans are a major source of income for the bank.

Now, if all your money is in a checking account, the bank really isn't allowed to lend this money out to other customers since you may come in and ask for it tomorrow. However, if you were to put your money into another type of account for a specified amount of time (more on these in a moment) the bank would know that they have at least that amount of time before you can ask for that money back. They may then loan it out to other customers while you earn your interest.

In general, if you are willing to leave your money in the bank longer, you'll receive a higher interest rate. (I say "in general" because there are times, as in 2006, when interest rates are as high or even higher on shorter term deposits. The "why" of this is beyond the scope of this book, but you do need to be aware that it sometimes happens.) So what exactly are your options for saving at a bank? Here is a rundown, in order of lowest interest rate to highest under normal circumstances.

Checking Accounts

We've pretty much been through this. What you need to know is that a checking account is not a savings account. If you want to put extra money aside, you need to move on to another account.

Savings Accounts

A savings account is very much like a checking account, but without the checks. The interest rate is slightly higher, but you still have daily access to the money in your account through an ATM or at the branch.

Money Market Accounts

A money market is best thought of as a high minimum deposit requirement savings account. Usually if you maintain a minimum balance (sometimes as low as $500 or as high as $10,000), the bank will pay you a higher interest rate. Some money market accounts will limit how many transfers or withdrawals you can make in a monthly period. If you need to have money available, but have no definite plans for it, a money market account may be a good choice.

Certificates of Deposit (CDs)

Certificates of deposit, or CDs, are deposit accounts in which you agree to let the bank have your money for a specific period of time. At the end of the time period, at renewal, you can choose to roll your money over into a new CD, or into any other deposit account of your choice. Obviously, you can also withdraw your money and do with it whatever you wish. Typical CD choices will be for 3 months, 6 months, 1 year, 18 months, 2 years, 3 years, 4 years, and 5 years. It's important to note that you will lose any interest earned, and in some cases some of your initial deposit, if you cash in your account early.

Individual Retirement Accounts (IRAs)

An IRA is really not an account type, but many people are misled by bank advertising that mentions IRA "accounts." IRA is a tax designation. Almost any savings or investment account other than artwork and collectable coins can be an IRA. Logistically, it is only a matter of filling out an application that states whether you want your account to be a "regular" account or an "IRA" account.

> **Certificates of deposit, or CDs,** are deposit accounts in which you commit your money to the bank for a certain amount of time and receive interest based on that time. For example, if you put $5,000 into a CD for 6 months, you may earn 6 percent interest. But if you put that same $5,000 into a CD for 12 months, you could earn 7 percent interest. During that time, however, you will not be able to withdraw the money, or you will pay a penalty fee to the bank.

Club Accounts

Some banks, and particularly credit unions, offer "club" accounts or something similar. Usually called Vacation Club, Holiday Club, Kids Club, or the like, these are accounts that are marketed as a savings vehicle for the named purpose. They may not offer any real benefit over a regular savings account, but they are still a great way to separate your savings from your regular budget money, and many banks offer the option to have the savings debited directly from your checking account before you're tempted to spend it. Even if you're saving for a down payment on a new car, if the "Vacation Club" account offers a better deal, use it to save for your car.

> **Unsolicited Advice**
>
> If you were to open an IRA at the bank (which you probably shouldn't—there are other, better options out there), you would then choose between the different accounts for the type of account you wish to designate as an IRA. A bank may have a special money market account just for IRAs, but it is still just a money market account. Got that?

Motivating Yourself to Save

Now you know why to save, and where to save, but *how* do you actually save? Same as with anything else—set a goal and a reward for yourself. Let's say that you want to save $10,000. You should first break that down into an annual goal, a monthly goal, and a per-paycheck goal. Then you should set up a reward for each time you meet your goal. It doesn't have to be big, but it should be something that recognizes the effort you've put in. If you're going to save over $1,000 a year by saving in advance for $10,000 versus paying off what you borrowed in advance, then you deserve a reward for your efforts.

When Saving Becomes Investing

Telling a financial planner that you are going to "invest" in a CD or other bank product is akin to dragging your fingernails across a chalkboard. Understanding the difference between saving and investing can make a big difference to your finances over a lifetime.

First, you need to define your goal; then, you must determine if you should save or invest to meet your goal. The advantage of saving is that when you want your money, you can get to it immediately, and you can be absolutely certain that you will get back at least what you put in and hopefully some interest. When you invest, you hope to receive a higher rate of return, but you *always* risk whether you will actually receive 100 percent of your investment in return, let alone a gain.

Read this next statement very carefully. Nothing will pay more than a bank deposit account and provide you the same level of safety and *liquidity* for your money. Absolutely nothing ever has, and nothing ever will. Remember earlier I said that whenever you enter into a business transaction, you should look at it from the other guy's point of view? Let's do that here.

> **Liquidity** is a term that refers to how available your money is after you make an investment. For example, a checking account is 100 percent liquid because you can easily remove your money at any time without penalty. Investments may be illiquid because of surrender charges, penalties for early withdrawal, or probable market fluctuations that make it unwise to withdraw your money at a certain time.

Say I knew for certain that if I had your money to invest I could make a 20 percent return on it. In this example, I also know that the best you can do at the bank is get a 5 percent return. What rate of return would I guarantee you if you brought your money to me instead of the bank? Do you think I'd give you the 20 percent? If I know the best you can do—guaranteed—is 5 percent, and my offering is guaranteed as well, why would I offer you much more than 5 percent? Maybe I'd offer you a little more because I'm not as big or well-known as the bank … perhaps 7 percent or 8 percent.

I probably wouldn't need to go much higher than that, and I wouldn't want to because every additional percentage point I give you is that much less profit for me. So remember, there is not and never will be a guaranteed safe investment that pays significantly more than a bank account.

So why invest? Simple. If you put all your money in the bank, it will be safe, but it won't make you much more. Remember that money has only one function: to buy stuff. And if you can't buy more with your money in the future due to inflation, you have really lost money.

Look at Table 5.5. In this case, the bank account yields 5 percent. Assuming that you pay about 25 percent of your income to taxes, you really aren't making any money after taxes and inflation. It doesn't do any good to assume that things will get better if the Fed only does this or that, or if one political party or the other controls government. Remember our discussion from earlier in the chapter about the function of banks. They take money from you and guarantee to give it back—but that's all they do. So in Table 5.5, you see what happens to a 5 percent gain on your savings. After taxes and inflation, you end up with a gain of zero. Bank interest rates may go up, but generally they only do so because inflation is going up, as well.

Table 5.5: Example of the effects of taxes and inflation on an investment of $10,000.	
Investment	$10,000
Interest at 5%	$500
Taxes at 25%	$125
After Tax Return	$375
Long-Term Inflation 3.75%	($375)
Net Gain	**$0**

So the answer to the question "Why invest?" is simple. You should invest to give your money a chance to make more money for you after taxes and inflation.

Banks Are for Saving, Not Investing

As soon as you actually accumulate some money, the customer service representative (CSR), formerly referred to as the "bank teller," will suggest that you move your money out of your deposit account and into something that might pay more. Or you will see ads on your bank's website or flyers in your statements for things such as annuities, mutual funds, or college savings plans. Remember this: banks are for banking and not for anything else. Here's why. The banking industry saw assets exodus traditional banking products in the late 1980s and '90s as interest rates plummeted and the stock market skyrocketed. Problem was that there was a legal separation between the banking, brokerage, and insurance industries. At one point, Congress felt that it was in the consumer's best interest to separate the industries. In the '80s and '90s they changed their minds and basically allowed each industry carte blanche access to each others' turf.

The problem, for the consumer, is that after decades of competing against each other, sales forces were supposed to now start selling products that they didn't really like and frankly knew very little about. For example, banks were always known for fixed-interest, guaranteed products such as CDs. Then all of a sudden bank managers were supposed to generate revenue by selling mutual funds, which were not guaranteed. With the market skyrocketing, this was seen as a great revenue generator for banks and credit unions. It was also a way to profit from money that would otherwise leave the bank entirely and go to brokerage companies as consumers flooded mutual fund companies with assets.

The problem is that banking culture is just not suited to provide advice. Bank management saw, and in most cases still see, mutual funds and annuities the way they see CDs—simply as a product for sale.

During this period I started an investment program and ran it for 10 years at a local financial institution. At that time I spent a fair amount of time networking and reading about trends, specifically in the niche of bank investment marketing. I terminated my contract for a very specific reason: I was given the choice to continue to bring in new clients at the expense of providing service to existing clients, or leave and focus my attention on existing clientele. I left.

Even if the intentions are good, the banking industry just doesn't understand the requirements of properly managing investment assets at the consumer level. Primarily, the investment division exists to generate revenue through "product sales." Banks want the revenue, but do not want the cost or liability exposure that actually comes with managing client money and providing investment advice. Basically, unless you have the net worth to be a customer of the bank's trust company (in most cases, at least $1 million), they want your commission dollars, but not the liability. They address this by selling products with no pretense of management.

A typical bank securities rep may have over 1,000 "customers." Do the math. With only about 220 working days per year, if a rep saw each client (or just reviewed the client's portfolio) once a year, they would have to go through 4.5 client portfolios a day. I reserve 2 hours per appointment, so that means a rep with 1,000 clients would need to spend 9 hours a day doing nothing but meeting with existing clients, leaving no time to generate new revenue. Obviously, it doesn't happen that way.

Think of it this way: in most cases, the bank is just a big middleman, soaking up fees so that you can have the "privilege" of buying their high-commissioned investment products. Even if the rep is employed by the bank, the investment division is still competing within the bank for customer assets. So because of the fairly low commission payouts to the rep, and lack of real expertise needed, banking reps are usually inexperienced in the industry. Banks are a great place to start a financial services career when a rep either doesn't have clients, or doesn't have the experience to work at an investment company. These reps typically deal with lower-net-worth clients; higher-net-worth clients are referred to the trust department for investment management. The fact is, just about any rep who starts out at the bank is inexperienced and unable to devote the proper amount of time to your portfolio.

Figure 5.2 shows investment representative employment change from 2004 to 2005. When choosing an investment representative or financial planner, you want to develop a relationship that lasts over time. The more your advisor knows about you, the better the advice she can give. Unfortunately, when financial reps change employers, clients are legally retained by their employer, making it difficult for clients to move with the rep. New companies may also offer different investment products so that a rep that has changed employers may not be able to service your account without selling and buying new investments, whether in your best interest or not. Bottom line: for consistency of a relationship, look where reps end up, at independent firms and as independent registered investment advisors. If reps don't feel they can do their job at a bank, as indicated by the high turnover, why would you want to put your money there?

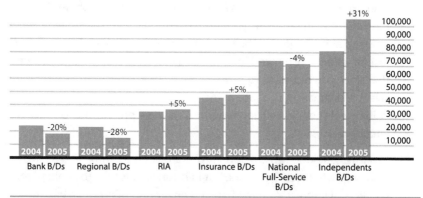

FIGURE 5.2: Investment representative change from 2004 to 2005.

Until banks learn that a mutual fund is not a CD and change their sales environment, attracting and retaining representatives will be a continuing problem.

So What Does This Mean to You?

You're starting out as a new investor, and frankly you don't have a lot of opportunities for great service anywhere. Some people assume that their bank is looking out for their best interest by at least screening the products that are offered. Bad assumption. Which mutual funds and annuities that are offered by your bank is often determined by how much revenue the investment company is willing to share with the bank. There is, in general, little or no correlation between quality investments and those that are offered by the bank. In fact, banks are notorious for selling high-commission, high-expense variable annuities when most would agree that a lower-cost mutual fund may be more appropriate.

What this means to you, then, is that you should not make your investments through a bank.

All investment reps, wherever they work, are held to a minimum standard of "appropriateness." Any investment sold must be appropriate for the client, but "appropriate" can be a pretty fuzzy concept. Here's an analogy.

Let's say that you are color blind, and you go into a clothing store and explain that you need a new suit. The salesperson sells you a bright red jacket, lime green blouse, purple skirt, and yellow pumps because they are overstocked with those items and he wants to get rid of them. After wearing your new suit to work, you return to the store and complain, "Everyone laughed at me at work." The salesperson replies, "I'm a salesperson, not a fashion expert. You asked for a suit and I sold you a suit." It can be argued that since you did in fact get what you asked for, it was an "appropriate" sale. Unfortunately, because of the brokerage industry, there are a lot of "color blind" people walking around with some pretty ugly "outfits." See what I mean?

In fairness, a good rep is a good rep wherever they work, and a bad rep is a bad rep wherever they work. But in business it is best to avoid potential conflicts of interest. And the banking environment is not an easy one to always do the best thing for your customer as an investment representative. For now, use your bank for banking. In Chapter 12, I'll explain the right way to invest and show you some options. And if you need a financial advisor, I'll also explain how to find a good one.

The Bottom Line

- Consider all the options before choosing a bank or credit union.

- Know what you need in savings accounts and how to differentiate among them.

- Brush up on banking self-defense to avoid unnecessary fees.

- Banks are for banking—saving and borrowing—not for investing.

The Ins and Outs of Borrowing

What You Will Learn

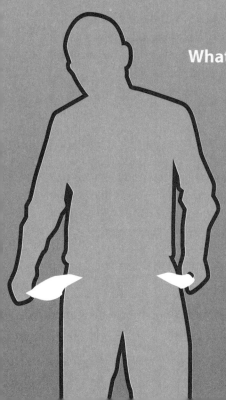

- How to make good financing decisions

- The pros and cons of different types of financing

- Different mortgage types, and how to make the best choice

- The true cost of borrowing

- How to borrow for big-ticket expenses, such as weddings

"Neither a borrower nor a lender be."—William Shakespeare

"[Cleveland] Browns [Football] owner Randy Lerner might be preparing to try another brand of football—English Premier League soccer. Sportinglife. com, an English website, estimates the Aston Villas [an English football team], worth approximately $105 million."—Bob Roberts, *Cleveland Plain Dealer*, July 25, 2006

(He actually did buy the team a couple of months after this headline was printed).

Will didn't get it quite right. There's apparently nothing wrong with being a lender. Al Lerner (Randy's deceased father) literally lived the American Dream. From a $75-a-week job in the 1950s, he went on to become one of the richest men in the world—the owner of the Cleveland Browns football team with a net worth estimated to be near $4.5 billion. How'd he do it? Primarily as president, and later as chairman and 10 percent owner, of MBNA Corporation.

Under Lerner, MBNA became the largest independent credit card issuer in the world. In 2005 they were acquired by Bank of America for $35 billion. Now Lerner's son, Randy, wants to own football teams on two continents, and is able to cough up $104 million to do it.

The lender has $4.5 billion, and what do you (the borrower) have? A cell phone that will be out of date in six months, a car that will lose half its value in three years, a catalogue of songs on your iPod that you won't listen to in two years … I hope you're getting the point.

Will got it half right.

Manage Your Debt Like a Stock Portfolio

Okay, I'm not going to tell you to never borrow money. And I've already gone over the cost of borrowing versus saving, but the fact is that you simply pay more for something when you borrow to buy it than when you buy it with cash. Inflation may reduce your cost in real dollars over time, but you still end up paying more.

Investing: The Reverse of Borrowing

The way to think about borrowing is the same way you should think about investing, but in reverse. By investing, you are putting off a nice lifestyle now for a better lifestyle in the future. By borrowing, you are buying a better lifestyle now and paying for it in the future, which reduces your ability for a better future lifestyle. When you invest, you want to maximize your interest or return to maximize your future lifestyle. When you borrow, you want to minimize your interest costs so as to minimize the effect it will have on your future lifestyle. It absolutely amazes me how people will get all worked up over which savings account pays 0.5 percent more, or which mutual fund is a little cheaper, but totally ignore the cost of their debt.

There is not necessarily anything wrong with borrowing today at the expense of tomorrow. The key is to make sure that tomorrow you will have a higher income, which will allow you to make your payments while still maintaining—and even improving—your lifestyle. As a Gen-Xer or Gen-Yer, as long as you're in the category that expects a rising income, there is no reason not to borrow against those future earnings. The key is "all things in moderation," which I think is a Ben Franklin quote. So let's look at some typical borrowing scenarios and the best way to go about it.

Financing Considerations

The biggie in this category is borrowing for a home, and unfortunately that has become pretty complex. The way to look at mortgage financing, and to some extent all financing, is to think of a four-legged stool. Each leg represents a part of the qualification process. One leg is your credit score, another is your income (which refers to both length of time on your job and your income relative to current and proposed debt), a third is any other liquid financial assets that you have, and the fourth is the amount of loan relative to the value of the property (loan-to-value ratio). A stool can stand on its own with four fairly strong legs or with three very strong legs, but not with just one or two legs. Lending approval is similar. You may not need all four areas to be perfect; one leg may be pretty weak, but the other three can compensate if they are strong. For instance, if you have a low credit score, you may still qualify for a good interest rate on a mortgage if you have a good income, several years on the job, and a sizeable down payment of about 25 percent or more. So let's look at each "leg" from the lender's viewpoint.

Credit Score

Your credit score is the single best indicator of how likely you are to make timely and complete payments on your loan. Period. Argue all you want, but the best thing you can do for your future financial life, short of winning the lottery, is to attain and maintain a high credit score. Opinions will vary on the definition of "high," and that definition will also vary based on the strength of the other criteria. But credit score is probably the one thing that you have the most control over. Shoot to maintain a 700 score at all times, over 740 when things are going well, and you'll be in good shape to borrow.

Income

Unfortunately, how long you've been at a job is a big factor, and one you may not have control over in terms of timing your major purchases. But do be aware that if you're looking at moving, or even buying a car, it is better to do so before changing jobs. The second factor in considering income is your monthly debt payments relative to your income. This has become less important as incomes vary so much. It means two very different things if your monthly income is $3,000 or $10,000 and you spend 30 percent of your income on debt. But a rule of thumb is that you should keep all your monthly debt payments to under 40 percent of your gross monthly income.

Liquid Assets

Liquid assets refers to other financial investments you have, the value of which means two things to a lender. First, having money in savings and investments means that if you get into financial trouble, say a few months of unemployment, you still have some assets to fall back on to keep payments current. It also means that you are not living completely paycheck to paycheck. Having no savings and applying for a loan that will increase your monthly debt-to-income ratio will raise a red flag with a lender. If you are barely making ends meet now, how do you expect to keep current with even higher payments?

Loan-to-Value Ratio

The lower the value of the loan relative to the value of the property, the easier it is to get the loan. A low loan to value means that you're paying 60 percent or maybe 70 percent of the value of the property. For example, if you're paying $100,000 for a starter home that's worth $200,000, you have a very low loan to value. Banks really don't want to repossess a property, but they like to know that if they must, they can get the full value of their money back by selling it. In addition, they know that the more money you have in equity, the less likely you are to walk away from a property.

Conventional Financing

With those considerations in mind, let's look at how to go about financing a new home. First, check out Table 6.1 below, which we first saw in Chapter 4. Without a doubt, the only mortgage loan you should consider is a 30-year loan (exceptions to follow). The first reason for this is inflation.

How Long to Finance

In the third column of Table 6.1, we start with a payment of $1,000 a month and show the value of that payment after adjusting for an assumed 3.5 percent inflation rate. Simply put, you are buying an asset that generally appreciates, a house, with an asset that depreciates, dollars. This is just a win-win situation all around.

Table 6.1: Mortgage payment in real dollars over 30 years.					
Age	Mortgage Year	Monthly Payment Real Dollars	Age	Mortgage Year	Monthly Payment Real Dollars
25	1	$1,000	40	16	$586
26	2	$965	41	17	$566
27	3	$931	42	18	$546
28	4	$899	43	19	$527
29	5	$867	44	20	$508
30	6	$837	45	21	$490
31	7	$808	46	22	$473
32	8	$779	47	23	$457
33	9	$752	48	24	$441
34	10	$726	49	25	$425
35	11	$700	50	26	$425
36	12	$676	51	27	$410
37	13	$652	52	28	$396

continues...

(Table 6.1 continued)

Age	Mortgage Year	Monthly Payment Real Dollars	Age	Mortgage Year	Monthly Payment Real Dollars
38	14	$629	53	29	$369
39	15	$607	54	30	$356

By the end of the loan payment period in year 30, your nominal $1,000 payment is only worth $356 in real dollars from the start of your loan. That means that it feels like you're paying $644 less than you were when you first bought your home, due to inflation and the fact that your money is now worth less.

Next let's look at taxes. Table 6.2 shows an amortization table for a 15-year mortgage. Based on a 6.5 percent interest rate, borrowing $150,000 would result in a monthly payment of $1,306.66. The third column breaks down the cumulative interest you would pay over the life of the loan. What many "advisors" fail to consider is the tax savings that you realize from your interest expense. This cumulative tax savings is shown in the next column. So after 15 years, your total cost would be ($1,306.66 × 180 payments) – ($25,559.70 of tax savings) = $209,639.10. This reduces your average monthly payment to $1,164.66, or about $150 a month less from tax savings, assuming a 30 percent tax rate.

Table 6.2: An amortization schedule for a 15-year mortgage.

15-Year Mortgage	
Loan amount	$150,000.00
Annual interest rate	6.50%
Monthly payment	$1,306.66
Total interest	$85,198.99

Year	Ending Balance	Cumulative Interest	Tax Savings	Net Payment
1	$143,890.18	$9,570.11	$2,871.03	
5	$115,075.68	$43,475.34	$13,042.60	
10	$66,781.72	$73,581.05	$22,074.31	
15	$0.00	$85,198.99	$25,559.70	$209,639.10

Now let's compare this to a 30-year mortgage (see Table 6.3). The table is exactly the same as the one you just saw, but I've added an extra column called "Investment Balance." To come up with the numbers in this column, I took the 15-year payment and subtracted the lower 30-year payment to come up with the difference of $358.56 a month. Then I assumed that we invested that difference at a 7 percent rate for 30 years. Let's compare the difference in our two loans at the end of 15 years.

Table 6.3: An amortization schedule for a 30-year mortgage.

30-Year Mortgage and Investment

Loan amount	$150,000.00
Annual interest rate	6.50%
Loan period in years	30
Monthly payment	$948.10
Total interest	$191,316.73

Year	Ending Balance	Cumulative Interest	Tax Savings	Net Payment	Investment Balance 7%
1	$148,323.41	$9,700.64	$2,910.19		$4,469.41
5	$140,416.47	$47,302.59	$14,190.78		$25,820.00
10	$127,164.19	$90,936.43	$27,280.93		$62,426.00
15	**$108,838.71**	**$129,497.08**	**$38,849.12**	**$131,808.88**	**$114,312.00**
20	$83,497.92	$161,042.41	$48,312.72		$187,873.00
25	$48,456.24	$182,886.85	$54,866.06		$292,154.00
30	$0.00	$191,316.73	$57,395.02	$283,920.98	$439,984.00

With the 15-year loan, we have a paid-off home with an after-tax cost of $209,639.10. With a 30-year mortgage, after 15 years we still owe $108,838.71. But we have only paid $131,808.88 of cumulative after-tax payments at this time. Remember, the difference in monthly payments has been invested and this has grown to $114,312.00, again assuming a constant 7 percent after-tax return. So if we really want to, we can pay off the mortgage with our investment fund in 15 years. Granted that whether or not we are ahead at this time depends on our rate of return on investment.

Let me take a minute to address the "invest" part of this decision. What you do with the extra cash flow is key to the success of the 30-year mortgage versus 15-year mortgage strategy.

The best choice for your investing would be to add the money to your 401(k) or other retirement plan. By doing so you never actually "see" the money, as it is deducted from your paycheck before you're paid, thus removing the temptation of spending it instead of investing it. But the primary reason is you gain two additional tax advantages. The first is that the additional money added to a retirement plan provides another tax deduction. This double tax savings—the additional tax advantage of a 30-year mortgage coupled with the before-tax savings of a retirement plan—has actually been termed a "tax arbitrage" strategy in a paper published by the Federal Reserve Bank of Chicago (*The Tradeoff between Mortgage Prepayments and Tax-Deferred Retirement Savings* by Gene Amromin, Jennifer Huang, and Clemens Sialm, May 2006). In their paper the authors assert that Americans are costing themselves as much as 1.5 billion dollars a year by choosing to shorten their mortgage amortization period, instead of fully funding their before-tax retirement plans. I'll discuss how this tax savings works in the next chapter when I address retirement plan investing.

The second advantage of retirement plan investing is that your investment grows tax-deferred. In other words, you pay no taxes on the interest or gains in your investment account. Instead, you defer your taxes until the money is actually withdrawn from the account, presumably in retirement at a lower tax rate. Not paying taxes on your gains makes it much easier to earn a net, or after-tax, rate of return of 7 percent or better.

Although not a tax strategy, another very important consideration is whether your employer offers a retirement plan where they match all or part of your contribution. If so, and you are not taking full advantage of the matching contribution, a longer mortgage allows you to take advantage of this "free" money by contributing to your retirement plan. If your employer is offering you money and you don't take advantage of it, that is akin to turning down a raise!

But this is not entirely a dollars-and-cents issue.

Thinking Ahead

When I ask people why they want a 15-year mortgage, most of them say that they want the security of a paid-off home in case they get laid off from their job, or become injured and unable to work. Now let's look at these two scenarios again, and determine which one provides more security. Who's to say that if you do get laid off it won't be for another 15 years? What if you were unemployed 10 years into your mortgage? With a 15-year loan, you would still need to find a way to come up with your $1,306.66 monthly payment without having a job. With the 30-year mortgage, you not only have a lower payment of $948.10, but you also have an investment account worth over $60,000. If you find yourself in financial trouble, wouldn't you rather have the $62,425 to pay your mortgage, as well as buy things like groceries?

Obviously, this would not be an option if you take my previous advice of investing your monthly savings entirely into a retirement account—at least without tax and penalty consequences. So the one thing we strongly urge when choosing a longer mortgage is to make sure you build up an adequate emergency fund before committing all your investments to a retirement plan. I'll be discussing investing more in the next chapter, and you will see how a conservative mutual fund investing strategy can help you build your reserve amount, and still realize a 7% after-tax rate of return.

Let's assume that life goes well and we find ourselves 15 years down the road with a decision to make: pay off the mortgage or keep making payments. First, going back to Table 6.1, look down 15 years and you see that our original payment is about 40 percent less due to inflation. So in Table 6.3, even though our payment is still $948, it will seem like less than $600 due to inflation. By the end of 30 years, you could have a paid-off home and $439,984.00 in investments.

As with all cash flow saving strategies, the goal is to end up with extra cash flow to invest, not spend. Unfortunately, too many times, people see extra cash flow and the first thought that comes to mind is, "great, now I can afford to buy…" You know yourself better than anyone else, and no one can be with you every day to make sure you make the right decisions. So do realize that although this makes dollars-and-cents sense, it will only make sense for you if you follow through and save or invest the cash flow savings. If you feel you lack the discipline, then you're better off with the "forced" savings strategy. In other words, go for the short-term 15-year mortgage instead. That way you know that in 15 years you will at least have a paid-off home. And that is better than 15 years left on a 30-year mortgage, and no savings or investments.

The Best Strategy: Investing the Difference

The best strategy in any type of financing is to buy what you could afford if you were using the more expensive finance option, then make your purchase using a less expensive option and invest the difference. For example, you might decide to buy a car based on the cost of a 4-year loan. Then do a 5- or 6-year loan, but invest the difference in payments to jump-start your investments. When buying a house, the best strategy may be to buy the house you can afford with a 15-year loan, but use a 30-year loan instead and, again, invest the difference.

Pros and Cons

30-Year Mortgage

Pros

- Maximizes the effects of inflation on future monthly payments.
- Maximizes the mortgage interest rate tax deduction.
- Provides cash flow to increase retirement savings (and more tax deductions) or other investment savings.

Con

- If you spend your cash flow savings, you will end up paying thousands of extra dollars in interest, and have nothing to show for it.

15-Year Mortgage

Pro

- Certainty. As long as you make your payments, you will have a paid-off home in 15 years.

Con

- The dollars and cents just don't add up. Your mortgage is most likely the cheapest money anyone will lend you, and the government currently offers tax incentives to borrow longer and invest for retirement. Take advantage of the incentives and use your money for better purposes.

At the beginning of the book, I related a story from a show in which they asked representatives of each generation what their main financial concerns were. For those in their 30s, the answer was saving for the kids' college and for retirement. Choosing a home based on a 15-year mortgage payment and actually using a 30-year mortgage and investing the rest can be a great solution to this dilemma. Many times in your 30s you are moving up from your original "starter" home. Once the kids have started in a school district it becomes harder for them to move emotionally, and for the parents to move financially. According to the U.S. Department of Agriculture, the average annual cost of raising a child in a dual-income household is nearly $5,500. Two kids cost basically the same as financing a $150,000 mortgage over 30 years! So even with a rising income, you may well be in the "house of your dreams" soon after children enter the picture.

When financing on a 30-year mortgage, many times couples will ask if they should make additional payments to accelerate their mortgage. All the same concepts apply as comparing 15-year and a 30-year mortgage. The answer is "no." The only time to consider accelerating your mortgage is if you already are putting everything away you need for retirement, funding college accounts if applicable, and sitting on a nice nest egg of noncommitted investment money for future needs and emergencies. And if you're in this position your income has probably put you in a pretty high tax bracket, and you will want the added tax benefits of the 30-year mortgage versus the 15-year mortgage anyway.

Saving and Investing Simultaneously

A few years ago a couple came in to go over options to pay for their children's college educations. During the appointment, I discovered that they had absolutely no debt, including no mortgage, and no investments because they had put everything they could toward paying off their debt. Their concern was over their two teenage children, one of whom was about to enter college. They had explored all the financing options, including financial aid and student loans, and were coming up short, but they were extremely proud of the fact that they had no debt.

Since I didn't have much to work with, I didn't see a need to "crunch some numbers" and get back to them with options. Basically all I could do was suggest that they pay as the children went along as much as possible since they had some extra cash flow, and take out a home equity loan for the balance. They were totally dumbfounded that I could recommend going into debt after they had worked so hard to be debt-free. The trouble was that they now had no way to educate their children.

I don't know what they ended up doing, but this is the potential predicament you wind up in if all your focus and resources go toward paying off debt. No matter where you are financially, it is imperative that you manage to save and invest at the same time as you service your debt. Without savings and investments, you will inevitably just end up in a position where you will need even more debt. Don't fool yourself—life never becomes less expensive!

Alternative Financing

Back in the "good old days," whenever that was, mortgage options were pretty much limited to the 15- and 30-year fixed-interest-rate mortgage. Today, as the number of finance companies proliferates, the resulting competition has brought forth a plethora of financing options. I'm sure I'm not aware of them all, and if I were I could probably fill a book just on explaining the ins and outs of all the various mortgage options. Suffice to say that the driving force behind most of these options is to make housing more affordable to more Americans, and the government's position is that home ownership is one of the best ways to create personal wealth. Like so many other government interventions, I think this one is about to backfire as well.

A Word of Warning

The government provides incentives to lenders for providing mortgage loans. They do this by providing uniform standards for loan approvals. Loans that meet these lending requirements are then packaged and sold to investors. This removes the default risk from the lender and places it on the investor. It also replaces the lender's capital, allowing them to make new loans. What this has done is allowed banks to provide mortgages to borrowers who would not otherwise qualify for a mortgage. These borrowers present too big of a risk to the bank on their own merits, either because of a past record of not paying their debts, slow payment on debts, or just questionable income that may not allow them to complete payments on their mortgage. While government agencies brag about their success in making home ownership a reality for more and more people, the result today is that foreclosures are also at record highs.

What does this have to do with you? If you can't afford your home with a traditional 15-year or 30-year mortgage, then maybe you should look for a less expensive home, rather than apply for one of the more "exotic" loan choices that follow. Best case, you realize that the smaller home is what was best for you anyway. Worst case, you have extra money, build up your savings and equity in your new home, and use both to step up to your dream home in a few years. Both outcomes seem a whole lot better than risking a foreclosure because you were allowed to stretch your resources to qualify for a loan. Remember, just because you qualify does not mean that you should sign that contract.

That said, there are always exceptions. Here is a rundown of the major types of alternative financing available, and when they may be appropriate.

Adjustable Rate Mortgage (ARM) Loans

As the name implies, the interest rates on these loans are adjustable, which means that what you pay will vary over time. Variable rate loans are usually offered at a "teaser rate." This lender gives you a low rate, guaranteed for a period of time that is less than the length of the loan.

When lenders think interest rates are low, they prefer to lend using an adjustable rate, hoping that as rates increase they will get more money back on their ARM loans. The lenders don't want to get stuck with low-interest-rate fixed loans in a rising-interest-rate environment. The opposite is true when lenders think rates are relatively high. With high rates the lender will want to lock in borrowers with fixed-interest-rate loan products. So when you look at ARMs, think like the lender. When ARM rates look extremely attractive, are lenders really giving you a good deal, or are they suckering you into a loan that will be in their best interest? Did I really need to ask that?

With that in mind, here are the major components of an ARM that you need to understand if considering this type of financing.

- ☐ **Initial Rate.** The initial rate is the rate that you will start out with. It is set by the lender and is somewhat arbitrary in that it is not dependant on other interest rates for how it is set. It will, however, almost always be set at a rate lower than conventional fixed-rate 30-year mortgages. Basically, if interest rates are low and fixed rates look attractive, ARMs will be set even lower to entice borrowers.

- ☐ **Adjustment Period.** The initial loan interest rate will be set for a period of time, typically one, three, or five years. After that period, the interest rate will adjust based on the term of the contract. After the initial adjustment period, the loan will readjust every period thereafter, as well.

- **Adjustment Limits.** At each adjustment period there will be a cap on how much higher the loan interest rate can actually rise. There will also be a cap for how much the interest rate can rise over the life of the loan. You will typically see this expressed as two numbers separated by a slash, such as 2/6. This would mean that the loan interest rate cannot increase by more than 2 percent each adjustment period and by no more than 6 percent over the life of the loan.

- **Index/Margin.** This is the single most important facet of an ARM and the least understood. First, the index is some type of published market interest rate that will determine your interest rate when your loan hits an adjustment period. Your new rate will equal the index rate plus a *margin*.

> The **margin** is fixed percentage points added to the index to compute the interest rate. The result will then be rounded to the nearest one-eighth of a percent. This will be your new interest rate.

The margin is very important because your payment will change based on your new interest rate. So the most important thing you want to look at is the history of the index your prospective loan is tied to.

Figure 6.1 is from Mortgage-x.com. It compares three common indexes used by lenders to determine interest rates on adjustable rate loans. Don't be scared off thinking that you need to actually understand what each of these are (although it wouldn't be a bad idea, it's not necessary). What you do need to know is that the *London Interbank Offered Rate Index (LIBOR rate)* is one of the most common used … and it's also the most volatile index. Notice how the LIBOR rate is the highest rate at the beginning and from October '95 through April '01, and again at the end of the time period. But never is it the lowest! Hmmmm, could this be a reason it is so popular with lenders? In general the *Cost of Funds Index (COFI)* rate is one of the slowest moving and least volatile, and if looking at an ARM, it would be my first preference for an index.

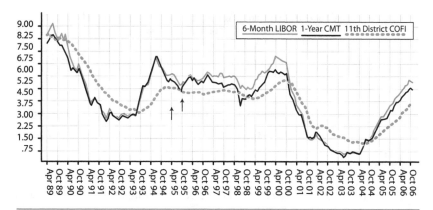

FIGURE 6.1: Comparison of the LIBOR and COFI indexes from October 1989 to October 2006.

For those of you who want to know, **The London Inter-bank Offered Rate Index (LIBOR)** is an average of the interest rates that major international banks charge each other to borrow U.S. dollars in the London money market. The LIBOR rate tends to move and adjust quite rapidly.

The Cost of Funds Index (COFI) is derived from the interest rate that banks pay on their deposit accounts, such as money market and short-term CD accounts. Since banks are reluctant to raise interest on what they pay to you, the COFI makes a great choice for the borrower when looking for an ARM.

Interest Rates

Does the interest rate you pay really matter that much? Take a look at Table 6.4. Here, I've used a $100,000 loan amortized over 30 years and compared monthly payments based on different interest rates. To understand how lenders try to manipulate borrowers into loans that are bad for the consumer but great for the lender, all you have to do is look at rates and loans issued over the last couple of years.

Table 6.4: Comparison of a 30-year mortgage payment at different interest rates.

Interest Rate	Monthly Payment	Interest Rate	Monthly Payment
2%	$370.00	7%	$665.00
3%	$422.00	8%	$734.00
4%	$477.00	9%	$805.00
5%	$537.00	10%	$878.00
6%	$600.00		

Despite historically low interest rates on fixed-rate mortgages, the number of ARMs issued has skyrocketed due to a combination of exceptionally low teaser rates on ARMs and rising housing costs in certain areas of the country. One of the reasons we are seeing record foreclosure rates now is that many borrowers were enticed with 1 and 2 percent starter rates on ARMs. Those loans are now rolling over to the contractual rate—the index and margin, at rates that are 7 percent and higher. You can see that people who stretched to get into their homes with a 2 percent interest rate are now facing monthly payments that are nearly double their original payments.

So if you do take out an adjustable rate mortgage, make sure you calculate worst-case scenarios for future rates and payments, and make an honest self-assessment as to whether that new payment will be affordable.

So When Do ARMs Make Sense?

Does it ever make sense to finance using an ARM? Yes, but first let me make it clear—it never, ever makes sense to use an ARM when that is the only way you can qualify for a mortgage on the property you are considering. Remember that historically, ARMs will be more attractive when overall market interest rates are low, meaning that lenders anticipate rising interest rates, which mean higher payments for you as your rate adjusts upwards.

That said, there are certain circumstances when an ARM may be a good financing choice. Here are three examples:

1. **Your home purchase will be temporary.** If you are in an area of rising home values and you know that you will relocate in a couple of years, then an ARM may be appropriate. On a traditional fixed-rate mortgage, you will pay down very little on the principal over the first

five years. During this time, the majority of your payment goes toward interest. For short-term financing, take advantage of the lower payment with an ARM.

2. **Low credit score.** If you currently have a low credit score, but expect to rectify that little problem, then you might want to finance using an ARM, knowing that you will refinance in a couple of years when you can qualify for a better fixed-rate loan.

> ### Unsolicited Advice
>
> If you are considering a short-term living situation, I would suggest looking at renting instead of buying. Remember that a mortgage comes with fairly significant up-front costs (more on that in a minute). Taking closing costs and realtor fees into consideration, a stay of five years or less would financially lean to renting versus buying.

3. **Rising income.** You might use a lower-rate ARM to get into the more expensive house you want now, knowing that your income will rise significantly in the next few years. For example, if you're about to finish a Master's degree and you know that upon completion you will automatically qualify for a promotion, you might want to consider an ARM.

4. **Market interest rates are at historic highs.** Back in the 1980s a 30-year mortgage hit a high of around 12 percent. At these rates it made sense to finance on an ARM as market interest rates declined. But even if you finance with a fixed-rate mortgage, remember that you can always refinance for a lower rate, as long as you maintain a good credit score. Shop for a bank or finance company that will waive a portion of your closing costs if you refinance with them down the road.

> When you **refinance,** you are simply paying off an existing loan with a new loan. A typical reason to refinance is for a lower interest rate. However, you can also apply for a larger loan than the balance of your current loan—this way, you pay off your current lender and have money left over for yourself. This is called a cash-out refinance.

Other Considerations

There are a few other variables in a loan that can cause some confusion, so let's go over the basics.

Down Payment Options

A rule of thumb is that you want to be able to put down 20 percent of the purchase price and finance 80 percent on a mortgage. The reason for this is that if you put less than 20 percent down, your lender will charge you private mortgage insurance, or PMI. PMI is an insurance policy in which you pay a premium that guarantees the lender they will not lose money if you should foreclose on your loan.

Basically, the lower the down payment, the higher the risk to the lender. If you put less than 20 percent down, PMI can be eliminated when the loan-to-value ratio drops below 80 percent. For example, if you buy a home with a 10 percent down payment, and after 4 years your home has appreciated to the point where the balance on your mortgage now represents 79 percent of the current value of your home, you should then be able to ask your lender to drop the PMI payment from your loan. You may want to check what the PMI removal procedure is with your lender prior to closing on a loan. You also only pay PMI on the amount that your loan is over 80 percent, so keep in mind that it will reduce your payment if you can put 17 percent down instead of just 10 percent, for example.

> **Unsolicited Advice**
>
> If you're questioning whether your home will appreciate, then I'd suggest renting or looking for a home in another neighborhood. There are now 95 percent loans available, but the interest rate is a little bit higher. So if at all possible, try to save up 10 percent of the home's value prior to purchase.

Aside from the PMI, I'm a fan of putting down the smallest down payment possible without affecting your interest rate. If you plan to stay in your home for a long time, say 10 years or more, a low interest rate should be your first concern. But with today's prices, I have a hard time recommending tying up more money than is strictly necessary for a down payment.

I'd rather invest the extra cash, and plan on eliminating PMI down the road after your home has appreciated.

For 2007, PMI is a deductible item on your taxes, along with your interest. Look for loans that offer the option to prepay your PMI to maximize the tax deduction.

Gift Money

You can have someone gift you the money for a down payment; however, the lender will require a letter from the giftor stating that the money is truly a gift, and not a loan. Lenders will not allow you to borrow for a down payment. The exception to this is that you can borrow from a 401(k) plan or life insurance cash value. The rationale is that you are not truly borrowing this money, since it is your own.

Points or No Points?

This is a source of ongoing debate and, in many cases, misinformation. First, you need to understand what a point is. A "point" in mortgage jargon represents 1 percent of the mortgage amount and is paid upfront at _closing_. Mortgage interest rates may be quoted with or without points. And this is where the confusion lies.

> **Closing** is the term used for the final meeting between you and the seller. It is where you actually sign the loan documents and the property title and money officially exchange hands.

The purpose of the points option is to allow you to "buy down" your interest rate, by paying a point or points up front. This is known as pre-paying interest.

Mortgage brokers are paid by the bank based on what interest rate the borrower pays. Let's use 5.5 percent as an example. The mortgage broker's commission would be paid based on any interest rate above 5.5 percent that the borrower agrees to pay. So let's say that two lenders are advertising a 6 percent interest rate. If that's all you look at, you would think that both places offer essentially the same loan. But upon application you find out that one of the lenders is offering a 6 percent loan, though only if you pay a point. If he is convincing in selling you on the idea that a point is normal at that interest rate, he will boost his commission at your expense. So points have been seen as a negative because unscrupulous lenders will tack on points simply as a way to boost their commissions.

The practice of misquoting rates now has been somewhat eliminated by regulators, at least legally. So be sure to read the fine print whenever comparing interest rates, because this is where lenders will boost their fees by adding points, or broker fees. It's important to note, however, that points can be a legitimate way to buy down your interest rate. Here's the way it works.

Lenders will "price," or set interest rates, on a 30-year mortgage based on the fact that the average mortgage lasts for approximately seven years. In other words, the average borrower will move or refinance their mortgage every seven years. This is why mortgage rates change more with adjustments in the interest rate paid on a 10-year Treasury bond than with the interest rate changes of a 30-year Treasury bond. So, when the lender prices a loan with a point, they base the new interest rate on the point compensating them for offering a lower rate for just seven years, not the full term of the loan.

So if you plan on being in your home for more than seven years and market interest rates seem to be average or low (meaning that there's less likelihood of refinancing soon), then you would want to pay a point to get a lower interest rate.

> Usually it does not benefit you to pay more than one point to buy down a rate. Lenders realize that some borrowers and good mortgage brokers are on to this strategy, and protect themselves from getting stuck for the long term with a low rate by making successive points less attractive.

The other thing to know about points is that points are 100 percent tax-deductible in the year paid, on a purchase. However, if refinancing, points are only deductible over the life of the loan, so they are far less valuable when refinancing. So, knowing this, here are some quick points to remember about mortgage points.

- When comparing mortgages, make sure that you are comparing interest rates based on paying the same number of points up front. Many loans are quoted without points or maybe with one point. Be careful of Internet sites that report "average" mortgage rates. Since these are averages of loans both with and without points, they will many times include some fraction of a point in the rate quoted.

▢ If you're planning on keeping your mortgage for more than seven years, paying a point may reduce your overall cost by reducing your interest rate.

▢ A point is definitely to your advantage when making a purchase, since points are tax-deductible in the year in which you get your mortgage. The deductibility also shortens the break-even point for paying a point to about five years from seven.

> There are several websites that offer calculators for comparing mortgages. One to check out is mortgage-x.com. But be careful when comparing different types of mortgages. I've yet to see a calculator that accounts for inflation, and few will account for taxes.

Conforming and Non-Conforming Loans

I hate to do this, because you're trying to process enough new information already, but there are two classifications of mortgages you need to know about. They are known as conforming and non-conforming loans.

Conforming refers to a mortgage that meets underwriting guidelines put out by a federal agency, usually FNMA (Fannie Mae). Mortgages are usually sold by the bank to a government agency that "bundles" up a group of mortgages and resells them to investors on Wall Street. Banks do this because they can generate fee income by originating the mortgage. Then, by selling the mortgage, they get their cash back so they can lend it again and make another fee.

Loans that don't meet FNMA guidelines and generally aren't resold are termed non-conforming. Although non-conforming loans are mostly thought of as being for people with poor credit, there are a number of reasons to finance with a non-conforming loan. At this point, what you need to know is that some mortgage brokers prefer to use a non-conforming lender, even for borrowers who would qualify for a conforming loan. So if you're applying for a mortgage loan and the broker says you don't qualify for the interest rate you expected, by law they must provide you with your credit score.

Know Your Credit Score

Remember that mortgage approval is based primarily on four things (the four "legs of the stool"): your credit score, length of time on job, the loan amount as a percentage of home value, and the value of any other investments or assets that you may own. Unfortunately, there is no formula to tell you how these all come into play in the underwriting process. But if you feel that your credit is in decent shape (if you have over a 600 score) and you have one other "leg" to stand on, you may well qualify for a conforming loan.

So until you find a mortgage lender whom you know you can trust or have prior experience with, be sure to look around. Unfortunately, when buying a home, timeliness is a consideration. Unscrupulous brokers will use this to their advantage and spring surprises on you at the last minute. Assuming that four weeks into the mortgage process it would be too late to start over, they may feel that they can stick you with higher fees without losing your business. Knowing your credit score gives you ammunition against any last-minute surprises.

Where to Go for Your Mortgage

This brings us to the question of where to go to get a mortgage. You pretty much have two choices: the bank (or credit union) or a mortgage broker. Let's look at the pros and cons of each.

The Bank

Although banks are becoming more creative, for the most part banks will offer the plain vanilla choices for a mortgage, usually the 30- and 15-year fixed-rate mortgages and several adjustable rate offerings. Almost always, the bank's loans will need to be underwritten to "conforming" standards. The main advantage of going to the bank is that you are far less likely to be ripped off by a bank than you are by a broker.

Typically, the bank will have a singular rate for each loan, with no negotiation other than the option to "buy down" your rate by paying a point. If you qualify for a conforming loan and are looking for the basic 30-year loan or an ARM that the bank offers, and if you are not overly financially savvy, then I have to recommend going with the bank. Pure and simple, the bank will not rip you off, and because their offerings are going to be pretty straightforward it will be easy for you to shop and compare rates and fees. Rates will vary from bank to bank, so be sure to get at least two quotes for comparison.

Credit unions may fall into the same category, but many credit unions are too small to effectively compete in the mortgage market. However, many do offer a limited choice of mortgages. Again, if they offer the terms you're looking for, they may have a lower fee structure than a bank or a broker. But be careful. Since most credit unions are too small to effectively run a mortgage company on their own, many will offer mortgages through a third party. Often this will raise the cost, as the mortgage company will pay some type of fee to the credit union for access to their members. So if you're looking at a credit union, make sure to ask if they lend "in-house" or if they use a third party. If they use a third party, you may still want to get their rates, but don't assume that you won't need to compare that rate with other lenders.

Mortgage Brokers

Why bother with a mortgage broker? Well, sometimes you'll have to. If you have credit problems, you're new on the job, you want a large loan relative to your income, are self-employed, or don't have a down payment, you may have to go to a mortgage broker to find a mortgage that you qualify for.

A good mortgage broker can provide valuable assistance in finding a loan when you can't get one anywhere else. But don't think mortgage brokers are just for people with credit problems. The primary advantage of a good mortgage broker is that they will be familiar with a large number of different mortgage programs from multiple lenders that can fit unique situations. And the best mortgage brokers will fit a loan to your unique situation.

Brokers are also valuable when your conforming loan is over about $150,000, at least here in the Midwest. That number may jump to $200,000 or above on the coasts and in the southeast. Here's why. Lenders pay brokers based on the interest rate they get when selling a mortgage. I have found that bank interest rates appear to be the equivalent of a brokered loan that pays the broker 1.5 percent of the loan amount, if the broker does the exact same loan as the bank. Now, some brokers like to specialize in people with bad credit, where they feel justified in charging 5 or 6 percent for a loan based on its difficulty. Some work with realtors and feel they should make the same 7 percent commission that the realtor charges. However, many mortgage brokers like to work with conforming loans because they are fast and easy.

In our area, a $2,000 to $2,500 commission is pretty typical for a broker working on a conforming loan. So if the loan is less than $150,000, a broker will need to raise the interest rate to make the same commission. On a higher loan, they can lower the interest rate and still maintain their commission. So borrowers looking for high-balance loans can really benefit from using an honest broker.

Compare Both

The best advice is to compare rates with two different lenders. Always get a quote from a bank, and then see if a mortgage broker can beat it. Ask for a _good faith estimate_ when you're quoted a rate that sounds like it may be the best offered. Do not get lazy and borrow from a broker just because he or she works with your realtor! I've seen some excessively high-cost loans sold this way. Unfortunately, too many people are just out to make a quick buck, and will take advantage of you if they think that you aren't going to shop and compare. Never, ever let a lender know that you aren't going to shop and compare rates. No matter who they are, it never hurts to give them some incentive to work in your best interest, not theirs.

So just where do you go when you need a mortgage? I wish it was an easy enough process to provide a set of steps for everyone to follow. But how your four components fit together will vary dramatically for different lenders. The following is a good rule of thumb, however.

1. **Get your credit score.** I've said it before, but I can't stress this enough. Knowing your credit score and your income and years on the same job, most lenders will be able to quote you terms for a mortgage and provide you with a good faith estimate.

2. **Go to your credit union, or find one you can join and go there.** If they offer the type of mortgage you are looking for, and keep the loan in-house, then ask for a good faith estimate. If they use a third party, you may as well ask for a GFE; you're already there, and at least the credit union is trying to give you a good deal.

A **good faith estimate** is a written document that will item-ize your costs to obtain credit. Some costs are not known up front, but the things you want to pay attention to and compare are:

- Interest rate and length of loan, usually expressed as number of payments.
- **Appraisal fee.** Most loans will require the property to be appraised by a professional appraiser.
- **Points.** Again not necessarily a bad thing, just make sure you are comparing apples to apples.
- **Broker fees.** Not a real fee and not necessary. The broker fee was created to avoid disclosing "points" when they were used just to jack up commissions.
- **Processing fee.** Another fee that we call a junk fee. In other words, a fee that has no relation to real costs and is just another way to boost commissions. A typi-cal processing fee should be under $500.
- **Yield spread premium (YSP).** This is how much a mortgage broker makes in commission for brokering your loan for a lender. Banks and mortgage com-panies do not have to disclose YSP. If you're using a broker, a reasonable YSP might be 1 percent to 2 percent of the loan amount.

3. **Once you have the GFE from the credit union, this is the deal to beat.** Call around to the local banks and see if any of them have a bet-ter rate. Make sure you are comparing the exact same program at each lender. When you have the best deal, call back and ask them to send you a GFE.

4. **Ask parents, co-workers, and relatives if they can recommend a mortgage broker.** If so, call the broker and ask what they can do for you. Since most mortgage brokers work on commission, they'll be anxious for the opportunity. However, I've run into many mortgage brokers that would rather not make anything if they can't make a large commission. Unless you're working with someone who was referred to you, if three of your four criteria are pretty solid, you may want to stay with the credit union or bank for your first mortgage. Once through the experience, you will be better qualified to determine whether the mortgage broker is offering a good deal the next time around.

5. **Beware of the Internet.** Understand that I buy just about everything except groceries over the Internet. In terms of Internet shopping, I was a very early adopter. But I'm not yet convinced that the Internet is the way to go for a mortgage. Although it can be a great place to shop for and compare rates and payments, I've yet to see an instance where the consumer really benefits.

> Also be sure to check with the Better Business Bureau in your area. The really bad mortgage brokers will rack up complaints quickly, and it's helpful to know who to stay away from.

That should give you enough information to make a good choice on your mortgage. One caution, though, is this: you're not buying a car, and hard negotiating is not expected. Good mortgage brokers and lenders are knowledgeable professionals. If you negotiate to the point of being obnoxious, you risk one of two things happening. One is that the person who truly has the best deal may no longer be willing to give it to you, and will quote you a high rate just to get rid of you. The second is that someone will take it upon him- or herself to make a fast buck at your expense. Remember that the good faith estimate is just that, an *estimate*. It is supposed to be close, but if at closing you find that your loan is several hundred or even several thousand dollars more than you expected, what are you going to do? Maybe two weeks before closing you'll hear "the interest rate changed and your new rate will be higher." If you're buying a home, you will lose out on the house and a security deposit if you walk away and try to go elsewhere at that point—you don't have time to start over and meet your closing deadline.

The unscrupulous in the industry know that you will have little choice but to go through with the mortgage. Is it unethical and illegal? Probably, but it does happen far too often. The Housing and Urban Development (HUD) has tried to pass a regulation that the GFE not be an estimate but a *guaranteed* statement of cost. Though the legislation never passed, a handful of mortgage companies have adopted a guaranteed quote of closing costs at application. Basically they guarantee that the GFE represents the most you will have to pay at closing. These companies deserve a shot at getting your business.

What Not to Do When Applying for a Mortgage

Wait! We're not quite done yet. The last step is what to do, or really what not to do, between the time you've completed an application and closing. Many loans, and homes, have been lost not due to bad lenders, but bad borrowers.

> Remember that the best investment advice is also appropriate when mortgage shopping: if it sounds too good to be true, it probably is. Mortgages offered by the originating lender are actually relatively competitive, with what are really pretty small differences in rates. But the amount of money a bank or broker wants to make for selling you that loan can vary tremendously.

While some problems arise because people just lie on the application (which is a really bad idea—virtually everything on a mortgage application is verified prior to approval by the lender), most times problems arise between the time the application is taken and closing just due to carelessness. Here are a few words of advice on what not to do between the time you apply for a loan and the closing.

- **Do not stop making payments on loans that are intended to be paid off or consolidated from the financing, no matter what the lender says.** The lender will pull your credit report a day or two before the closing, and new late payments could easily nix the deal.

- **Do not change jobs.** One of the criteria for loan approval is typically time on the job. Taking a new job could nix the deal. Lenders will verify employment within a day or two of closing.

- **Do not lie to emphasize your income.** Many times I've seen self-employed people claim a certain income at the time of application. But after the loan process has started they bring in the required tax returns, which show substantially less income than that which was stated.

- **Do not lose important documents.** Sometimes the borrower cannot find documents such as a divorce decree, bank statements, verification of a gift used for down payment, disability award letter … and the deal is off.

Borrowing for Big-Ticket Items

There really isn't a good way to ever borrow, unless you can convince someone else to pay back your loans for you. Remember that by borrowing you are consuming today at the expense of your financial future. Little expenses don't seem like much, but they add up. And big payments can rob you of a lot of lifestyle that you may regret giving up down the road.

But again, things come up that we do need to borrow for. And, hopefully, pay raises will come. But making smart borrowing decisions today will make a big financial difference tomorrow. I think I've spent about as much time as I can on buying a home, and have pretty well addressed car buying in a previous chapter. The basic rule is to spend less than you can afford. You will receive far less satisfaction from your purchase if you regret it every month for years ahead when you try and keep up with all the other bills. The golden rule of borrowing is to always continue to save something, even when you're trying to pay off your debts.

The Best Approach: A Home Equity Loan

So what's the best approach to borrowing? The answer is kind of like the answer to the question of how you get your first job when all the help-wanted ads say "Experience required." The best way to borrow is on a home equity loan, which means that you must first acquire equity in your home, either from paying down your mortgage or through appreciation of the property.

Building home equity does not happen overnight, but it is a big advantage of home ownership versus renting. It works like this. Typically, a bank will give you a line of credit based on the difference between the value of your home (or a portion of the value, typically 90 percent) and the balance on your mortgage. Just like with a credit card, you can borrow all or part of your limit. As you pay down the loan balance, you recreate credit that you can turn around and borrow again.

Home equity loans have two advantages over other financing. Because you are using your home as collateral, the bank is fairly comfortable that you will pay them back. If you don't, they can literally take your home away through foreclosure. So because home equity loans are considered less risky to the bank, they are more likely to offer a lower interest rate on these loans than they would on _unsecured debt_. Another benefit of home equity loans is the fact that the interest that you pay the lender may provide a tax deduction as mortgage interest. (Check with your tax preparer to see if this applies in your situation.) So usually the best way to borrow for big-ticket items is by using a home equity loan if you can. Interest rates will be half as much, if not a quarter, as what you may pay on a credit card based on national averages.

> **Unsecured debt** is money borrowed without pledging any specific collateral in return.

Credit Cards

If you don't have a home, or if your home is too new for you to have enough equity to be eligible for a home equity loan, then you have to consider other options. Although some credit unions and banks will still offer unsecured loans, most have foregone the option in favor of another form of lending: credit cards. Although rates can be reasonable on credit cards as long as you have good credit, the interest rates and costs can skyrocket if you let your credit score slip, or miss even one payment. So remember, without a home and home equity to borrow against, the best way to minimize your cost is to maintain a good credit score.

The True Cost of Debt: The Wedding Example

As a society, we have a terrible case of "keeping up with the Joneses." And nowhere does this manifest itself more than in the American wedding.

Weddings just have an element of every force that conspires to get us to spend too much, and usually come at the worst possible financial times for the participants. (As a note of disclosure, as the father of two daughters, I have a bit of a bias in this discussion.) But bias or not, the reality is that between the Hollywood weddings, the advertising media, and the wedding industry, weddings have become one of the most ridiculous over-expenditures in American life.

Now I fully understand that I may have to eat these words, but let's try to sidestep the emotions for a moment and take on a hint of rationality. A friend of mine, whose daughter is getting married in a few months, mentioned that his wife is prepping him for the occasion by leaving wedding-related articles for him to read. In his readings he has discovered that the average wedding now costs about $30,000. According to Money. cnn.com, more than $125 billion was spent in the wedding industry in 2005. With this kind of money at stake, let's see what a wedding really costs. (And although I'm picking on the cost of a wedding, the same analysis holds up no matter what you run up your debt on. It is just one more opportunity to stress what the true cost of debt is.)

First, the best way to pay for a wedding is to plan ahead—way ahead. If you were able to save $275 a month for seven years at 7 percent interest, you would end up with $29,700. So your cost would be $23,100 and your earnings would add nearly $7,000 to your total. Compare that to Table 6.5 below, which shows your monthly payment, total payments, and interest costs if you were to finance $30,000 at various interest rates.

Table 6.5: Cost to borrow $30,000 for a wedding.

Interest Rate	Monthly Payment	Total Payments	Total Interest
9%	$482.67	$40,544.28	$10,544.28
10%	$498.04	$41,835.36	$11,835.36
12%	$529.58	$44,484.72	$14,484.72
14%	$562.20	$47,224.80	$17,224.80
16%	$595.86	$50,052.24	$20,052.24
20%	$666.19	$55,959.96	$25,959.96

Even at a reasonable interest rate of 9 percent, if you borrow 100 percent of the cost of the "average wedding," you would not only pay $10,500 more than the actual cost, you would pay over $17,000 more than if you were able to plan ahead and save for seven years.

Statistically the average wedding costs more for a one-time event than most people have managed to save in a working lifetime in their 401(k)s. $30,000 may not seem like too much—the cost of a nice car or two—and now it is more common for costs to be shared by both sets of parents and the children themselves, but look at the opportunity cost surrounding the timing of the expenditure. If the parents can afford to pay for a $30,000 wedding, they could afford to instead add to their 401(k). A $500-a-month contribution for just 10 years could add $100,000 to their retirement nest egg.

If the wedding couple themselves are paying for the wedding, why in the world would they want to take on so much debt at such an early stage of life? Since we're playing with averages here, you either are still paying on, or maybe just paid off, $40,000 of combined college debt, have two car loans, and have either bought or are planning to buy a home, and you will probably add another $10,000 to your debt on furnishings and accessories for that new home. Do you want to spend the next 20 years whining about how you can't get ahead because of all your debt? Whew, now that's an ugly future! But for many, it's not too far from reality.

> **Unsolicited Advice**
>
> Even "modest" weddings can cost a lot, and some debt may be necessary. Just be careful of the advertising hype, try not to feel that you have to outdo what someone else did, and do what's best for you and your family. But just so you know, if you wrote that $30,000 check to an investment account, instead of to the wedding planner, videographer, photographer, bar, band, etc., it could be worth over a quarter-million dollars by the time you and your sweetheart make it to retirement!

Borrowing to Start a Business

I just wanted to add this because some of you will want to forego corporate life and strike out on your own. And I guarantee that you will be frustrated by the lack of borrowing resources for the budding entrepreneur.

First, there is no money from anywhere for someone who has no money on his or her own. You may have heard of the Small Business Administration (SBA). And, yes, they give loans to businesses. But they underwrite them the same way any loan is underwritten. They will want to see you commit a good amount of your own capital, have a written business plan, and see that their money is buying real assets to use for collateral.

At this point, you may be asking why you would need an SBA loan if you had all those things—which would be a fair question. The reality is that most new businesses that need capital systematically accumulate credit cards, and will use cash advances on those cards to finance their new business. Happens all the time. Some are successful and some fail, but that is what risk and reward are all about. Look, no one ever got rich "working for the man." Sure, *some* doctors, and *some* lawyers, and *some* corporate types make a pretty good buck. And many, many small business owners do what they do for the love of their vocation or for the independence … but a whole bunch of business owners do it because they want the financial opportunity.

I was just at a conference and struck up a conversation with a young man (under 35) outside a restaurant. Through the course of conversation I came to find out that he co-owns a major real estate development company, which he started right out of college. Is he lucky? Does he have super-special skills? Is he a trust-fund baby? Hardly. He grew up in a town of 1,000 people, his parents were not rich (in fact, he put himself through college), and for funding he borrowed $25,000 on his credit cards to get started. Gutsy. But often that's what it takes—taking on debt, along with lots of hard work.

But borrowing *to improve* your future is a 180-degree difference from borrowing *from* your future. Would I rather go $25,000 in debt and try to build a financial future than spend $25,000 on something that will be consumed in one day, one week, or even over three or four years? You bet. With one, there is a chance of you significantly improving your future standard of living; with the other, there is a 100 percent certainty that you are lowering your future standard of living. Now which path looks the most risky?

How Not to Borrow: Borrowing from Your 401(k)

Borrowing from your 401(k) should be a last resort for important expenses such as medical bills or, in some instances, to help buy a home if that makes financial sense.

You should never tap your 401(k) for expenses such as cars, vacations, weddings, or other big-ticket items that are all about diminishing returns. Here's why: you will be on the hook to pay yourself back with interest, and by taking a chunk of your retirement money out for some period of time, you forfeit the growth that could have occurred on that money plus the money left in the account. A larger balance can compound faster than a smaller one.

Plus, if you leave your company while the loan is outstanding, you may be asked to pay it back as soon as you leave or soon after. Otherwise, the money will be treated as a distribution, subject to income tax and possibly a 10 percent early withdrawal penalty. For example, I have a client who had a sizeable loan outstanding on his 401(k). One day when he arrived at work there was yellow tape across the front door barring admittance. The company had gone bankrupt without any forewarning. As a result, my client's loan on his 401(k) became taxable income, with a 10 percent penalty.

Remember, your 401(k) plan is your retirement, not a savings account. If you think you need the money now, think about how much more you'll need it when you don't have a job, and no desire to get one when you're supposed to be retired. 401(k) loans are tax traps, and worse, they can jeopardize your retirement.

The Bottom Line

- The mortgage process is complicated, but well worth the effort to shop and compare.

- Use inflation and tax deductions to lower the cost of home ownership.

- The "best way to borrow" really comes down to you and your credit score. If you don't keep a good credit score, you will pay dearly in higher interest rates when you need to borrow.

- By planning ahead and strengthening "the four legs of the stool" prior to borrowing, you can save yourself considerable interest costs by qualifying for the best interest rates.

Insuring Your Stuff

What You Will Learn

- What insurance does and how it is priced

- What the different types of insurance are, and how to choose the one you need

- Why it's important to understand your coverage before it's too late

Okay, so the last few chapters have focused on paying off your debt so you can increase your wealth, increasing your wealth so you can get more stuff, and the best way of getting that stuff. So now what? Well, now that you've got it … you need to protect it. How do we do it? Well, with insurance, of course.

The Purpose of Insurance

Mary Hart was selected as co-host for the popular *Entertainment Tonight* TV show in 1982. The story goes that, after ascending to this position, she took out a million-dollar life insurance policy … on her legs. During the show, Hart would sit on a stool in a rather short skirt, with her legs crossed, and entertain us. For those of you too young to remember, Hart was (and still is) an extremely attractive woman with equally attractive legs. But what would have happened to that profitable career of hers had those "assets" been damaged? Ms. Hart, or her agent, knew that if anything happened to her legs, she would be out of a job. Now, I can't vouch for the accuracy of this story, but it does serve to demonstrate the purpose of insurance.

> This type of "career insurance" is actually pretty common. Many college athletes buy policies that insure them against a career-ending injury before they become professionals.

Many people would wonder why Mary Hart would waste money on insuring her legs, when the odds of anything happening to her would be very small. After all, wouldn't the *premium* be high for such a large insurance policy?

> The **premium** is the amount of money paid to the insurance company for coverage. Generally, payments are made monthly, quarterly, semiannually, or annually.

The answer is this: Hart knew that if something did happen, and here's the key—no matter how small the odds—she would be out of a lucrative job. In fact, she probably felt that her ability to get any high-paying job comparable to hosting *Entertainment Tonight* would be jeopardized. In other words, she made a decision to buy insurance based not on the *probability* of something happening to her legs, but on the consequences that would result if something did happen. She felt in that case, she would need additional resources (an insurance check) if this were to happen to her. From the insurance company's standpoint, the premium was probably relatively low, even on such a large amount, because the probability of something happening to her legs was equally low.

> **Probability** is the mathematical odds of an event happening. It is a step that is used to determine the premium for insurance.

Insurance premiums are based on the probability of something happening and the potential size of the claim. Unfortunately, the more expensive that insurance is, the more likely it is that you will need it. For example, a policy that insures against a career-ending injury would be much more expensive for a professional football player than for a professional golfer, just because the risk of serious injury is so much higher for a football player. This is a very important concept, and one that we will use throughout this chapter. See Table 7.1 below.

Table 7.1: Sample equation that illustrates how insurance premiums are calculated.

Amount of Insurance		Probability of Event		Premium*
$100,000	×	50%	=	$50,000

*In practice, the premium would also include costs for overhead, commissions, profits, and so on, but for our purposes in this chapter, we will consider the actual insurance benefit to be only cost, unless stated otherwise.

From this table, we can see that if we want to insure something for $50,000 and the odds are 50/50 on whether an event will happen in any given year that will allow us to file a claim, then the insurance company must charge 50 percent of the insurance amount for a premium. In other words, with a 50/50 chance of losing their money each year, the insurance company must recoup what they expect to pay out every two years.

A Little Bit of History

Life insurance industry statistics show that the "average" American is underinsured. From what I know, it's not from lack of effort. Insurance products generally pay a very high commission, and there are plenty of insurance agents in need of a sale. It seems that attitude and ignorance are the main culprits for the underinsurance problem. So let's look at a little history to better understand the need for insurance.

Until relatively recent history, say the A.D. 1400s or so, people just didn't understand the concept of probability. For most of civilization, things just happened due to the unpredictability of nature. For example, the odds of being hit by lightning are by observation very low. Man, however, didn't consider the odds when out walking in a thunderstorm. You were either struck by lightning or you weren't. Your odds were 50/50. And most importantly, there was nothing you could do to change the outcome. Either your number was up, or it wasn't.

This began to change rapidly in the seventeenth century among scholars and businesspeople in Europe. Trade was growing. Ships were setting sail for Africa and the Far East. Fortunes were being made. But some were troubled because some of those same fortunes were being lost due to storms and pirates.

In the 1690s, a man by the name of Edward Lloyd opened a coffee house on Tower Street in London. The coffee house became a popular place among merchants to gather and share information gleaned from their voyages. By sharing information on the best routes to take, ports with friendly natives and supplies, likely weather conditions, and such, sailors and businesspeople hoped to lower the risk to their ships and cargo when undertaking these long voyages. Eventually, a group of men pooled their resources and began to _underwrite_ such voyages. In 1871, Lloyd's of London was incorporated to "underwrite maritime insurance." By studying past voyages, the underwriters would determine the probability of a successful voyage and charge a premium based on their conclusions. And thus the modern insurance industry was born. It allowed businesspeople to undertake great risks that they otherwise couldn't afford to take.

Many businesspeople at that time could not afford to take risks on their own. It would take all their personal wealth to put together a boat and crew to sail off on a trading voyage to Africa or the Far East, so loss of a ship would mean being financially wiped out. But due to the potential for profit, these businesspeople could afford to pay some of their income, in the form of an insurance premium, so that others would assume all or most of their financial risk.

> To **underwrite** means to assume financial responsibility in exchange for payment of a premium. In the case of maritime insurance, Lloyd's of London would reimburse the costs if the ship were lost at sea or struck by some other natural disaster.

What Does It Mean for You?

Now how can we apply this to you and modern times? Very simply, if you own property (and no, it doesn't have to be a trading ship), and couldn't afford to replace it if it were lost or damaged, you need insurance. If you have debts that someone else will be responsible for if you should die, you need insurance. And if others rely on you for their income, then you also probably need insurance.

Whether we like it or not, it's necessary. During most of your life you will probably have at least one—and more likely several—insurance policies at any one time. Making the right buying decision (and knowing when not to buy) can save you thousands of dollars over your lifetime. The right decision can protect your job, your income, and your property. And if you should need money due to an accident or injury, the service provided by your insurance company can be invaluable. With something this important, you don't want to leave the purchasing decision up to your emotions or misinformation … right?

What You Need to Know

Simply put, insurance allows us to undertake risky activity that we would otherwise avoid. By understanding this concept, we can better understand and evaluate insurance decisions. As long as the market for insurance is competitive and policy terms and conditions are fully disclosed, then premiums will be based on the probability that you will file a claim and the amount of potential loss to the insurance company. In other words, you do not need to determine whether the odds of something happening justify buying insurance. Your job is to determine the consequences if something *were* to happen. If you are unable or unwilling to deal with those consequences, then you need insurance. And the premium you pay will reflect the odds.

The other thing to know is that the insurance industry is not a perfect example of an open competitive industry. Premiums will, in fact, vary greatly between companies for the same types of insurance. It may be because the regulators care more about the insurance companies than the consumer, or because they themselves don't know the product well enough to understand it. Certain insurance carriers have less interest than others in actually selling certain types of insurance, so they actually price their product high to intentionally minimize sales. Other times, insurance companies have captive agents that have no choice but to sell their product if they wish to make a living. Some insurance companies feel that this gives them the opportunity to charge higher rates than they could otherwise, if their product had to compete for "shelf space" with independent agents.

So, with all this in mind, let's look at a couple of examples of different types of insurance that you may need, how you should best go about evaluating your needs, and how you can purchase a product.

Some caveats before we start: First, the insurance industry is regulated primarily at the state level, so some rules and restrictions may vary in your state. Second, the industry divides insurance licensing into two broad categories: *personal insurance* and *property and casualty (P&C) insurance*.

> **Personal insurance** includes life insurance and annuities, disability and long-term care insurance, and health insurance. **Property and casualty insurance** includes auto insurance, homeowner's and renter's insurance, and various business insurance products.

Although there is considerable overlap between the two, financial planners will generally only work with the personal lines, and health insurance is handled by specialists in business and group insurance plans. The P&C agents are generally "encouraged" by their insurance carriers to sell life and annuities, but I would strongly suggest you seek out two separate agents and work with a specialist in each area. Part of my rationale is that life insurance is the most stable, predictable line of insurance. Most companies that sell primarily life insurance will carry high ratings from insurance rating services like A.M. Best or Moody's. On the other hand, it is much harder for a P&C company to maintain the highest insurance ratings. Things like earthquakes, hurricanes, and tornadoes are much less predictable than human mortality. These company ratings rate the financial strength of the company, which does not necessarily correlate to the quality of their product. So I suggest buying life insurance from life insurance companies and P&C insurance from primarily P&C insurance companies.

In my opinion, you do not need to know, nor should you know, all the ins and outs of the insurance industry. Insurance agents make nice commissions on the policies they sell you. It is their job to know the best products, determine your needs, and recommend products accordingly. In other words, just as with investment salespeople, you should make them earn their commissions. A good agent will not be offended by this concept. In fact, a good agent would much rather design a program that fits your needs than risk improper coverage. All you need to know is enough information to tell whether the insurance recommendations fit your needs or the agent's.

Car Insurance

Most likely, your first experience with insurance will be auto insurance. Fortunately, auto insurance is actually a fairly straightforward purchase. To an auto insurance company, it is not a question of *if* you will be in an accident. It's a question of *when*.

Statistically, you will be involved in an auto accident once every eight years. And we know that with a high probability of an accident, you're going to be facing high premiums unless you can do something to affect those odds. So let's look at the different parts of an auto policy so we can figure out how to keep your premiums low.

Policy Breakdown

An auto insurance policy insures four different things:

- Property damage to your car

- Property damage done to the other vehicle or property involved in the accident

- Personal damage done to yourself and your passengers

- Personal damage done to the occupants of the other vehicle

So the two ways to reduce your premiums are to be part of a statistical group that has an accident less than every eight years, and to reduce the potential liability to the insurance company when you do have an accident. Remember that averages are just that—averages. For everyone who has an accident every six years, someone else only has an accident every ten years. That's where the eight-year average comes in.

How to Get the Best Rates

So what can you do to get what are termed "good driver" discounts, or receive the best rates? Let's check it out.

Keep your grades up. If you are a new driver, there is very little you can do to reduce your insurance rates. But one thing you can qualify for is a reduction based on good grades if you're still in high school or college. Insurance companies have found that there is an obvious correlation among safe driving, overall responsibility, and good grades.

Try to be included on a family policy. Generally, your rates will be cheaper if you can be included on your parents' policy. They may already receive a discount for their past good driving experience and for having multiple policies with the same carrier. I've heard of parents who don't want their children on their own policy, because they're afraid that the accidents of an inexperienced driver could permanently damage their record. This is not a worry, as insurance rates are determined by the driver and the type of car. A higher rate or poorer driving record of one driver will not affect the rates of the other drivers on the same policy.

Maintain a good credit score. As if you haven't heard this one a few times! But as you now know, your credit score affects more than just your cost to borrow money. It affects your ability to rent an apartment, get a job, and get auto insurance. A credit score may not be a deciding factor in auto insurance, but it is a factor that's included in an overall rating system. And since males are considered "junior drivers" until age 30, and females until age 25, you don't need anything else that may cost you more money to drive, do you?

Practice good driving habits. I know being young and driving fast seems like an American tradition. But besides being stupid and dangerous, it can also nail you in your pocket book. In Ohio you do get a "pass" with your first ticket, but once you move out of the lowest premium band, you can easily be looking at a 45 percent increase in premiums. That's a hefty price to pay for a lead foot or a little showing off.

> It never hurts to shop around for rates, even if you're eligible to be added to a family policy. One thing I've discovered about insurance companies is that some companies price a new policy to a minor prohibitively high to avoid having to add young drivers at all. Don't think that an insurance company will cut you any slack just because your mom and dad have been insured with them for 30 years. You may want to start with your parents' policy, but as with any major purchase, a few extra phone calls will never hurt.

Minimum Cost, Not Minimal Coverage

Another way to keep your premiums down is to raise your _deductible_. Remember that the insurance company knows you will be in an accident. Fortunately for everyone, most accidents fit into the fender-bender category, which means that no one is hurt and the cars involved sustain fairly minor damage. So if you have a little money in savings and your insurance policy won't have to cover the cost of this type of accident, you can lower your premiums fairly dramatically by raising your deductible.

To lower your premiums, you should have at least a $500 deductible, and $1,000 would be even better, if you can afford it. Generally, setting your deductible above $1,000 doesn't save enough in premiums to offset the added financial risk that you take on. Be sure to compare costs from several different auto insurance companies. Again, this is what a good agent is for. If she can't tell you where the cost benefit analysis peaks in your favor, then move on to another agent who can.

If the expense of a high deductible is too hard to come up with, you could always apply for a credit card just to cover your deductible. Remember that the insurance company statistics say you will have an accident once every eight years. If you need to charge $1,000 to cover your deductible and your credit card interest rate is 11 percent, it would only cost you $16 a month to pay off that $1,000 in 8 years … just in time for your next accident!

> The **deductible** is simply how much you have to pay out of your pocket before the insurance company starts to kick in their share. If you have an accident that causes $1,000 in damage and you have a $500 deductible, you will be responsible for the first $500 before the insurance company kicks in their share (in this case, the other $500).

But compare that $16 a month to pay off the credit card to how much you save by increasing your deductible to $1,000. Don't accept a higher limit even if the credit company offers it, and don't use the card unless an accident actually occurs. Not only would it be disastrous to be short on credit should the need arise, but having an available line of credit with no outstanding debt will help, not hurt, your credit score. If necessary, you could always put it in a baggie of water and keep it in the freezer to avoid any other use. Sounds crazy, but sometimes it's the only thing that works!

Liability Limits

Each state determines what the minimum amount of insurance liability limits are to drive in their states. But here are the pros and cons of purchasing minimum coverage.

If you're considered a "junior" driver, you are already paying dearly for any policy, and a minimum coverage policy will be significantly lower in premium. A minimum coverage policy will insure your car for its value (this is also required by your bank if you have a loan on your car or are leasing). The policy will also pay for damages to the other vehicle. But while full coverage might pay about $100,000 for an individual's injuries, a minimal policy may only pay $10,000. As you get older (and because you're following the advice in this book), you will have accumulated some wealth, so you will want to increase your coverage to protect your personal assets should you cause an accident and be sued.

Because the purpose of insurance is to provide you with protection against financial loss, minimal coverage is adequate as long as you don't have much to lose in terms of finances. But on the other hand, you need to have coverage on your policy as well that will protect you and your car if you are in an accident caused by drivers with no insurance, or with minimal coverage for themselves. This is called coverage for uninsured/underinsured motorists.

> Before deciding on coverage limits, get a quote on the difference between minimum coverage and higher limits. If you have maintained a good driving record, the difference in premium may be nominal. Think about whether you would want to have financial coverage if you were to be so unfortunate as to cause an accident where someone was injured.

Health Insurance

There is probably no insurance that is more controversial today than health insurance. We spend more money on medical services than any other country in the world, yet we're not first in terms of life expectancy. In fact, based on a new study by the World Health Organization (WHO), the United States ranks 24th worldwide in life expectancy. This ranking is based on a system that subtracts expected years of disability from actual life expectancy. In other words, it's a "healthy life expectancy" ranking—how long a person can expect to live before age and illness affect his or her lifestyle.

As our population ages, more and more of our taxes will be required to maintain government health insurance programs. Private employers will continue to shift a higher percentage of rising medical costs arising from an aging workforce onto employees. What does this have to do with your personal health insurance? This: you will be paying more, not only for your health insurance coverage, but also for the underfunded government programs. It will be in your best interest to do everything you can to minimize your personal health-care costs and to understand the federal health-care system, as you will inevitably face future political decisions based on health insurance issues.

Let's start with the assumption that you have health insurance offered through your job. The first thing to know is that you do want to opt for the coverage no matter what the cost. For young single males, premiums for even the most comprehensive plans should be fairly low, likely under $100 a month. For women, unfortunately, premiums will be nearly 50 percent more due to the addition of maternity coverage. Again, go back to the reason for insurance—to protect you from incurring a cost that you cannot bear on your own.

Now, you may be wondering if you're young and healthy and not planning on a pregnancy, why bother with health insurance? First, I think that if you went through the hospital and asked how many people actually planned on being there, you'd find very few. Things happen constantly that we have no control over, and since premiums take care of the probability of something happening, you only need to ascertain the financial conse-quences. Considering that one of the top reasons cited for filing bank-ruptcy is overwhelming medical bills, I think that the need for insurance is obvious. If something should happen—and things *do* happen—then you need to be prepared. You don't want to create a financial hole that can be impossible to climb out of, or wreck your credit with a bankruptcy.

All Those Acronyms: PPOs, HSAs, HMOs ...

You need to get health insurance. You might as well accept it. So let's get started learning the terminology.

- **Premium.** For our purposes, the premium is the cost of coverage to the policyholder. It may not be the actual cost of coverage, but the cost after the employer's contribution.

- **Co-pay.** The amount of the premium required to be paid by the policy-holder. The co-pay may be stated as a percentage of the total or as a dollar amount. The co-pay amount will vary for different services such as prescriptions, eye care, and hospitalization.

- **Cafeteria plan.** This is a type of benefit plan where policyholders can select from a variety of benefits typically including health insurance, life insurance, disability insurance, and more. Generally the employee is given a dollar amount to spend by the employer for any combina-tion of benefits. The main advantage is that the "income" needed to buy the benefits is non-taxable. Any additional costs will be paid by the policyholder before tax deductions, which lowers your taxable income. (This is a good thing; more on this in the tax chapter.)

- **Section 125 plan.** Section 125 refers to an IRS code that allows any premiums paid for health insurance by the policyholder to be deduct-ed from the policyholder's paycheck on a before-tax basis. This also lowers your taxable income.

◻ **Preferred Provider Network (PPO).** To keep premiums down, some insurance companies have a group of physicians, health-care providers, and facilities that agree to reduced rates in return for having patients directed to them through a PPO. Typically, premiums are lower for using providers in the PPO network.

◻ **Deductible.** Just like with any other insurance, your deductible is how much you need to pay before the insurance company kicks in. Plans with very high deductibles may be called Health Savings Accounts, or HSAs.

◻ **Health Maintenance Organization (HMO).** This is a form of health insurance that has a range of coverage on a group basis. A group of doctors and other medical professionals offer care through the HMO for a flat monthly rate with no deductible. However, only visits to professionals within the HMO network are covered by the policy. All visits, prescriptions, and other care must be cleared by the HMO in order to be covered. A primary physician within the HMO handles referrals for care.

An HSA is a great choice if you're young and healthy. Basically, you pay into the plan an amount that would be similar to the premium in a high-cost, full-service plan, but your premium is divided into two parts. One pays your health insurance premium for a high-deductible plan. The remaining amount goes into a tax-deferred savings account. If you require medical care, you can withdraw money from the savings portion to pay your deductible amounts. If you don't use the savings amount it can stay in the tax-deferred savings or investment account until needed. If money remains at retirement it can then be pulled out, penalty-free, as a supplement to other retirement savings.

There are so many health-care companies and variations of benefits that it is impossible to tell everyone what to do. But here are a few rules of thumb to follow. If you're young, healthy, and single or married with no kids, use an HSA if available. If you're married with kids, stick with a traditional plan. If the budget is tight, PPOs can be a great cost-saver. HMOs will offer the largest savings. However, be aware that most of the controversy surrounding health insurance is due to HMOs.

HMOs share one characteristic, and that is pre-certification. This means that you will need approval for most medical treatment before it's given. You will also be required to use doctors and facilities within the network, similar to a PPO. The problems arise when the HMO does not approve treatment. Now, they can't just say "no" because they don't want to pay. The question only arises for procedures that are considered unnecessary or experimental. While we certainly hope that no one ever finds themselves in these circumstances, just be aware that things do happen. One drawback of HMOs and PPOs is that you are required to use providers within their networks or pay a substantially higher amount for the treatment. If you do not live in a large urban area with a wide range of quality health-care providers available, this could be a concern.

> **Unsolicited Advice**
>
> If you're not on a budget, or if you find that your income is growing and you have more than one health-care option, consider moving up to a full-coverage plan. The freedom to chose your doctor and receive treatment without the stress of preauthorization can be a blessing when you're sick.

Short-Term Medical Policies

So what if you're between jobs or just graduated from college? Two answers. First, many insurance agents will have access to a short-term medical policy. The way these work is that you choose the time period you want to be insured for, usually from one month up to six months, then pay the premium up front for the entire period. Coverage for these programs is very basic and is really only intended to provide "catastrophic" coverage. There is no option for prescription coverage, doctor visit co-pays, or any other feature you might look for in a company plan. This is why the premium is very low, even if you choose coverage for several months. But what this type of coverage does do is provide protection against personal financial catastrophe should you fall ill or be in an accident while unemployed. This is great stop-gap coverage, and I wish employers would help to make employees aware of its availability when they terminate employment, because the other choice, if you are leaving a company that did provide health coverage, is to continue your coverage under COBRA. And this is not such a great choice.

Congress passed the landmark Consolidated Omnibus Budget Reconciliation Act (COBRA) health benefit provisions in 1986. The health-care provision provides that if you are covered under a group health plan and separate from service, you are entitled to continue your coverage for up to 18 months. The catch is you will have to pay 100 percent of the actual premium, including the amount that your employer was paying on your behalf. Also, businesses must employ more than 20 people to fall under COBRA. For more information on COBRA, the Department of Labor has a nice list of FAQ's at their website: www.dol.gov/ebsa/faqs/faq_consumer_cobra.html.

No Coverage: A Disaster Waiting to Happen?

Have you heard the expression SOL? If not, don't worry about it. If so, don't worry—it's really not that bad, as long as you're healthy. If your employer doesn't offer coverage, or if you are self-employed with no employees, you will need to apply for an individual policy.

The problem with individual policies is that insurance companies can turn you down or charge premiums that may make coverage cost-prohibitive. And that is very important to understand. Many younger people in this situation will elect to not pay for health insurance on the basis that they can get it later. But later may be too late. If you do find yourself with an illness now, you might not be able to get coverage later. Aside from the obvious suspects such as diabetes, cancer, or a heart condition, there are so many bizarre illnesses out there that pop up unpredictably, it can be a real concern. And once diagnosed with these pre-existing conditions, you may not be able to receive coverage on an individual basis.

This is another area that will vary between states, but there are two options. In Ohio, once or twice a year, group health insurers in the state offer an open enrollment period where they must accept all applicants. But premiums are very high, as the insurance company knows that they will be accepting people with medical conditions and the associated claims. Check with your state insurance department for rules and options where you live. The second option is to consider a job with an employer that does offer health coverage, because when you join with a group plan, you cannot be turned down.

Being self-employed is one of those cracks in the system that needs a fix. Once you have a group plan, you can change from one group plan to another and be guaranteed acceptance into the group. However, if you have an individual plan, and later add employees and would like to offer a group plan, you are not guaranteed acceptance into the group coming from an individual plan. So it is best to offer a group plan as soon as possible so you will be guaranteed coverage. Individual plans are usually noncancelable, but premium increases can make maintaining the policy prohibitive.

Varied Rates

In Table 7.2 I've included sample rates from one major health insurance carrier. These are rates based on a $1,000 monthly deductible and are the best rates offered for this plan, meaning that this assumes a very healthy group. Do not assume that you will be able to find comparable rates, because rates vary dramatically based on size, health, and geographic location of the group. (I've seen rates that are 200 times greater than those shown in this table! I'm including them mainly so you can see what the total cost of your health insurance could be.)

		Table 7.2: Sample Medical Age Rated Table.		
Age (Male)	Employee	Employee + Spouse	Employee + Children	Employee + Family
< 25	$84.01	$311.45	$266.87	$552.84
25–29	$96.30	$346.27	$279.16	$587.66
30–34	$114.75	$370.87	$290.63	$605.35
35–39	$141.37	$407.73	$265.52	$573.26
40–44	$176.20	$452.81	$300.55	$613.75
45–49	$235.63	$528.63	$359.98	$689.55
50–54	$311.44	$659.77	$426.59	$794.76
55–59	$426.18	$835.98	$553.45	$985.20
60–64	$551.18	$1,042.92	$695.16	$1,192.45

Sample rates for illustrative purposes only. Not an offer to sell. May not represent actual rates.

Typically, the employer will pay half of the employee rate. If you are thinking of going the self-employed route, this should give you an idea of how much you will need to budget for your health care.

Homeowner's Insurance

It's pretty easy to take for granted your homeowner's policy. And with a claim being filed on average only once every 12 years, there isn't much cause to think about it. Premiums are usually paid with the mortgage company, so with homeowner's insurance it can be a case of "out of sight, out of mind." But this can be a big mistake, as the residents and former residents of Mississippi and Louisiana discovered in the wake of Hurricane Katrina. Many people who apparently thought they had coverage to protect them from a loss due to hurricane damage have discovered that their damage claims are being denied. The insurance companies claim that hurricane damage is specifically defined as "wind damage." Since many homes were damaged by water, which is covered under flood insurance, the policyholders' claims are being denied. According to an article in the *Wall Street Journal*, the first court case regarding this issue was settled in favor of the insurer.

Without knowing any details, I can say that the insurance company has a valid point in denying claims for damages due to water damage in the wake of Hurricane Katrina. Since New Orleans sits below sea level, I would imagine that a private insurance company would not even issue a policy in New Orleans that would cover water damage. The probability of what happened would be too great of a risk for an insurance company to take on. And insurance companies would know that should a flood occur it would likely cause citywide damage, not just damage to an isolated house or neighborhood.

Now, this does not in any way address the issue of whether the residents had reason to believe they would have been covered due to intentional or unintentional remarks by the sales agents. But this much is clear: if the residents had understood their policies and demanded explanations from their agents, a great deal of financial heartbreak could have been eliminated.

What You Need to Do

It's hard to go through an entire homeowner's policy and discuss every provision. What I would recommend is that you sit down with an agent (it's usually better if you use the one you have your car insured with, as you may get a discount for having both policies with the same company) and have him or her explain the policy to you. Start with the most expensive, comprehensive policy you can buy. Each provision or rider will be itemized out with the associated premium. Look at each item and have the agent explain what it covers and whether there are other options. If it's not necessary, delete it and work your way down to a policy that is as affordable and as comprehensive as you need it to be. This may not sound like a thrilling evening, but as you can see from the unfortunate circumstances of Hurricane Katrina, it is important to know your coverage.

Tenant's (or Renter's) Insurance

Tenant's insurance is purchased when you are renting a residence. Many people don't understand the importance of a tenant's policy; they think that it only covers the loss of their personal belongings from theft or maybe fire. And while that may be reason enough to look into a tenant's policy, that's not all it does. Actually, the most important part of a tenant's policy is the fact that it covers your landlord's property should something you do—or fail to do—damage the premises. It also protects you against the unfortunate consequences should someone get hurt while in your home.

This is no small thing, and tenant's insurance should be carefully considered by anyone who rents a home. Policies are typically less expensive than homeowner's policies, but can be invaluable in case of emergency.

What You Need to Do

For a tenant's policy, I would recommend that you do the same thing as you would if you owned your home: sit down with an agent, usually the one you have your car insured with, and have him or her explain the policy to you. Make sure that you start with the most comprehensive policy you can buy and go through each provision to see whether it's something you feel you need. With the agent's help, you can work your way down to a policy that's as affordable and as comprehensive as you need it to be.

Basically, now that you have some "stuff" that's important to you, whether it's your home, your car, or even just your health, you'll want to make sure that it's protected. Go out and insure it. It's that simple.

The Bottom Line

- The best way to keep your auto insurance premiums low is a combination of qualifying for the best insurance rates and keeping your deductibles high.

- Medical insurance is a must-have—it's not an optional benefit.

- It's essential to work with an agent to make sure that you understand the benefits on your homeowner's or renter's insurance policy.

Now That You Know You Should, Here's How to Do It: Investing in Your 401(k)

What You Will Learn

- Why a 401(k) is more than just a savings plan

- What they will try to tell you and why it's wrong

- The stages of investing

- A simple investment model to follow for once-a-year maintenance

Live Long and Prosper ... If You Have the Cash

I was listening to one of the morning news programs the other day while I was getting ready for work. They were asking various people of different age groups what their biggest financial concerns were.

The 20-something person said, "Paying off my college loans."

The 30-something couple's response was, "Funding college for our kids and saving for retirement."

The 40-something gentleman? "Doing a better job saving for my retirement."

The 50-something woman said, "I know I'm behind others my age in saving for retirement, but I don't know how to catch up."

And finally the retired couple: "We're worried about outliving our retirement savings."

So there you have it. Once you're out of your 20s or early 30s, you can bet that you will spend the rest of your life worrying about retirement! There are two things you can do about that. Either do nothing now, because your 20s are your last chance to not have to worry about retirement, or do a little bit now to help alleviate worries, and create some significant wealth. Tough choice?

What Is a 401(k)?

The _401(k) plan_ has become the retirement plan of choice for most of America. Originally, they were considered "savings plans" and in many cases seen as a supplement to the _corporate pension plan._ This is probably the biggest reason that so many Baby Boomers have not saved adequately for retirement. No one really explained that the 401(k) is not a savings plan, but an income replacement plan. And replacing your income for 30, or even 40, years of retirement takes a pretty big lump of money, even if you expect to live on a modest income.

In terms of retirement, we Baby Boomers are somewhat of a 'tweener generation. Our parents' generation was the generation of long-term employment, the 30-and-out crowd. (This refers to the idea that after 30 years of working for the same company, there would be a nice pension for them to retire on. After a few years on the rocking chair on the front porch they were expected to "move on out.") But many things conspired to put an end to this idyllic picture, one of which was that life expectancies have been gradually increasing almost since the dawn of man. This is great for us, but not so good for pension accounting.

> A **corporate pension plan** is technically a defined benefit plan. It defines what your benefit will be at retirement based on factors such as your age, years of service, and pre-retirement earnings. The company's contribution is determined annually based on the projected amount of the pension that that they will have to pay out.
>
> On the other hand, a **401(k) plan** is called a defined contribution plan because your contribution is a set, predetermined amount that you control (typically a percentage of your pay). The outcome, or how much you have at retirement, is affected by your investment results and amount of contribution.

How much money you need for retirement (or a corporation needs to have put aside to fund your retirement pension) depends on three things: the rate of return on investments, the amount of each pension payment, and how long you will likely live. This issue of increasing longevity was pretty easy to ignore in the 1980s and 1990s as the stock market experienced its greatest run in U.S. history, but it must be faced by your generation. To understand the dual roles of life expectancy and stock market returns, let me just briefly explain how pension plans work. This is very important to know, so you fully understand that your 401(k) is *it*. It is your retirement plan, not just a savings plan. And to fully understand the responsibility that has been thrust upon you, you must understand the difference.

The old-fashioned pension, the one that would pay you an income for the rest of your life after retirement, was the expectation of the post–World War II generation. Today pensions are becoming increasingly rare—for the most part, only government agencies or extremely large corporations offer them. The reason boils down to pensions having become a financial burden to companies, a burden that was not foreseen just a few years ago.

While a 401(k) plan receives most of the attention, there are several other defined contribution plans that can be offered by employers. While there will be differences, most of what is covered in this chapter will apply to these plans as well:

- Simple IRA
- SEP (Simplified Employee Pension Plan) or SARSEP (Salary Reduction SEP)
- Profit Sharing or Money Purchase Plan, (commonly referred to as Keogh Plans)

Basically, a pension plan is designed to pay a worker a monthly income for the rest of his or her life based on his or her working income before retirement and how long he or she stayed at the same company. During an employee's working career, the company is obligated to set aside money that will fund this future obligation. Obviously, the longer a retiree lived, the more the company would need to pay out. And while life expectancy was showing a dramatic increase over the last couple of decades, the stock market was also on a roll. So in many cases corporations did not even have to add money to their pension plans for several years. The existing balance from many companies' investments was growing so fast that the stock market gains were sufficient to continue to meet rising annual funding obligations. This all came to a quick halt during the market downturn from 2000 through 2002. During this period, the stock market lost about 50 percent of its value (based on the *Standard & Poor's 500* stock index).

The **Standard & Poor's 500 (S&P 500)** is an index made up of 500 blue-chip stocks, or shares of established companies with steady records of profits and dividends and a high probability of continued earnings. This index is commonly used to measure stock market performance.

And many individual stocks plummeted even more. The result was that U.S. pension plans in general became grossly underfunded. The Pension Benefit Guaranty Corporation, the federal agency that insures these private-sector defined-benefit pension plans, had a surplus of $9.7 billion at the end of 2000 but a deficit of $11.2 billion at the end of 2003. Pension plan underfunding stood at more than $350 billion in 2005, and in August 2006

Congress passed a bill requiring that all pension funds, except those in the airline industry, must have their funding caught up in seven years. The idea was that this would reduce the amount of future claims that will be made against the Pension Benefit Guaranty Corporation. (This is necessary because the PBGC doesn't have an extra $350 billion lying around. Well, actually, they do. As a U.S. government retirement agency, Congress can just elect to tax us a little more, to bail out the agency … along with bailing out the underfunded public pensions, like Social Security.)

In other words, current retirees and future retirees (your parents) are accumulating a huge bill that will soon be presented to Uncle Sam to fund our retirement. And you will be the working stiffs who get to foot the tax bill. So on top of a higher tax bill, government regulation will likely create the end result of fewer pension plans. This is because the simple solution for companies that can't afford to get their funding up to required levels will be to do the only thing they can—get rid of them. And the reason you need to understand this is because unlike your parents and grandparents, you will likely be the one responsible for financing your retirement. All the risk that used to be placed on companies to adequately fund your retirement is being dumped onto your shoulders.

Or, more appropriately, onto your paycheck. And without the raise, too.

Congratulations, You're Now a CFO

The risk of being able to afford to fund a pension plan, the commitment to properly funding it, and the responsibility of investing it are all on your shoulders now. Think of it this way: you have now assumed the position and responsibility of what entire departments at large corporations were hired to do. You are the Chief Financial Officer (CFO) of your pension plan. According to Salary.com, the median expected salary for a typical CFO in the United States is $279,815. Do you think your company will have the courtesy to increase your salary for taking on this added responsibility? My guess is no.

All this explains the psychological difference between a 401(k) as a savings plan and as a pension plan. For your grandparents' generation a 401(k) was just a tax-deferred savings plan, a supplement to retirement. For you and your generation, the 401(k) *is* your retirement plan. That is a realization that most of your parents have not made, or have made too late. $100,000 is a lot in a savings plan, but it's not even a fraction of what's necessary in a pension plan. Let's take a look and see what a couple million will do.

Investing Early Makes a Difference

Okay, let's up the ante a little bit here. Let's say that you are an upwardly mobile professional or semi-professional. By the time you retire you expect that you will be making $120,000 a year based on what your boss's boss's boss is now making. By then you'll be packing away bucks in your 401(k) and paying a ton in taxes to keep Social Security and Medicare alive, so I'll assume that you are actually living on about $90,000 a year in today's dollars right before you retire. If you want to keep this income level in retirement, here's what you'll need.

Table 8.1: Amount of money needed for retirement at age 65.	
Current age	25
Retirement	65
Current income goal	$90,000
Projected retirement income at 3.5% inflation	$389,294
Lump sum needed	$7,785,880

I'm going to pause now and just let that sink in for a moment. And be assured that last number is $7,785,880—it is not a typo. More than 7 million dollars.

I'm assuming that you withdraw 5 percent of your balance each year to live on after retirement, and you wish to leave the balance intact for your heirs. Now, you might say, "Forget the kids, I want to spend what I have!" It's really not a big difference, and considering that your life expectancy could easily reach 120 over the next 40 years, you really want to keep your cash intact anyway.

This is the real difference between a savings plan and a retirement plan. Now you know why they say "a million dollars just isn't what it used to be!"

You *Can* Take It with You

So how did we get hoodwinked into this 401(k) business anyway? Well, actually, we asked for it. As the company/worker relationship has changed from the "30-and-out" model, workers tended to change jobs more frequently. And because the old defined-benefit pension plans assumed that you put in your time and retired from the same company you started with (and that you had to be around 62 to retire, or maybe as early as 55 if you had put in 30 years of service), pension plans were lost as employees changed jobs more frequently.

With 401(k)s we have the ability to take our retirement money with us, even if we change jobs often. And after only a few years (usually between five and seven), you even get to take the company's matching money with you when you go, according to a *vesting schedule*. This *transportability* feature has been a huge selling point for 401(k) plans. When you leave, you can either *roll over* the money into your new employer's plan, or into an IRA, or take the money as cash (but with penalties and taxes paid).

A **vesting schedule** refers to a period of time over which the employer's contribution to your 401(k) account becomes yours, even if you leave the company. A typical example would be that 20 percent of the employer's contribution becomes yours over each of the first five years of your employment.

Transportability means that you own the money in your 401(k) plan. If you leave your current employer you can take 100 percent of the money you contributed, along with that money's earnings, with you.

A **rollover** means that your balance in the 401(k) plan can be moved into another 401(k) plan or an IRA without paying taxes or penalties on the balance.

There is a limit to this transportability feature, however. If you take your balance as cash, you will pay taxes on the amount in your account, as well as a 10 percent additional penalty. (To calculate the tax liability, you add the distribution amount to your regular income for the year. Then calculate the tax on that amount.)

If you leave your job and decide to take your 401(k) as cash instead of rolling it into another 401(k) or an IRA, the employer is required to withhold 20 percent of the balance. This is not necessarily what you will actually owe. (For example, in 2006 if your taxable income, including the distribution, was between $30,651 and $74,200 and you were single, your taxes on the distribution would actually have been 25 percent plus the 10 percent penalty.)

Start Small and Be Smart

So how in the world do I expect you to save over $7 million throughout the course of your career? Well, there are a lot of variables at work here that will affect how much you can save. First, remember how in Chapter 1 I said that it is common for older people to pack away a ton of money in their last few years of work? In Table 8.1, you would have actually been earning nearly $520,000 a year prior to retiring. It would be reasonable that you could be putting $200,000, or more, of that away each year for the last 5 to 10 years before you retired. You'll also probably be working longer. I mentioned a 120-year life expectancy, and I was being serious.

With our conspicuous consumption, we Baby Boomers have driven the United States (and to some extent the global economy) since our births. But more importantly, we've driven the search to prolong life. Now that we have started to make serious progress in living longer, we're seeing the not-so-pleasant consequences—an increase of rheumatoid arthritis, Alzheimer's disease, diabetes ... all brought on because we're living longer. So the focus of medicine has now turned from extending life at all cost to extending the quality of life. Medicine is finally starting to prevent instead of just reacting—by the time you retire, you could have a personal nano-bot running around inside of you constantly providing feedback on your health. Problems could be fixed internally by your nanobot MD.

But a longer life means a longer working career. I hate to say it, but if you're 30 now, plan on working until you're 70, at least. The good news is that time is a great ally in building wealth. In investing there is a Rule of 72. If you divide your investment rate of return into 72, the answer is how long it will take for your money to double. (For example, a 10 percent rate of return means your money will double every 7.2 years; at 8 percent, your money doubles in 9 years.) So in our previous table, if retirement age was at 72 instead of 65, our investor would only need half the savings by age 65. (In other words, $3.9 million will grow to $7.8 million in the additional 7.2 years with a 10 percent rate of return.)

As I've already said, the best strategy for you is to start early, even if you start small—and to be smart.

Take Advantage of Company Matching

With most 401(k) plans, the employer will match all or a portion of the employees' contributions. In addition, any money you put into the account yourself will reduce your income before taxes are calculated—ultimately saving you money at tax time. Take a look at our revised monthly budget with this information added.

Table 8.2: Revised sample budget that includes a contribution to a 401(k) account.	
Gross Income	$2,500.00
Deductions	
Social Security	$155.00
Medicare	$36.25
Federal	$275.00
State	$77.44
City	$18.86
401(k)	$150.00
Employer	$75.00
Health	$40.00
Net Income	**$1,747.45**

If you look at Table 8.2, you'll see I added a $150 contribution to a 401(k) plan. Also notice that Net Income only drops by $132.55. This is because the federal, state, and city tax liability were also reduced since the 401(k) contribution lowered the taxable income. (Unfortunately, Social Security and Medicare deductions are not affected by the 401(k) contribution.) So if we add it up, by simply making a contribution of 6 percent of the pay in this example, we gained a $75.00 employer contribution and a $17.45 tax savings. That's $92.45 of benefits on a $150 investment. Now that is being smart about your money!

Also, look at the tax tables given earlier. This example is based on the second-lowest tax bracket. The tax advantages are magnified tremendously as you work your way up to that $150,000-a-year salary.

401(k) Investment Strategies

Most 401(k) plans today offer employees a selection of _mutual funds_ that they can direct their money into. At the onset of these plans there was some reluctance on the part of employers to offer them to their employees. One of the concerns was who was responsible if an employee made a bad investment decision? Is the employee solely responsible or would liability fall back onto the employer?

> A **mutual fund** is a type of collective investment that pools money from many different investors and invests the money in stocks, bonds, short-term money-market instruments, and/or other securities.

The Department of Labor (DOL), which oversees all types of pension plans, made a very important ruling. They ruled that if employers followed a set of guidelines that included providing employees with the proper information necessary to make good investment decisions, then liability for investment performance would lie solely with the employee.

Now, on paper this sounds pretty good. The reality is that the information in many cases is so confusing that about 25 percent of eligible employees choose to not to invest at all. The educational materials, and DOL guidelines tend to focus on the "risk level" of the employee. So someone who fills out a questionnaire that shows they have little tolerance for stock market ups and downs will be guided toward a more conservative portfolio, which historically generates a lower return. The trouble with this strategy is that a 401(k) is your retirement plan, and should therefore be designed to accumulate enough money for your retirement. Instead, left to individual preferences, investments are all over the risk spectrum because people invest based on emotion instead of reason.

As an investor in your 20s or 30s, your portfolio should be full of high-risk investments because of their long-term horizon, right? And it stands to reason that the older worker, who has saved too little and is running out of time, should invest conservatively because he or she "can't afford to lose anything."

Wrong.

Let's talk for a moment about the inaccuracies of these assumptions. I know that for most of you, it's very tempting to skip to the end of this chapter and get right to the "What exactly should I do?" section. (By the way, what I'll tell you is extremely simple and requires action only once a year!) But please don't jump to the end. Research on investor psychology tells us this: if you just skip down, you may follow my advice for a while. But sooner or later, you'll read another book or article, or someone at work will tell you another way you "should" be doing it. You'll think that the new way sounds better and move on to the next idea or system. And you will continue to do this for years, until at some point you'll be fed up and seek professional help, which could potentially be a disastrous decision (more on that later). On the other hand, if you actually understand what you're doing, you will have the confidence to stay the course. So if you can just stick with me for the rest of this one chapter, and understand what you are going to do, you won't have to jump from fund to fund, or system to system, because you will be able to see through appealing (but bad) advice. And if the mood should strike, and you want to do some analysis on your own, I'll be giving you a pretty good path that you can follow to do your own homework.

What Exactly Are They Telling Me?

Throughout history mathematics has been considered the "pure science," in the sense that numbers don't lie. $1 + 1$ will forever and always equal 2, and it's pretty hard to argue otherwise. It took mathematical formulas for Copernicus to convince the world that the Earth did, in fact, go around the sun. (It was also mathematics that saved Copernicus from the nasty medieval fate that awaited others who dared to challenge the beliefs of the times.)

But my industry is a bit contradictory when it comes to the use of mathematics. On the one hand the math needed for financial planning computations is a little more complex than what's needed to balance a checkbook (which, as we found out, only about half of us do). And the math needed to formulate investment strategies is a lot more complex … yet many of us don't understand it. To see where I'm going with this let me tell you a story about a young lady we'll call Jane.

I had run an ad at Wright State University looking for an intern, noting that the job could lead to a full-time position after training. WSU is our local state university, and they happen to have been one of the first universities in the country to offer a degree in financial services. Overall, I can say that I've been pretty impressed with many of their graduates. So I call one, named Jane, in for an interview. One of my first questions is, "So why did you major in financial services?" I figured I'd get one of the typical answers, "it's challenging," "to help others," whatever. But instead I got, "Well, I really wanted to be a finance major, but there's this one finance class you have to take that's really hard. There's a lot of math. You don't have to take it in the financial services program, so I switched to that." True story.

So presumably Jane is somewhere out in the world, helping people like you achieve financial success—even though she was incapable, or at least unwilling, to understand the math necessary to do basic finance! That's scary, but it is also the financial services industry. You see, much of the bad advice given in our industry, even by well-meaning advisors, could be avoided if the advisor would "just run the numbers" for themselves.

Unfortunately, there are absolutely no qualifications necessary to become a "financial planner." To get into financial planning one just needs to enter the workforce and demonstrate an ability to convince people to do business with one's firm. The most financially successful people in this industry are frequently (but thank goodness not exclusively) good salespeople who may or may not have any actual financial skills at all.

Now let me backtrack just a bit before I get into too much trouble here. A person doesn't necessarily need any specific degree or background to be a good financial planner. But being a good investment advisor is a whole different thing. Financial planning is what we've been doing so far in this book. A few future value calculations, some statistics, and good organizational skills can all go a long way, especially if most of it is done by computer. So it is far more important to understand the financial planning concepts than it is to actually understand calculations. Armed with the experience necessary to obtain a Certified Financial Planner designation (CFP), and the understanding of a few basic concepts, a financial planner can do a great job of planning.

Understanding Risk

Let's start with the risk questionnaire. Every 401(k) plan that I've seen has had a risk questionnaire or analysis that asks questions that you score yourself on. Based on your score, which tells your risk tolerance, you will be classified as a certain type of investor. But the risk questionnaire is rather silly, because whenever I ask a prospective client how much money they want to make I always get the same answer: "As much as possible." When I ask how much are they willing to lose, they respond, "None." Doesn't matter what age you are, where you are in life, or what your goals are; the answer is always the same. We all want to make as much as we can with no risk. And this is where the whole concept of modern investing (it's called Modern Portfolio Theory, or MPT) completely falls apart.

> **Modern Portfolio Theory (MPT)** really isn't modern at all. Today's investment models, from 401(k)s to large institutional portfolios, are governed by the tenets of MPT. MPT is really a compilation of three works; the first was done in 1959, the next in 1963, and the final work was published in 1981.

Although the works that make up the MPT were very accomplished academically, their application to the real world is somewhat of a stretch. Each of these works attempted to make sense of hundreds of thousands of historical data points for stocks, bonds, and Treasury bonds without the availability of a modern computer. Therefore, many assumptions had to be made to make the data workable with the technology—or lack thereof—of the day.

So without going through an academic dissection of MPT, here is what you need to know:

- The current application of MPT is not an application at all. Most of what is done today, citing MPT, is contradicted by what the original authors actually said.

- As interpreted, MPT says that you can design a portfolio based on a given rate of return and a predictable level of risk. In other words, if you want a higher return, all you need to do is take on higher risk. If you want to avoid risk, well, then you will be avoiding return as well.

What a bunch of bull! Look, investing isn't like baking bread. The purveyors of MPT would have you believe that all you have to do is turn up the heat (higher risk) on the oven and your bread will get done faster (higher return). But if you know anything about baking you know that this method results in a burnt ball of goo. And that's exactly what "aggressive" investors in technology stocks have come out with over the last seven years—a burnt ball of goo.

Figure 8.1 is a graph of the NASDAQ since 1974 from www.finance.yahoo.com. Back in the 1990s, many of the new technology companies were listed on the NASDAQ. Typically, a company would move to "the Big Board" (the New York Stock Exchange) as they grew in size. But starting in the 1990s companies such as Microsoft and Intel decided to stick with their NASDAQ listing. As such, the NASDAQ became synonymous with technology stocks. Since many of these companies were new, but with exciting prospects, the NASDAQ became somewhat synonymous with high-risk, high-reward investing. And as you can see, in the second half of the 1990s the value of the NASDAQ, driven by tech stocks, rose to incredible heights. During this period, the MPT advocates were in their heyday. The market worked exactly as predicted; higher risk (new technology companies) did in fact provide higher returns.

> Originally an acronym for National Association of Securities Dealers Automated Quotations, **NASDAQ** is an index representing the return of stocks that are traded on the NASDAQ exchange.

But look what has happened to the index from 2000 on. In March 2000, the index peaked at just over 5132; it finished 2006 at 2415.29. That is 53 percent below its high, over six and a half years later! In fact, the last time the NASDAQ was below 2400 was in January of 1999. So an aggressive investor who invested in the NASDAQ in January 1999 and has held on the way the buy-and-holders tell you to has had roughly a 0 percent total return for over 7.5 years. Where is the higher return associated with the high risk? That investor would have made more money in a savings account in a bank, and would also have had no risk.

Now if you had invested in the NASDAQ at the worst possible time, in March of 2000, you would have a 53 percent loss at the end of 2006. So you're probably thinking that it would take a 53 percent gain to get back to even, right? Wrong. In fact, if the index is at 2415 and the peak was 5132, it would take more than a 110 percent return to get back to the all-time high. How long will a buy-and-hold investor have to wait to see that kind of gain? I don't have a crystal ball, but I'll tell you that more than doubling your return does not happen overnight.

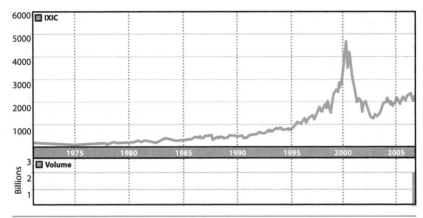

Figure 8.1: A chart of the NASDAQ index from 1998–2006. (Yahoo.com)

The First Rule of Investing: Don't Lose Money!

This is the problem with so-called "aggressive" investing. To put it simply, the industry tends to define *aggressive* in terms of volatility. The wider the range of returns, from the highs to the lows, the more "aggressive" an investment is said to be. But somewhere in this definition is an assumption that the higher highs will offset the lower lows and produce better returns. Unfortunately, the math just doesn't work out that way. Here's what I mean. Take a look at the example in Table 8.3.

Table 8.3: An example of "aggressive" vs. "sensible" investing.
(This information is not representative of actual investment returns.)

Annual Return	Joe Aggressive	Susie Sensible
Year 1	20.00%	10.00%
Year 2	−5.00%	10.00%
Year 3	17.00%	10.00%
Year 4	18.00%	10.00%
Year 5	0.00%	10.00%
Total Return	50.00%	50.00%
Average Annual Return	10.00%	10.00%
Growth of $1,000	**$1,573.88**	**$1,610.51**

Here we have two investors, Joe Aggressive and Susie Sensible. They have both filled out their risk questionnaires, and Joe decides that an aggressive growth mutual fund fits his needs. Susie, although young, chooses to be more cautious.

Joe's investment has three very good years, and two not-so-good years. (For the proper perspective on this, the S&P 500 index will lose 20 percent of its value one year out of five.) So based on history, Joe is pretty lucky. His worst year is –5 percent and he had one year of no gain. Susie, on the other hand, cruises along at 10 percent each year. Both have a 50 percent cumulative rate of return. Both have an average rate of return of 10 percent a year. But look at how much money each of them has at the end of five years! Assuming that they both started with $1,000, Joe now has $1,573.88 and Susie has $1,610.51.

So even though Joe took more risk, he has less money. Now there's not a huge difference in their ending amounts, but compounding that difference over a working career can add up to real money.

Wait, that still doesn't explain the difference, right? How can two investments with the same average annual return come up with different accumulated values? Let me show you. Take a look at Table 8.4.

Table 8.4: An example of negative compounding.	
Investment	**Rates of Return**
Year 1	+50%
Year 2	–50%
Average	0%
Return on Investment	–25%

For example, if you start with $10,000 and make 50 percent, you will have $15,000. Lose 50 percent and you will have $7,500, or 25 percent less than what you started with. This is what I call _negative compounding_.

> **Negative compounding** refers to the fact that if you have a negative return on an investment, it takes a larger percentage gain just to get back to even.

You have now learned the first rule of investing: Don't lose money! The mathematics, which never lie, work against you. Any loss requires a larger gain to bring your working capital back to its original level. The definition of risk is that a large loss is not followed by a big enough gain to have made the loss worthwhile.

Increasing Risk/Volatility Assumptions

Based on the assumed relationships, we would think, and are in fact led to believe, that mutual funds that invest in small companies will outperform mutual funds that invest in big companies. And that mutual funds that buy growth companies will outperform mutual funds that buy value companies. And that low-return funds will be less volatile than high-return funds. Let's see what history tells us.

In Table 8.5 are the results reported in a paper written by professors Samuel L. Tibbs, Stanley G. Eakins, and me titled "Profitability of Style Index Momentum." The paper is written to explore the value of a specific trading strategy, the switching between investment styles as it applies to mutual fund investing. The chart below ranks different investment indexes, first by volatility and second by rate of return.

Table 8.5: Style index risk and return rankings.			
Investment Index	Risk Ranking	Return Ranking	Actual Returns
Small-Cap Growth	1	5	9.84%
Mid-Cap Growth	2	4	10.88%
Small-Cap Value	3	1	16.09%
Large-Cap Growth	4	6	8.69%
Mid-Cap Value	5	2	14.75%
Large-Cap Value	6	3	12.26%

Russell Indexes from 1972-2005
Risk Ranking using Standard Deviation
Average Annual Returns from 1972-2005

While the rankings are pretty much as expected when looking at risk rankings in terms of the size of stocks in the index, the relationship is nearly opposite of what is expected when looking at the return rankings. And value indexes ranked as both the least volatile and the highest return over the time period studied, with Mid-Cap and Large-Cap Value showing the least volatility and nearly the highest return characteristics.

Does this mean value always beats growth? No, of course not, but it does consistently. In another paper written by Craig L. Israelsen titled "How

Often Does Value Beat Growth?" and published at Horsesmouth.com, he answers his own question by saying "62% of the time for large caps, 71% of the time for mid caps, and 90% of the time for small caps ...." Professor Israelson's conclusions are based on five-year rolling returns using data from 1980 through 2004.

Just a sampling of studies of actual data strongly supports the claim that risk, as defined by volatility, does not necessarily translate to higher returns over the long run. In fact, average annual returns for the more volatile asset classes are significantly lower than the returns from safer, less volatile investments. The implications are pretty straightforward. You can be a successful investor on your own by adopting a very simple, low-risk strategy.

Aggressive or Conservative ... or Neither?

So now you're wondering, if I'm not an aggressive investor, what am I? Shouldn't I be taking more risk than, say, my dad or grandfather? The answer to that, at least for now, is "No, not really."

Keep repeating the mantra, "Good investing is not losing money, good investing is not losing money ...." You see, to me there really is no such thing as an aggressive investor at this level. Because without spending time on really understanding the markets (which still gives no guarantee), you will for the foreseeable future be a buy-and-hold investor. In other words, I want to set you up with a system to invest your 401(k) while simultaneously giving you the best opportunity for growth and the lowest probability of a major loss. All this, without having any great secret knowledge or having to take much time to do it!

What's in It for Them?

"Why would you diversify your investments if you knew what you are doing?"

—Warren Buffett

For all the talk and allure, the stock market does not typically make poor people rich. Instead, it tends to make rich people richer or rich people poorer!

For those of you not familiar with the name, Warren Buffett is one of the richest men in the world—and one of the few people in history to have accumulated massive wealth through investing. This accomplishment is a true testament to Mr. Buffett's talent in stock investing. The one thing I learned early in business is if you want to succeed, follow in the steps of someone who has actually done what they talk about. Warren Buffett has certainly "walked the walk," not just "talked the talk."

It's just not that easy to make money through investments. You have to understand the market, financial statistics, how the economy affects the value of investments, and have a very good understanding of investor psychology, as well. In addition to that, you need probably the biggest ingredient of investment success—a whole lot of humility. Unfortunately, these are not the attributes of the average financial planner or stockbroker.

Most people in the industry, even those who really want to do the right thing, are brainwashed by a mutual fund industry that sees success as the ability to gather and retain your assets. The industry fosters an attitude that it doesn't really matter what you invest in, just as long as you invest. To this end, the "education" from the mutual funds and brokerage industries tells you to diversify. In other words, no matter what is happening in the market, to the economy, in politics, you've been advised to stay invested in a little bit of everything at all times.

Now, let's think about this. Who does this advice really benefit? The investment industry, the mutual fund companies, and the brokerage firms make money from your assets, or the amount of money they have under management. In other words, the more money invested, the better off they are.

So what does that mean? An industry that is based on you, the investor, investing your money and never taking it out of your investments (i.e., buy and hold), and a retail sales force that gets paid for bringing in new assets, no matter what the market conditions may be. The primary form of compensation for retail investment people is commissions. On a commissioned transaction, the broker is paid all or most of their compensation when you invest. So there is little incentive to service existing clients, and strong incentive to bring in new clients … and their assets.

In other words, the entire industry is one giant conflict of interest, based on bringing in assets and ignoring your existing investments while trying to gather more of your assets. The financial services industry is dominated by players whose best interest is served by you investing your money, keeping it where it is, and receiving little if any service after the sale.

Now, on its own this isn't so surprising; many industries are structured this way. When was the last time you bought anything and were truly happy with the service after the sale? But the problem in this case is that the very people who have a selfish interest in your money are also the people who are providing most of the "advice" you receive on how to invest. We don't just let the foxes to tell us how to guard the henhouse, but we rely on them to do so! I'm not saying this to put anyone down. I'm saying this so you understand what you're faced with.

Let's go back for a minute to the concept of risk tolerance as a basis for investing. With this concept different investments are scored from 1 to 9 based on their expected return, and separately again from 1 to 9 based on their expected risk (see Figure 8.2). Let's say you score a 5 for risk. There are then two ways to invest.

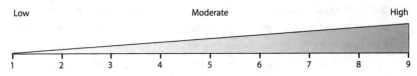

FIGURE 8.2: A standard risk scale, with 1 being low risk tolerance, 5 being moderate, and 9 being a high tolerance for risk.

One way would be to invest as you see in the figure. The pie chart in Figure 8.3 is from a real insurance company's brochure and represents the holdings of one of their investment funds. With this approach, you simply buy a little of everything (in this case, quite literally a little of everything). By definition, if you bought equal amounts of each investment, you would end up with the average return and average risk of the group. So let's say you end up at 5 on our scale. This is a great sales pitch, because it looks a lot more complicated than it really is, and salespeople can show off using pretty, multicolored pie charts.

I have some problems with this concept, though. One, as I just mentioned, is that if you buy and hold a whole bunch of investments, you end up with average risk and average return. Why should you, as an investor, spend your hard-earned money on fees and commissions for average returns? The second problem is, again by definition, if our average is a 5, then half of our investments are underperforming, and half of our investments are being subjected to more risk than average, with the idea being that your only concern is your "portfolio."

I don't find this consistent with reality. For example, if you have $20,000 invested, 1 percent (or $200) would be in "Small Company Growth," which would be about a 5 on a return scale and a 9 on a risk scale. My question is, why bother? If you're looking at this as a portfolio, or at the whole $20,000, then what difference can it possibly make to have $200 out of $20,000 in one fund? Whether that fund "booms" or "busts" is rather irrelevant since it makes up only 1 percent of the portfolio. Thus my quote from Warren Buffett—diversification is only necessary when you really don't know what the heck it is you are doing. And dividing a portfolio into 44 different funds goes well beyond necessary diversification.

So again I ask, if the insurance company doesn't know what they are doing (Warren Buffett's words, not mine), then why pay them a fee to manage your money for you? Since insurance companies and mutual fund companies are the biggest providers of 401(k) plans, this is the type of advice you will be receiving on how you should invest your funds.

So what is your alternative? Doesn't it make sense that if you want something with a risk level of 5, you just invest in an investment that is representative of a 5 risk level? And wouldn't you be even better off if the expected return level was even higher than a 5? Yes, it does. And that's where we're heading. Take a look at Figure 8.3.

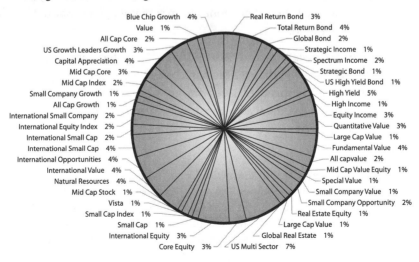

FIGURE 8.3: Sample pie chart showing diversification.

Do as They Do, Not as They Say

Whenever I give talks on financial planning, I try to explain to my audience that in any business dealing you have to look at what is in it for the other guy. And no matter how much trust and confidence you may have in him, you have to "follow the money." In other words, if you're expecting someone to do something other than what is in his financial best interest, sooner or later you're likely to get burned.

What you need to do is see through the "self interest" advice of the financial services industry, and learn to do as they do, not as they say. So before we get back to your 401(k) plan, let's look at the players in the financial services industry and how they affect the investment advice you get.

The retail, or consumer, side of the financial services industry can be broken down into three generalized groups:

Salespeople with very little knowledge or real skills. These are the people you need to avoid like the plague. Their idea of financial planning is what product has the highest commission to maximize their own financial planning.

Financial planners. These are the dedicated people who enjoy doing planning work. Their business model is based on developing a life plan for their clients. Unfortunately, most planners make their money by charging fees or commissions for investing your money. So while they may be good at planning, they make their money from something they may not be that good at: investing.

Registered investment advisors (RIAs). RIAs are fee-based investment managers. Most will charge a fee based on assets under management. As independent advisors they have a *fiduciary* responsibility to work in your best interest. Most, if not all, advisors who focus on investment management will be RIAs.

> **Fiduciary** is defined by the Certified Financial Board of Standards as follows: "[Acting] in good faith, with the care an ordinarily prudent person in a like position would exercise under similar circumstances; and in a manner he or she reasonably believes to be in the best interests of the client."

The investment industry providers, the mutual fund companies, variable annuity companies, and the variable life insurance companies all rely on financial planners and financial salespeople to sell their products. That means the purveyors of these products have to come up with a story that is simple enough for the average financial salesperson/planner to understand so they can sound smart when they pitch the goods to you. So catchphrases like "risk analysis," "diversification," and "style analysis" are all thrown around like they mean something more than they do. And you end up with what I call "pie-chart investing," as you saw in Figure 8.1. So it boils down to this: the mutual fund industry is the biggest culprit behind the greatest misinformation campaign in U.S. history. And since mutual funds are the investment vehicle of choice among most 401(k) plans, you need to understand what they tell you, why they tell you that, and what you really need to do to create the wealth you will need.

Stages of Investing

In investing there are three distinct stages: building a portfolio, maintaining a portfolio, and withdrawing from a portfolio. In each stage, volatility plays a different role.

While building a portfolio, you can take advantage of the same volatility that hurt Joe Aggressive earlier. Understand that when you put money into your 401(k) plan, you are buying shares of a mutual fund. The value of your account is the number of shares you own times the value of each share. So building your retirement nest egg is akin to building your house one brick at a time. What if you were going to build a house in, say, 10 years, and you were going to start buying bricks now? To make it budget-friendly you'd send the brickyard a little (say, $200) at a time. Wouldn't you be thrilled every time the bricks went on sale? Investing in your 401(k) is no different. Look at the example in Table 8.6.

Table 8.6: The effect of volatility in a sample investment.

Dollars invested	Price per share	Number of shares	Value
$200	$10	20	$200
$200	$8	25	$360
$200	$10	20	$650
Total invested	**Rate of return**	**Total shares**	**Value**
$600	0%	65	$650

Look at what volatility has done for us now. We have invested a total of $600, we've had a 0 percent rate of return (the beginning share price and ending share price were the same at $10), but we have actually made money, ending with $650 for our $600 investment!

So while we want to avoid risk like the plague, when we have invested a pot of money at once and want it to grow, volatility becomes our friend when we are *dollar cost averaging* into a fund.

> **Dollar cost averaging** refers to investing the same sum of money regularly over time. This allows you to take advantage of dips in the price of a security to accumulate more shares.

Step-by-Step Formula for 401(k) Success

Now you're confused. Do you want a conservative fund or an aggressive one? you wonder.

The answer is both. And here is how I want you to get it.

Step 1. Look at the investment options in your 401(k). Most plans will categorize your funds for you. If not, just look at the names of your funds. Most funds will describe their investing style in their name. Look for a fund with any of these terms in its name: Small-Cap Value, Aggressive Growth, Mid-Cap Growth, or Microcap Growth. Avoid any funds with the following terms in their names: Foreign, Technology, New, Science, or Select. Not that there aren't times to own these funds or that they are not "good" funds; they may well be. But our goal here is both effectiveness and simplicity.

Step 2. The next fund you want will be described in one of the following ways, and I've listed these in order of preference, so stop when you find a fund that matches: Dividend Growth, Large Value, Mid-Cap Value, Equity Income. If there is more than one fund in the top category, make your choice based on the fund with the best 10-year return. If no fund has been around that long, go for the best return for the longest period given.

Step 3. Log onto your plan website and you will have a few more decisions to make. First, choose the fund that you want your contributions to go into. (That will be the fund you came up with in Step 1; we'll call that your Buy fund.) Second, direct any employer matching contributions into the same fund. Third, if you have already been contributing to your plan, move your entire balance into the fund you chose in Step 2 (we'll call this your Hold fund).

Step 4. On an annual basis, and this is very important, I want you to move all the money that has accumulated in your Buy fund, the one where the new contributions are going, into the Hold fund. A good time to make this move, so you remember, is whenever you file your tax return for the year. Historically, the first quarter of the year is one of the strongest times for the stock market. Due to New Year optimism, pension plans being funded, and contributions to IRAs, cash flows into the market are usually strong. You may have heard the saying "Buy in November and go away in May." By holding the aggressive fund through the first quarter of the year, you will take advantage of this stock market *seasonality*. And by switching accumulated values in the Buy fund into the more conservative Hold fund, you are better protecting what you've accumulated from a market drop.

> **Seasonality** in investing is a theory that investment returns are consistently better or worse at certain times of the year or month, or even during the week.

Whether you are a conservative or aggressive investor, dollar cost averaging works best with a more volatile fund. And no matter what type of investor you are, you want to do what will work best for you. So we pick a fund like Joe Aggressive's fund for your contributions and company match. Due to the fund's volatility, you will have more opportunities to accumulate your shares while "on sale." On the upside, aggressive funds will provide a shot in the arm to your portfolio in very good markets. And as you get older and your annual contributions become a smaller percentage of your account, a drop in your Buy fund will have less impact. When your other fund looks stodgy, this fund should shine.

By doing this you will better protect what you have accumulated each year by moving it into a more conservative (read: less volatile, not necessarily lower return) fund. But I've also added a fourth funding source for your retirement: dividends.

Make Your Investments Accumulate More Wealth

We all could use a little free money. I've already shown you that you have three sources of funding going into your 401(k) plan. The first is your own contributions—this is the tough one. But in return for your fiscal responsibility, a typical employer will match some of your contribution with their own for your second source. Third is the tax break you get from the IRS. Remember that your contributions are added on a pre-tax basis, which means that your contributions don't count as income when figuring your income tax. Here, I've used the same table from Chapter 1 but I've added a fourth contribution source, dividends.

Table 8.7: Dividend payments in a sample investment.			
Contribution	**$ Amount**	**% of Income**	**$ Invested**
Employee	$2,400	6%	$2,400
Less tax savings	$600	1.5%	
Net employee cost	$1,800	4.5%	
Employer match		3%	$1,200
Dividends		2.5%	$1,000
Totals	$1,800	11.6%	$5,100

ASSUMPTIONS: *$40,000 ANNUAL INCOME*
EMPLOYEE CONTRIBUTES 6% OF PAY
EMPLOYER MATCHES $.50 FOR EVERY DOLLAR THE EMPLOYEE CONTRIBUTES, UP TO THE FIRST 6%
ACCUMULATED BALANCE IN THE PLAN IS $50,000
THE INVESTMENT FUND PAYS A 3% ANNUAL DIVIDEND

> **Dividends** are money that some companies pay out of their earnings to their shareholders, or someone who owns shares of that company's stock.

By re-investing dividends, you are taking advantage of the first wonder of the financial world: compound interest.

> **Compound interest** is the process of earning interest on your interest. In this case, your dividends will buy more mutual fund shares, which pay more dividends, which buy more shares …

Now this might not be where you are now, and it will take some time to accumulate $50,000 in your 401(k), but these numbers should be pretty effective in convincing you of the opportunity you have if you just take advantage of it.

We've already gone over the tax benefits and employer match, so now I'll explain the dividend contribution. Companies have three things they can do with their earnings. They can reinvest in the business by buying or adding to capacity (land and buildings) or by spending it on research and development. They can save the money for future expenditures. Or they can pay it out as a dividend to their shareholders.

This is one reason we use a large value or equity income fund. Companies that fit into these categories are large and established. Typically, they don't grow extremely fast, but they do grow consistently. And since management can plan on steady growth, they feel comfortable committing a piece of their earnings to shareholder dividends. Again, don't be fooled into thinking you can't make money with these companies, or that I'm just too old to understand growth or technology companies. One thing I've learned is if you want to be successful, do what successful people do. And the mutual funds in these categories have one thing in common: their investment managers will use methodologies most closely resembling those of Warren Buffett.

Buffett's investment success can be summed up pretty simply: buy stocks of good companies at a good price. And by investing in a mutual fund with a similar philosophy, if not the exact same strategy, you can have the fund you buy add a significant contribution to your 401(k) every year through dividends. In my example, your own investments are adding 2.5 percent of your pay into the fund, and buying more shares for you. And that is how to get rich—make your investments accumulate more wealth for you!

Q&A: Let's Address the "Buts"

A full discussion of all the various investment strategies you could use is well beyond the scope of this book. But I do want to take time now to address some common "buts." (I'll also touch more on investment ideas in the next chapter.)

Q: *Everyone says that I should diversify. If I only own two funds, am I diversified enough?*

A: The "everyone" you refer to is mostly the mutual fund companies and their army of financial product salespeople. It is unquestionably in the best interest of the mutual fund industry for you to diversify into many mutual funds. But if you diversify more, you spread your money around lots of funds, which hides the bad performance of some of them. You also spread your return around, which by definition gives you an "average" of all your holdings—the good, the bad, and the worst. History and experience show that as long as your returns remain average you are unlikely to sell your funds and go somewhere else. I'm trying to show you how to be above average.

The idea of diversification is to avoid the risk of an individual company. In every article I've ever read on diversification, spreading your money among 25 or 35 stocks is deemed adequate to properly diversify. Holding two mutual funds is plenty of diversification if those funds are properly chosen as described in this chapter.

Q: *What should I do when foreign stocks, or small caps, or some other category is doing better?*

A: Nothing. I fully understand that, based on history, your Hold fund may never be the top-performing fund of all your plan mutual fund choices for the year. But what I also know is that based on history, it is equally unlikely to be your worst either.

Q: *In different years some of my fund options do really well. Isn't there a way to move from fund to fund to find the best?*

A: Yes, sort of. The industry will call this "market timing" and tell you how bad it is and how it won't work. I don't call it "market timing"; I call it "investment management." Since most financial salespeople/planners are unable or unwilling to develop investment models on their own, they stick with the diversify buy-and-hold system. There definitely are ways to move among funds to increase returns. However, this book is for those of you who are really at the early stages of work and life in general. You have too many other things to do with your time than to try to figure out how to outguess the market. If advanced investing really does interest you, a good place to start is in the appendixes at the end of this book. One note, though: if you choose to ignore this advice, do your experimenting with your Buy fund, not your Hold fund. You'll do less damage this way!

The Bottom Line

- You don't need to go through a bunch of steps and questionnaires before investing in your 401(k).

- The number-one rule of investing is "Don't lose money."

- A successful 401(k) investment strategy can require only one day a year to maintain.

Real Estate Investing

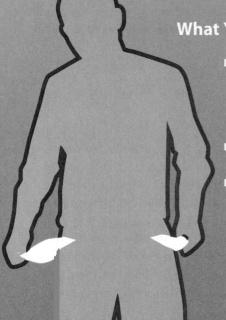

What You Will Learn

- Understand the many options when choosing to become a real estate investor

- Evaluate purchase options

- Decide when to be a landlord and when to sell

I'm looking at a flyer I received from the Ohio Real Estate Investors Association (OREIA) for their annual conference. The conference covers three full days with special pre- and post-conference seminars. Looks like there are about 20 different presenters and about 25 different sessions covering topics from short sales to investing in mobile home parks (don't laugh—mobile home parks can be cash cows!). The presenters look like a varied group as well; young, old, men, women, all ethnicities—more diversity than I've seen in 20 years of attending security industry conferences. In short, a pretty good cross-section of Americans. And it seems like they all know something important: that it doesn't take the grandiose plans of Donald Trump to improve your net worth with real estate.

Real estate investing isn't like other types of investing. Some of the most successful real estate investors I know probably haven't worn a suit since the last wedding they attended. There are no glass ceilings or degree requirements in real estate investing, and you can easily start out on a part-time basis. Oh, and the best thing of all is that with good credit (there I go again), you can get started with little or even no money of your own.

So why isn't everybody a real estate investor? Risk, hassle, fear of the unknown … take your pick. Real estate investing is not for everyone. It does take time. There are numerous strategies, financing options, and of course legal complexities involved in real estate investing. Just like in stock market investing, there are many ways to analyze the market. There's always the "get rich quick" hype, and lots of different strategies to distract the potential investor from the goal. But sometimes you have to just jump in and get started.

If I Knew Then What I Know Now, I'd Be in Real Estate

This is not going to be a complete primer on how to invest in real estate. There are probably thousands of books on the subject, and there are far too many things you should know if you really want to be an expert. But probably the best strategy is to use the knowledge you've gained here, an understanding of your own local market, and a desire to begin a profitable venture to jump in and buy your first property. The OREIA is the state chapter of a national organization, and in Ohio alone there are 27 local chapters. The best thing to do is find an organization near you and join. There is absolutely no better teacher than those who are already doing successfully what you want to do. The voice of experience beats a book or seminar any day.

The catchphrase in financial planning these days is "wealth management," but few firms live up to the billing. Most financial planners will tell you that since your home is one of your biggest assets, you already own plenty of real estate, and you therefore need to bulk up on stocks and bonds to balance your portfolio. The reality is that few "wealth managers" make money on real estate, but they do on stocks and bonds, and the problem with their argument is that a home is rarely a financial asset. It is a roof over your head. As such, it is unlikely that you will liquidate it one day to generate income.

True, in some instances it is possible to sell your home at the time of retirement and move to a smaller place. And in other instances, relocating from a high-priced area to one with lower property values will allow you to cash in a portion of your home equity to add to your available funds at retirement. If you find yourself in one of those situations, then certainly a percentage of your home equity can be considered an investment. But for most Americans, retirement means staying close to home, where familiarity and family are priorities. In that case, downsizing usually means upgrading in age and amenities, which translates to higher cost. While a house is a good tax deduction and can provide a cheap way to borrow, it is not an asset. I'd caution against taking advice that says otherwise.

Creating Wealth with Someone Else's Money

Investment real estate—that is, a house or property that you own but do not live in—is the only investment where you use someone else's money to create wealth. This shoots a great big hole in most diversification theories. Don't get me wrong, there are downsides, and obviously traditional investment portfolios are a major asset for most people. But if you feel "trapped" at your current income level, don't feel that your income allows you to accomplish what you want, and are willing to invest time and effort into creating wealth, then real estate investing may be for you.

So where do you start? That depends mostly on your strategy. Real estate investing typically involves one of two strategies: either purchasing property and renting it to those who can't or don't want to buy for themselves; or, just like in stock investing, buy low and sell high. In real estate vernacular, this is called *flipping* the property.

> **Flipping** refers to the practice of buying a property below market value and selling it quickly for a profit. Flipping usually involves "fix-up" costs to bring the home up to market value.

Rental Properties

I'll start with buying property with the idea of renting it for a period of time, either for cash flow or to ultimately own the property for personal use. Many times, my clients become landlords by default—usually when they inherit a property and choose to rent it instead of selling. But whether by default or choice, the moneynomics of being a landlord are the same. When you rent out a property, you are in a position of having someone else buy an asset for you.

So let's look at a few guidelines to get started with. First, I'll start with the easiest purchase decision. Can you buy a property and pay the mortgage, taxes, insurance, and upkeep costs from the tenant's rent? If so, what are you waiting for? Many real estate investors will say that you need immediate cash flow, meaning that your rental income should actually exceed your mortgage costs to make a purchase worthwhile. I'm certainly not going to argue the point, but I think it greatly narrows your opportunity. Let's look at an example.

Is the Return Worth the Hassle?

In Table 9.1 I've laid out a hypothetical scenario. Let's assume that you purchase a property for $100,000 by putting $20,000 down and financing 80 percent of the value. (This is a conservative loan scenario, and we'll discuss other options shortly.) All the rules of getting a residential mortgage, which we discussed in Chapter 6, apply to this situation as well. You'll want to borrow for as long as possible; in this case, inflation will work twice in your favor: first, as your mortgage payment remains fixed, its true cost is declining as inflation erodes the value of the dollar. Second, if you look at the rent column, rent starts at $750 a month and is increased annually with inflation as well.

You'll notice that initially your cash flow is actually negative; rent is $9,000 but your costs are $10,462, which leaves a shortfall of $1,462 a year. A bad investment? Not quite, because this is where it gets fun, an example of moneynomics at its finest. Notice that in the second column the value of your property increases every year. Now, on a year-to-year basis, this is not always the case. But even if you look at the current depreciation in home values, it is only a correction of grossly overinflated appreciation of the last several years. I will bet that if you take the 10-year period from 2000 to 2010, most residential real estate will have shown at least a 3 to 4 percent growth rate, which will likely be representative of inflation for that period. But while your real estate is increasing in value, the government assumes that it actually declines in value, and lets you take a tax deduction for this "loss"! Now this gets exciting! In fact, it's a real opportunity for revenge.

Table 9.1: Table showing cash flow for a $100,000 rental property.

Year	Property Value	Mortgage Balance	Annual Cost	Annual Tax Savings	Net Cost	Annual Rent	Net Income
1	$100,000	$80,000	$10,462	$5,309	$5,153	$9,000	$3,847
2	$104,000	$79,263	$10,612	$5,293	$5,319	$9,360	$4,041
3	$108,160	$79,263	$10,768	$5,276	$5,493	$9,734	$4,242
4	$112,486	$77,611	$10,931	$5,257	$5,674	$10,124	$4,450
5	$116.986	$76,688	$11,099	$5,237	$5,862	$10,529	$4,666
6	$121,665	$75,694	$11,275	$5,215	$6,060	$10,950	$4,890
7	$126,532	$74,622	$11,457	$5,192	$6,265	$11,388	$5,123
8	$131,593	$73,467	$11,647	$5,167	$6,480	$11,843	$5,363
9	$136,857	$72,223	$11,845	$5,140	$6,705	$12,317	$5,612
10	$142,331	$70,881	$12,050	$5,111	$6,939	$12,810	$5,871
15	$173,168	$62,442	$13,206	$4,927	$8,279	$15,585	$7,306
20	$210,685	$50,177	$14,613	$4,661	$9,952	$18,962	$9,009
25	$256,330	$32,352	$16,325	$4,273	$12,052	$23,070	$11,018
30	$311,865	$6,448	$18,407	$74	$18,333	$28,068	$9,735

According to the IRS, residential real estate loses its value in a "straight line" over 27.5 years. That means that you divide your original purchase price by 27.5, and take the resulting amount—in this case $3,636 per year—as an income tax deduction called "depreciation." On top of that, you get to deduct your mortgage interest, for a total first-year tax deduction of $5,309. So now your negative cash flow has turned into a $3,847 positive cash flow. Thank you, IRS!

If you look at the last column in Table 9.1, you'll see that your annual net income increases every year, except for years 25 through 30. This is because you lose your depreciation deduction after 27.5 years—but this is quickly offset with increases in rent.

Opportunity Cost

But we're not done yet! Whenever you look at an investment's return to determine whether it's a good investment, you must look at what your money could have earned if you had done something else with it. This is known as _opportunity cost._

> **Opportunity cost** is the cost of passing up the next best investment choice when making an investment decision.

With this hypothetical purchase, I assumed that you put 20 percent down on the property and financed 80 percent. So our cost in financial terms is $20,000. To properly evaluate this investment, we need to look at what else we could have done with $20,000 instead. Take a look at Table 9.2. This is what many "financial planners" will show you (if they can figure out how to do the math).

Table 9.2: Value of $20,000 if invested.		
Year	**Invest $20,000 at 10%**	**Property Value**
1	$20,000	$100,000
2	$22,000	$104,000
3	$24,000	$108,160
4	$26,620	$112,486
5	$29,282	$116,986
6	$32,210	$121,665
7	$35,431	$126,532
8	$38,974	$131,593
9	$42,872	$136,857
10	$47,159	$142,331
15	$75,950	$173,168
20	$122,318	$210,685
25	$196,995	$256,330
30	$317,262	$311,865

If our analysis stopped here, then it would seem like a wash. We'd get the same result whether we invested our $20,000 in the stock market (assuming a 10 percent after-tax return) or to bought real estate. The investment property would be worth $311,865, and the $20,000 invested at 10 percent would be worth $317,262. The decision would seem to come down to whether the net cash flow, from the Net Income column in Table 9.1, is worth the hassle factor of being a landlord. True. But let's also look at a better analysis of opportunity cost.

If we kept the $20,000 invested for the whole 30 years, then a true comparison would include not only the value of our rental property after 30 years, but also the value of investing our hypothetical net cash flow every year as well. Let's look at Table 9.3. Here we have the net income from our rental property in the first column. The second and third columns show the value of investing the net income each year, at the beginning of the year, at 5 percent and 10 percent, respectively. The last column is the $20,000 invested at 10 percent from Table 9.2.

Table 9.3: Opportunity Cost Analysis.

Year	Net Income	Invest 5%	Invest 10%	Invest $20,000 at 10%
1	$3,847	$4,039	$4,231	$20,000
2	$4,041	$8,483	$13,986	$22,000
3	$4,242	$13,361	$30,082	$24,200
4	$4,450	$18,702	$53,662	$26,620
5	$4,666	$24,537	$86,019	$29,282
6	$4,890	$30,898	$128,609	$32,210
7	$5,123	$37,822	$183,074	$35,431
8	$5,363	$45,344	$251,260	$38,974
9	$5,612	$53,505	$335,242	$42,872
10	$5,871	$62,344	$437,344	$47,159
15	$7,306	$118,347	$1,322,577	$75,950
20	$9,009	$199,033	$3,213,365	$122,318
25	$11,018	$312,905	$6,920,192	$196,995
30	$9,735	$461,102	$13,794,285	$317,262

Yes, that number in the third column is over $13 million—all generated from investing the cash flow from just one rental property valued at $100,000. At this point, I don't think you'd care if the rental burned to the ground! And that's not all. Other expenses related to your purchase can also provide added tax deductions. Take a look at the following deprecia-tion list, taken from IRS tax instructions.

- Refrigerators, ranges, dishwashers, carpeting, furniture—5 years
- Land improvements (sidewalks, fences, landscaping shrubbery, septic systems, water pipes)—15 years
- Computers and peripherals—5 years
- Typewriters, adding machines, copiers—5 years
- Automobiles and trucks under 13,000 lbs.—5 years
- Office furniture (desks, chairs, file cabinets, etc.)—7 years
- Residential rental property building—27.5 years
- Nonresidential rental property—39 years

These items provide a tax deduction over the listed number of years. For example, if you buy a refrigerator for your rental property, you can deduct the cost, in equal amounts, over a 5-year period. In addition, smaller items (such as paint or plumbing supplies) can be deducted immediately if used to maintain the property. One caution, however: landlord tax rules are a maze. Be sure to find a CPA experienced in working with other landlords before you buy your first property.

The Benefits

Let's look at the opportunities that come from this one rental purchase.

Cash flow. Tired of living paycheck to paycheck? Try adding a property to your portfolio that consistently generates income on a monthly basis. And, unlike with your paycheck, you can count on getting a raise. Tenants expect rents to increase.

Retirement income. Getting by, but can't come up with money for your 401(k)? Try rolling your profits from just one rental property into your 401(k) or other retirement account. $13 million from someone else's money—and only $20,000 of your own—ain't so bad.

Becoming a mogul. Why stop at one? After just five years you have over $40,000 of equity in your property and $20,000 in your investment account, assuming an after-tax, 5-percent return. Why not use it to buy another two or three properties?

Get the point? Thanks to two economic certainties, inflation and taxes, real estate is the shortest and surest path to accumulating real wealth, for anybody. The example I gave is about as unassuming as it gets. No special skills are involved, no luck is needed, no sitting through sheriff's sales or auctions is required. Just find a decent property in a good school district, buy it with an easy-to-find, 80 percent loan-to-value mortgage, and throw a "For Rent" sign in the front yard. And read up on ways to ensure that you get a decent tenant!

The Assumptions

Before proceeding I should probably explain the three basic assumptions you need to make if you decide to invest in real estate.

1. Inflation will continue at or higher than historic rates.

2. Tax advantages of owning real estate will continue.

3. Demand for housing in general, and rental property specifically, will remain strong.

I've pretty well covered the inflation issue a time or two already. But specifically in housing, here are the numbers. The U.S. population was 200 million in 1967. It took 39 years to grow by 50 percent to 300 million in 2006. If the population grows another 50 percent in the next 39 years, by 2045 the U.S. population will be 450 million. I know demographers expect a slowing growth rate, and predict we'll only hit about 400 million by that time. Much depends on immigration trends. But either way, U.S. population growth will continue, and with that growth the one absolutely sure thing that everyone needs is a home. And many will choose to rent that home.

Barring a major overhaul of the entire tax system, I would say that tax advantages for real estate are pretty safe. The home builders, bankers, mortgage lenders, and realtors all make up a pretty powerful lobby group, and all would rebel at the thought of anything that would discourage a vibrant housing market. And the government has always taken the position that home ownership and a strong housing market need to be encouraged. Not that changes won't be made, but the beauty of real estate is that you own a real asset that has real value. If you should decide, for any reason, that you no longer want to be a landlord, then you always have the option to sell.

Vacation Properties

Many people assume that they can get a cheap vacation by buying a vacation home for personal use, renting it a out for a few weeks, and getting all the tax advantages of a rental property. Not quite; the IRS is on to that one.

The Rules

The rules are quite complicated (no surprise there), and need to be reviewed carefully if you're looking into purchasing a vacation home. But basically, the determinant revolves around 14 days of use. If you use the property for more than 14 days and rent it for more than 14 days, you prorate deductions between personal use and as an offset against income. But you are limited to residence deductions—no depreciation is allowed. You can offset all your income if you have enough deductions, but you cannot show a loss. The only way to fully use a vacation home as an investment property for tax purposes is to use the property for fewer than 14 days per year. This doesn't leave much time for vacationing, considering the hassles of landlording from a distance. However, if you find yourself one day closing in on retirement, having a vacation home is a great way to have someone else pay for your future retirement home.

If you're considering the purchase of a second home, review the rules closely and make sure that you don't get in over your head, assuming that you can sell the home quickly at a higher price. While good properties in good locations always seem to be in demand, no property is impervious to market cycles and economic turns.

When it comes to the IRS, an extra warning can never hurt. If you do invest in a vacation home, never try to take the full deduction and use your property more than 14 days, thinking that you won't get caught. If the IRS audits your return, they will likely check things like electric and water consumption when the property was supposed to be empty.

Flipping Properties

While being a landlord may have traditionally had a blue collar image, flipping has gone mainstream. There are several TV shows on just this type of investment out now, and one of these, appropriately named *Flip This House*, offers flip tips at www.aetv.com/flipthishouse.

While buying property at the right price certainly helps the economics of the deal when renting, it is absolutely essential to flipping. Notice that I avoided saying "cheap" or "low," and instead used the term "right." I did so because this is an area that has some commonality with stock investing, except that your style is probably more dictated by demographics than personal preference. In most normal markets, the idea is to buy low and sell high. But in some markets, you'll have no choice but to buy high and sell higher, which is similar to growth investing in the stock market. And as with stocks, this growth style comes with a lot more risk.

Although real estate prices might not move quite as fast as the stock market, a change in sentiment, interest rates, or a new, hotter market can all knock 10 percent or more off the value of a property in a very short time. So although most of the sexy side of flipping focuses on expensive houses in fast-growing markets with six-figure profits, a much more realistic approach is to focus on ways to buy property cheaply instead of counting on rapidly rising prices.

While there are far too many buying strategies to fully cover each one, real estate is unique in that in many cases you are going to be buying someone's home, and you want to do so at the lowest possible price. But because you are buying homes, there are some unique opportunities out there that you need to have a basic understanding of.

The Fixer-Upper

The most common way to buy real estate cheap is to buy a fixer-upper. Most home buyers, when looking for a new home, want a house that is in move-in condition. Buying a home is a major financial undertaking for most people, and no one wants to save up for years and make payments that represent a major chunk of their paycheck on a home that is in disrepair. This can provide an investor with a great buying opportunity.

Homes can be found in most markets in every condition, from completely dilapidated to just needing minor cosmetic work. Obviously, the more work the home needs, the greater the opportunity to make a profit. However, don't discount the idea of purchasing homes that only need a little TLC as a way to turn a quick profit. Especially in higher-end and newer neighborhoods, homes can sit for months just because of an odd choice in carpet or wall colors.

What you want to look for are homes in nice neighborhoods that usually turn over quickly, but are just not selling. In this case, you should see if the home has any interior items that can be replaced inexpensively—preferably without hiring contractors. Also go over the exterior. Realtors cite exterior appearance, or "curb appeal," as a key factor for a quick sale. Since your potential profit margin may be slim, you may want to contact the seller directly and let him or her know that if the realtor's contract expires without the home selling, you would be interested in purchasing the property.

Let's say that you are looking at a $190,000 property that should sell for $200,000. Typical realtor fees will be 6 to 7 percent of the selling price. In this case, based on a $190,000 sale price, the owner would owe the realtor $11,400. If the home hasn't sold during the realtor's contract, which is usually for 90 days, you would offer something less than the asking price. Even in a normal market, a seller would expect to lower their price by say 3 to 4 percent. But since the house hasn't sold, you could ask the seller to come down a full 10 percent, or another $19,000. You could also make a list of items that need to be fixed and add the repair costs, if done by a professional contractor, to your proposed discount. Let's say that you come up with another $10,000 for paint and new carpeting. In all, you would offer $40,400 less than the current asking price. If your fix-up costs run $10,000, and you can turn around and sell the property at the original asking price, you would pocket around $30,000 for your trouble. Not bad if everything goes smoothly.

But first you'll want to make sure that the property only needs cosmetic surgery, not a major bypass. If major work is needed, you should find out ASAP whether the owner is willing to further decrease the price to compensate for repair work. Be sure to hire your own home inspector to inspect the property.

Next, ask yourself if you are ready, willing, and, most importantly, able to do the work yourself if the home needs major repairs. While contractors might be necessary for some work, it is rare that you can buy a home that is on the market for a low enough price to be able to pay professional contractors to do your rehab work for you. At a minimum, you should be prepared to paint and plant. But don't be discouraged—I've heard many stories of investors making a nice little profit in just a couple of months by planting some nice bushes and flowers and painting a few rooms.

Once finished with your rehab work, it is imperative that you sell quickly. Remember that every month that goes by is another mortgage and insurance payment out of your pocket. You may have noticed that in the example above I did not include an allowance for a realtor fee to sell your property. That's because a realtor's fee can kill a profit margin. So what many flippers do is sell the property on their own. These properties are known in the industry as FSBOs (pronounced FIZ-bos), or properties that are for sale by owner.

Sheriff's Sales

Sheriff's sales are offered when the owner of a property did not pay the mortgage company, their taxes, or both. In these situations, the owner is evicted and the properties are auctioned off to the public. One of the problems with buying a property at a sheriff's sale is that the buyer is not given access to the home for any type of inspection prior to the sale. This means that the buyer must make sure to pay way under market value to offset the risk of expensive repairs. Think of it this way: in a best-case scenario the person being evicted did nothing to maintain the property. In the worst case, he or she may have done intentional damage to the property. The process of going from eviction notice to auction can be eight months to a year, depending on where you live. A lot can be done to a house in eight months.

Sheriff's sales are frequently touted in the infomercials as sure ways to profit in real estate. It does happen, but here's the downside. Many times the home is being foreclosed on due to nonpayment of a mortgage, which means that the bank is being stuck with a house that it doesn't want. Over the last several years mortgage companies have been lending a higher and higher percentage of a home's value to buyers, which has resulted in less home equity. It also means that the original buyer probably paid private mortgage insurance on the loan. So here is what happens.

The bank's mortgage on the property being auctioned is likely to be from 90 percent to over 100 percent of the property's value. Since buyers are looking for a bargain, no one is going place a bid that high at an auction, so the bank ends up bidding for their own house, and eventually wins the bid. The bank then hires a realtor, who puts the property up for sale at fair market value. At this point, it is okay to sell for less than what was owed, because the PMI will kick in and pay the difference between what the bank receives from the sale and the balance on the unpaid mortgage. So now, instead of a "distressed" property selling at auction, you have a bank selling a house in a traditional manner, meaning that they are likely to get a traditional price.

Now, does this mean that auctions are a waste of time? Not necessarily. There is always the possibility that a property is being auctioned with a low enough loan value that the bank is not a factor in the bidding. How aggressive a bank is in bidding will also depend on the local real estate market. In a seller's market, the bank is more likely to bid, thinking that they can do much better selling the property themselves. But when the market turns soft, as it has recently, banks will likely be much more interested in just getting out of the property.

Since a mortgage lender will lose everything in a sheriff's sale for nonpayment of taxes, they will likely buy the property themselves. But it's more likely that a home with a mortgage and back taxes won't make it to auction. Knowing that they will lose everything if it does, the lender will raise payments to the homeowner and force them to escrow their tax payments. This way the property may still end up in auction, but for nonpayment of the mortgage instead of taxes.

A home could also be paid off in terms of mortgage, but offered at auction for failure to pay property taxes. In this case, the property is guaranteed to be free of all encumbrances after sale. It's possible to find quality properties at tax sales, but it's rare.

Auctions may be an avenue to pursue in order to buy low-priced real estate, but don't expect properties to fall on your lap for "pennies on the dollar," as they say. Do expect to spend a fair amount of time bidding before actually buying a property. Not surprisingly, when I hear success stories from auction buyers, they are usually full-time professionals in the real estate flipping or rental business. Most part-timers will look for less time-consuming strategies.

The Short Sale

Another popular strategy touted by get-rich-quick gurus is the short sale. The way this works is that you buy a property directly from the home-owner after a foreclosure has started but before the sheriff's sale. Here you are trying to accomplish two things: first, to convince the owner to sell you the property prior to foreclosure, which keeps a foreclosure off their credit report; and second, to convince the bank to take less than what is owed.

Think of it this way: although it does happen, no one really wants their home to be foreclosed on if they could sell it for more than they owe on the mortgage. But what you typically have is someone who financed 95 percent or even 100 percent of the purchase price when they purchased the home. Due to financial problems, possibly loss of a job, medical bills, or an adjustable rate mortgage that just shot up in interest rate and payment, the owner can't afford the home any longer, and the current market value is now below what the owner paid for the house.

This sounds like a no-brainer. You negotiate the price in advance with the mortgage company. In theory, they will take a discounted price to avoid having the home on their hands for months without receiving payments while going through the auction process, foreclosure, and resale. And since you have negotiated a price that's below market value, it is possible for you to purchase the house with no money down and still have instant equity in the property. And the owner gets to walk away without the fore-closure on their credit report. Sound too good to be true? Well, maybe.

In this case, the problem isn't with the plan—it's getting the other players to go along with it. Again, you'd think this would be a no-brainer for the original owner, but my understanding is that people in foreclosure are generally pretty skeptical of this solution. After the notice of foreclosure hits the county website with a sheriff's sale notice, legitimate real estate investors and hucksters alike come out of the woodwork to take advan-tage of the soon-to-be homeless. So getting in front of the homeowner to pitch a short sale may be the toughest part. And if they are simply in over their heads with multiple bills, it is also likely that they will file bankruptcy to avoid the foreclosure.

In short sales you also run into bank bureaucracy that may make no sense at all. Many times you'll find that the bank will go through the foreclosure process, an auction, and regular resale, no matter how much sense a short sale appears to make. My guess is that without going through the whole process they may be unable to file a claim on the PMI insurance if it was carried on the loan. Before spending a great deal of time, you may want to call local lenders and see what their policies are regarding short sales. If you don't get anywhere, it doesn't mean to give up—it just means that it may be a bit harder than the Internet ads and infomercials will make it out to be. There are plenty of nonlocal mortgage lenders that will do business in your area through various mortgage brokers, and these may be more accommodating to the idea of cutting their losses quickly through a short sale.

Again, a lot depends on your timing. In a soft market, banks will be much more willing to deal rather than be stuck with the real estate. If you're willing to hold on for a while and rent the property or do a rent-to-own contract while waiting for the market to turn, a soft market in real estate, just like in the stock market, is a buying opportunity.

A recent client of our mortgage company purchased a five-year-old home for $125,000 in a short sale. It had originally sold for $185,000. The home had been 100 percent financed by the original owner and they were unprepared for the payments when their adjustable rate mortgage adjusted upward. The new owners can rent the house for the next four or five years, break even on cash flow, and hopefully sell the home for over $200,000 for a nice profit, considering that they had zero of their own money tied up in the transaction.

How to Buy Real Estate

So you're ready to buy, but where do you get started? As I said before, it just takes a little time and commitment to learning to make buying real estate and being a landlord work. If you research rent in your area, determine how much mortgage you can get for what your fair market rent is, add in taxes, insurance, and a little extra, you'll do okay. The fact is that someone else is buying you an asset. The advantage of this strategy is that there isn't a lot of risk involved. You can walk through a house, have it inspected, even run "For Rent" ads before you close. That leaves little room for surprises.

If the house you are looking to buy has been sitting for a while and needs a little TLC, all the better. If you're buying good, solid real estate in a good neighborhood, you should be able to sell and get out without getting hurt too badly, even in a worst-case scenario. Plus, a "safe" property gives you the opportunity for a little on-the-job training.

> Be careful about buying property where the rent is substantially below the cash flow in the hope that the property will appreciate enough to make up the difference. Many investors have been caught this way in what were fast-appreciating markets, but values have started to turn down. Just like stock buying, if you're jumping on a trend you have to get in early. Those who arrive late to the party are likely to be disappointed.

Decide whether real estate investing is really something to dive into before spending too much time and energy on finding the really good deals. There are plenty of other people competing for the really good properties as well. I hate to break it to you, but the "secrets" of real estate investing really aren't secrets anymore!

Three Steps to Buying Success

But if you really want to go for it, buy really cheap, and you can make thousands in just a couple months. There are two ways to do this. One way is to spend lots of money on seminar material and Internet courses. The other is to follow these steps. Now, you don't need to do everything here, but the more work you're willing to do, the better deal you may find. Again, just like in stock buying, the more homework you do up front, the more likely your success.

Step 1. Go to your county's website and look for a link to either the "Sheriff's Page" or "Sheriff's Sales." Click on the list of properties, then the details. You will see a list of all the properties on the docket for auction in the next several weeks, and the results of the past few auctions. Usually, the site will be divided into two sections: foreclosures for mortgage nonpayment and foreclosures for taxes. This is the information that dozens of websites will provide to you for free.

Step 2. From here you can go to the County Auditor's web page and find out the owner's address, mailing address, and a description of the property. This is information that you will have to start paying for on the various real estate websites, but it can be free if you just look for it. You'll find a lot more to go on as far as how big the house is, the number of bedrooms and bathrooms, and so on. If you're pursuing a short sale, you'll also need to find the owner's contact information.

Step 3. One last thing you need to do is check out the property at the website of the County Recorder's Office. By searching by the owner's name, property description, or address, you can find the property and a list of all _liens_ that have been filed against the property.

If you follow these steps, you will find many potential properties for purchase, but you will be competing with other investors. Remember that sometimes things are cheap for a good reason, and a modest profit may be better than a possible large profit that comes with a lot of risk.

> A **lien** is a claim against the property for a debt owed to another individual. A common example is a contractor's lien. When a homeowner contracts with an individual or business to do work on the home and doesn't make full payment on the work, the contractor may file a lien against the property. When the house is sold, lien holders are paid before proceeds are distributed to the property. Liens are paid in full before the property changes hands.

Another Buying "Secret"

If you're willing to put in some more time, here is one more "secret" to know about. And if you just subscribe to my newsletter for $199 ... okay, just kidding, but this is the stuff that is available for free that I've seen as "only available with paid subscription" on the Internet.

If you go to the Clerk of Courts web page within your county's website, there will be a list of all civil actions filed. This will be everything in civil court, from cases against stalkers to divorce filings to credit card companies filing for nonpayment. But what we're looking for are mortgage delinquencies—civil actions that are being filed by a mortgage company. What is being recorded is that a letter has gone out to a homeowner via certified mail, on that date, notifying them that their lender is going to start foreclosure proceedings.

The owner's name will be on this site, and you can now backtrack through the other county pages to find out more about the property. For example, at the Auditor's page you can get a historical record of ownership. From this you may find that the owner is deceased and that ownership has transferred to a relative or to the estate. And maybe they can't or don't want to make mortgage payments. In this case, they may be willing to accept just about any offer that gets them out from under the property and mortgage liability.

If you record the last case number, you can come back to the website each day, start at the last case number you viewed, and go forward. You'll then see a list of all new actions for the day. You will know before the homeowner does that he or she is about to be foreclosed on. The advantage of this extra step is that the foreclosure notice will likely precede the notice of a sheriff's sale by months, depending on your county.

Earlier I mentioned that by going through the sheriff's sale you will likely be competing with many other investors, since sheriff's sales are listed in the newspaper as well as on the Internet. By going to the County Clerk of Courts web page, you'll get a jump on much of your competition.

If you find that you are in financial trouble and may have your home foreclosed on, be careful about accepting a short sale yourself. Loan forgiveness is generally considered income by the IRS. If you borrow $10,000 from someone and they say that you don't need to pay them back, that is the same thing as receiving $10,000 of income because they will likely write off the bad debt as an income tax deduction. So if the bank agrees to take a lower amount than what is owed to avoid foreclosure, it is possible that they will issue you a 1099 tax form. So before things get this bad, sell the property, get a second job, do whatever you can. But if foreclosure is unavoidable, seek professional advice from a CPA and/or a bankruptcy attorney.

Financing FYI

The real estate lending business has changed quite a lot in the past few years. Not too long ago, if you wanted to buy investment property, you had to have 20 or even 30 percent down to buy non-owner-occupied housing. Today, there are far too many options to begin to describe them. The best advice is to contact two or three mortgage brokers (and here you do want mortgage brokers, not banks) and talk to them about buying investment properties. Find someone who not only sounds knowledgeable, but also shows an interest in working with you. In my office our mortgage company's manager will work with investors to find properties, structure deals, and of course arrange financing. He will generally offset any consulting fees against financing commissions when the deal is finished.

A good mortgage broker can save you thousands on your transactions. The biggest question you want answered is whether they are willing and able to use different lenders. Different lenders will have different programs depending on the situation. You need someone willing to find the best lending options for your circumstances.

Don't be put off by high interest rates. There is considerably more risk to the lender when financing investment properties versus homes. Lenders know that it's a lot easier to walk away from an investment property than your home. Risk also increases the more that is lent relative to the home value. Lending 100 percent of a property's value means that the lender will surely lose money if they foreclose in the first several years of the mortgage.

When borrowing for investments, think in terms of dollars, not percentages. It doesn't matter if the best interest rate you can get is 10 percent when home mortgages are at 6 percent. What matters is the total dollar cost to do the deal versus the payoff. If you're planning to rent out the property, can the rent cover the mortgage payment and other expenses? If so, that's all you need to worry about.

Naturally, you'll want to shop for the best terms since interest rates do affect profits, but what I'm saying is don't nix a deal because you think the interest rate is too high. Run the numbers before making a decision.

Back in the early 1990s, junk bonds were the Wall Street investment du jour. Market interest rates were still very high, with mortgage rates above 10 percent. Some of these junk bonds were paying 18 percent or more. So why would a major corporation be willing to pay a stupidly high interest rate like 18 percent? The simple answer is, if that's the best they can do and they feel they can make more than 18 percent with the capital they raise, then it is a good business decision.

Sell It or Rent It?

Once you've acquired an investment property, you can either sell it or rent it. There are definitely pros and cons to both. Selling for a quick buck is great, except that to make more money you have to do it all over again. Renting may be the slow way to get rich, but in a short period of time you can accumulate enough properties so that at some point they can generate cash flow without requiring you to be constantly buying and selling.

Clients tell me either that they love or hate being a landlord—there doesn't seem to be much in between. If you have good tenants who pay their rent and don't abuse the property, renting is great. Or if you have enough properties and can budget for a management company that takes on all the headaches for a percentage, being a landlord can still be a great business.

On the other hand, a series of nonpaying tenants, damaged properties, and places that remain empty for months between tenants is not only a financial drain, but an emotional one as well. The saying, "I'd rather be lucky than good" applies itself well to the real estate business. As with so many things in life, if it was easy everyone would be doing it. But from what I've seen and experienced after a few years of a learning curve, people who are still at it don't regret it.

For Sale!

No matter what you choose to do with your property, you should be aware of the ins and outs of selling. Selling a property is much more than putting up a sign in the front yard. But if your house is in a neighborhood with several other homes for sale, hopefully by realtors, you can count on the traffic they will generate to create some attention for your property as well.

Many times an agent who has a property for sale in the same neighborhood will contact a FSBO seller and offer a reduced commission if they sell the property for you. But whatever you pay, a realtor's fee comes out of your profit, so the best bet is to sell the property yourself. Fortunately, there is a lot of help out there to do so successfully.

First, drive around your neighborhood and look for signs for other properties for sale by owner. Many times signs will be provided by mortgage companies that help FSBO sellers, hoping to pick up the financing for the buyer. The other source of assistance is the Internet. By simply typing in "FSBO" on Google, I got over 40 million websites! One of the most popular is forsalebyowner.com. For a nominal fee (relative to a realtor's commission), this company provides all the services and advice necessary to sell your home on your own. What you should take into consideration for pricing, though, is that you need to leave enough room that, if necessary, you could hire a realtor and get out with at least a small profit.

Of course, risk can be lowered by buying property at prices even further below what should be considered fair market value. One client of mine came in to roll over his 401(k) because he and his wife had decided that their part-time real estate business was ready to go full-time. They found a neighborhood where they could buy homes for about $20,000, spend about $20,000 in fix-up costs, and sell the properties for about $70,000 on rent-to-own contracts. Without involving permanent construction help, they felt comfortable doing one house a month. Not bad; no boss, no time clock. The way this worked is that they would get a loan from a *hard-line lender* for the purchase and fix-up, so they had no out-of-pocket costs. After they made the improvements, they refinanced based on the appraised value of the home, which was now around $70,000. On a *cash-out refinance*, they easily got 90 percent of the appraised value, or $63,000. Based on their business plan, this gave them a pre-tax income of over $20,000 a month, plus a little cash flow from the rental income.

Finding properties this far under market value may not be that easy, but there are probably a lot more of them in your city or town than you think.

A **hard-line lender** is a private lender who provides short-term financing based on purchase price and estimated fix-up costs. Closing costs are low, but the interest rate is high (10 to 12 percent in today's market). They also limit the loan to no more than 50 or 60 percent of the estimated appraised value when the rehab is completed.

A **cash-out refinance** is when you refinance a loan for a higher amount than the original mortgage. In this case, the new loan pays off the $40,000 loan for purchase and fix-up and provides the owner a cash-out amount of about $23,000, less costs.

The Bottom Line

- Real estate investing can be the great economic equalizer. It does not take high academic achievement, exceptional skills, or even a lot of money to create personal wealth in real estate. But it does take time and hard work.

- Getting "great deals" helps, but is not necessary for a real estate investment to be profitable.

- Using someone else's money and the power of inflation is a great way to compound investment returns.

Insuring Yourself

What You Will Learn

- Why you need life insurance

- An easy way to determine how much life insurance you need

- How to determine what type of life insurance you should buy

Most of you are probably thinking that insurance is one of the worst topics that you could possibly spend your time reading about. But it is necessary, and you picked up this book to learn all you could about planning your financial future, right? And look at it this way, sooner or later you'll be approached by someone you went to high school with, a guy you know from church, a family member, or some woman from a social group you belong to who will try to sell you a life insurance policy. This is because insurance companies like to recruit people with a large circle of friends and associates. And the first thing a new agent is required to do is make a list of 100 of their closest "friends" and contact them about buying life insurance.

Being one of those friends, you're going to feel uncomfortable saying no. Instead, you'll listen to their pitch and because they've been well trained to sell their product, you'll feel guilty if you don't buy. And you'll end up with a policy that you may or may not need. But you'll continue to pay premiums on it for the next 20 years, or until your "friend" leaves the business—whichever comes first. Unless you read the rest of this chapter. In the pages ahead you'll discover how to determine how much life insurance you'll need, and get some valuable tips on buying the right type of policy.

Actually, It's Income Insurance

Life insurance is an important purchase. As we learned earlier, insurance allows you to take risks. And despite its name, life insurance insures your income, not your life. So life insurance allows you to take risks with your income that you couldn't, or shouldn't, without it. But don't worry, the risky behavior refers to financial risks, not bodily risks.

Life insurance allows you to accumulate debts and know that you are not burdening your kids if you should die before those debts are paid off. In other words, what you need to look at is what you have bought today (or plan on buying in the future) that someone will need to continue to pay for if you were to pass on. For example, could your spouse afford to make house payments without your income? Would your kids be able to afford college? If you're single, did someone co-sign a loan for you that they could get stuck with? If so, then someone besides yourself is counting on your income, and you need life insurance.

Figuring It Out

Life insurance can be the simplest insurance from one standpoint—filing a claim. With many insurance claims there are arguments over who's responsible, how much damage was done, the right way to get things fixed, or whether something is fixed or replaced. But with life insurance it's pretty straightforward—you're either dead, or you're not! But buying life insurance and knowing what you're getting is another story. So let's jump right in and calculate your coverage needs.

There are several calculators for life insurance needs on the web, but the one I've used is at www.bankrate.com/brm/insurance-advisers/life-insurance.asp. Whichever calculator you use, the necessary steps will be the same. Here is the information you will need and the steps to take.

Step 1. Add up the expenses that your death will incur. Funeral costs, the cost of moving your things out of an apartment, lost income for a spouse who takes time off from work …. I know, this isn't a pleasant thought. If you want to ballpark the number, I would suggest starting with at least $20,000. If you are married with kids, make it $50,000.

Step 2. Add up the balance on all your debts that someone else will be responsible for after your death. This protects a co-signer, as well as your spouse and family.

If you're single with no dependents, you're done! Skip down to Step 6. If not, go on to Step 3.

Step 3. If you're married and your spouse works, would his or her own income be sufficient if all debts were paid?

If the answer is yes, you're done! Skip down to Step 6. If not, go on to Step 4.

Step 4. If your spouse doesn't work or needs additional income, how much does he or she need? Take out a calculator; divide the additional annual income he or she needs by .05. (This is the sum of money required to provide the income needed assuming a 5% withdrawal rate. This is the same as calculating how much you need to retire on.)

Step 5. Do you want to leave some extra money for your kids' college educations, weddings, emergency cash …? If so, how much?

Step 6. Add up your answers and subtract any financial resources you already have that can be used. (Add in savings and investment accounts, but not retirement accounts, if you're married.) The result is how much life insurance you need. Pretty simple, isn't it?

And if you're still confused, here's the last step ...

Step 7. See an insurance agent and have him or her do the calculations for you!

If you do decide to see an agent, you can check his or her work if you already have the results from the 6 previous steps to make sure that the payment isn't inflated. Typically, the higher the death benefit, the higher the agent's commission will be. To my knowledge every life insurance product on the market pays a commission, and every agent has, or should have, a life needs calculator on their computer. Make them do the work. If someone is going to get paid for selling you a policy there is nothing wrong with expecting them to work for it.

If you see an *independent agent* or financial planner, he or she can even shop around at several companies for the best product and premiums. And even if you choose an independent agent, be sure to continue to shop around. Companies that market their products to independent agents do so in one of two ways: by offering the best product, or by offering the highest commission. Unfortunately, far too many insurance salespeople, whether they call themselves agents or planners or advisors or whatever, look at the commission instead of the product.

And don't forget to make sure that the agent actually does the calculations; many agents' idea of how much life insurance you need is how much you can afford. I'll have more tips later, but first we have to decide the big question: term or cash value insurance?

> An **independent agent** works for a private company that represents many different insurance companies. Just remember, while it may seem smart to go to a big company with a well-known name to buy insurance, you've heard of them for a reason. Someone has to pay for all that advertising!

Is Buying Term Really "Sticking It to the Man"?

You've probably seen the commercial where a well-dressed gentleman is sitting at his desk in front of an impressive skyline. Next to him stands a younger man, obviously a subordinate. The gentleman at the desk says he is going to "stick it to the man." The younger gentleman responds, "But you *are* the man." I don't know what the commercial is for, but I guess the point is that the gentleman enjoys sticking it to the man so much, that he isn't bothered by the fact that he is sticking it to himself. It's a funny idea, and memorable, too.

> ## Unsolicited Advice
>
> Whenever phrases such as "obscene profits," "greedy cor-
> porations," or "at the expense of the little guy" are being
> thrown around, be very skeptical of the source. These are
> great slogans to grab headlines, but if the accusations are
> true (and sometimes they are!), it should be easy to back
> them up with real numbers instead of emotional rhetoric.

We all love the underdog. The advertising execs are well aware of this and use it consistently to sell their products. Remember the long-running "We're number two, so we try harder" campaign used by the car rental company Avis? In the life insurance business, term life insurance has taken over the "stick it to the man" position. Rarely promoted by insurance agents due to the low commissions paid compared to traditional whole life policies, the media jumped on the bandwagon in the late 1980s, and up cropped a group of "anti-insurance insurance companies" that promoted cheap term insurance over the higher premium, whole life, or universal life policies.

Now, there is a lot to be said for term life insurance. But because of the publicity, I often see consumers asking for term without any idea of what it is they are buying. And too many industry experts are willing to jump on the bandwagon, or just don't understand the issue well enough to explain it to you.

I was reading another financial planning guide the other day and the author said that you should "just buy term life insurance. Period." The explanation was that with a typical cash value policy, the insurance company likes to make about three times as much profit from your premiums as what they will pay out in a death benefit. No other explanation. But not only is that statement simplistic, it's also shortsighted.

> Usually the least expensive alternative, **term life insurance** offers coverage for a specified period, such as 10 years, with an option to renew. Premiums are paid throughout this time, but generally increase as the policyholder grows older.
>
> Also known as ordinary, standard, or permanent life insurance, **whole life policies** remain in effect during the insured's entire lifetime, provided that premiums are paid as specified. This type of insurance also builds a savings element (called the cash value).
>
> **Universal life insurance** is a combination of the two, offering the protection of a conventional term insurance policy as well as the flexibility of changing the amount or timing of premium payments.

Let's Do the Math

Check out the math on that statement. Let's say that you take out a life insurance policy at age 30. Your life expectancy is around 80, so you could end up with a policy that is in force for 50 years. In return for insuring you from Day 1 (you could be run over by a bus the day after your policy is issued and your beneficiary would receive a check even before the insurance company cashed your first premium check) through the last day of Year 50, the insurance company makes a profit of three times your premium over 50 years, if you live that long.

By comparison, the way I figure it, if you have a 30-year mortgage at an interest rate of 7 percent, you'll pay about 2.5 times the cost of your home to the bank in total payments over just 30 years. So is the insurance company making three times your payments, for considerably more risk (if you don't make your mortgage payments, the mortgage company gets your house—what does the insurance company get if you don't make your payments?), really worth discounting the notion of cash value life insurance altogether? Do the same pundits tell you not to finance a home because you'll pay the bank 2.5 times the value of your home? Of course not.

So why the double standard? Well, I can come up with two possibilities. The first is that it's easy to pander to the common way of thinking; insurance companies are bad so they're easy to pick on. The second possibility is that life insurance is just very complicated. And rather than try to explain it, it's easier to shoot off a couple of sound bites. Whichever the case, I'm going to buck the trend.

So let me explain what term and cash value really mean when we talk about life insurance.

> I had a client we'll call Mr. Smith. Mr. Smith made about $90,000 a year. His wife didn't work, and he had two children under 10 years old. Their mortgage and debts were about $250,000. Mr. Smith came in for an appointment because he had a term life insurance policy that was going to end in a few months and he wanted to replace it. Trouble was, after Mr. Smith took out his original policy, he was diagnosed with type 1 diabetes. He was now uninsurable for any type of life insurance. In his case, "just buy term, period" backfired. Had he known that there was a family history of diabetes, he could have taken out a cash value policy when he was able and still would have had insurance.
>
> Remember that life insurance allows us to take on financial risks that we would otherwise avoid. Should Mr. Smith have taken on $250,000 of debt if he'd known that he'd be uninsurable? Knowing that if he were to pass away, his wife and family would most certainly lose their home and any other assets that they may have accumulated?

Life Insurance 101

Okay, I know why you wouldn't sign up for this class if it was offered in school. Your eyelids are getting heavy just reading that title, right? But I have done this presentation hundreds of times. It takes less than 10 minutes in person. Bear with me; in the next 10 minutes you can save thousands of dollars and gain peace of mind if you have debts, are married, and/or have children who depend on your income. Because, as we saw in the case of Mr. Smith, "just buy term, period" can be really bad advice in certain circumstances.

The first life insurance ever offered was in fact what we would today call term life insurance.

Breakdown of Term Life Insurance

Let's look at Figure 10.1. Original term insurance is actually very simple. For a given death benefit, say $100,000, the premium (what you pay) and the cost of insurance or COI (what the insurance company expects to pay out to policyholders in the form of a death benefit plus their overhead expenses) are equal. So, as age and likelihood of death increases, the premium and COI increases. Makes sense, right?

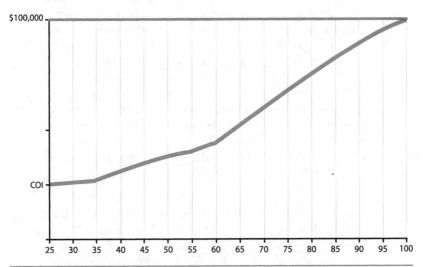

FIGURE 10.1: Term life insurance premium and benefit by age.

Let's look at an example. In this case, I'm ignoring administrative costs and commission expenses: if 100 25-year-olds are insured for $100,000, and the insurance company expects 1 out of 100 to die in the first year, then everyone must pay $1,000 (100 policyholders × $1,000 premium = $100,000 of benefit paid) of premium so there is enough money to pay the death benefit. The next year, there are only 99 insureds remaining. If the insurance company again expects 1 of the insureds to pass, then the premium increases to $100,000 ÷ 99, or $1,010.

As you saw in Figure 10.1, the insurance company does not expect anyone to live past age 100. So if just one of our original insureds turns 99 years old and still wants insurance, the premium would be $100,000. (The probability of paying a claim 100 percent × the insurance amount of $100,000 = the premium.) This is an example of what is called *annually renewable term life insurance*. In other words, each year, if the insureds want to renew the policy, they can, by simply paying the higher premium. Usually, however, the insurance company will set a limit on how many times the policy can be renewed.

The problem with this scenario is that as you age and your mortality increases, the premium rises—slowly at first and then very quickly as you pass middle age. In other words, when you are most likely to die, premiums become very expensive. This is why most policies will lapse, or be discontinued, before paying a claim. Since less than 2 percent of all issued term policies will ever pay a claim, the premiums are very low.

> **Mortality** is the likelihood of death in a given year, usually stated as a percentage. This is the opposite of *life expectancy* which is the age to which an individual or group of individuals is expected to live. Mortality and life expectancy increase each year!

So you see my confusion as to how buying term life can be equated with "sticking it to the man." By comparison, auto insurers expect to pay a claim every seven years, and whole life policies expect 100 percent of policies to eventually pay a death benefit. However, because it is cheap, term insurance is often seen as ideal for young people. And because it's simple, it is embraced by the financial "experts."

However, term insurance, as the name implies, is purchased for a specific period of time, or term, typically between 5 and up to 30 years. At the end of that period you have no more insurance. Most policies will allow a policyholder to renew the policy for another period of time, but the guaranteed premiums will be prohibitively high. The insurer realizes that the incentive to renew the policy will be strongest for those who have developed a health problem during the original policy term. And since they really don't want to actually pay a claim, they make it nearly impossible to afford.

> The industry has made term insurance more budget-friendly by offering level term policies. Here, the insurance company averages out the premiums for the life of the policy and bills the insured a level (equal) premium for all or part of the length of the policy.

Breakdown of Cash Value Life Insurance

Because term life insurance premiums rise as we age, many people stop renewing their policy just when they (well, actually, their heirs) are most likely to benefit. For this reason it was actually the consumer who demanded a level term for life or a permanent policy that a policyholder could actually hold until death, no matter what the age. And thus was born whole life insurance. For all the negatives surrounding whole life insurance (its image, which is well deserved, is that of being very expensive), one good thing that can be said is that if you pay your premiums as scheduled, you will have insurance until you die, and your beneficiaries will receive the benefit.

You may have heard life insurance referred to as universal life, variable life, adjustable life, or whole life. These are all forms of _cash value_ life insurance. Let's take a quick look, because fundamentally they all work the same. Check out Figure 10.2.

> **Cash value** refers to a type of life insurance in which part of the premium is used to pay the premium itself. The rest is deposited into a cash value account that earns interest for the policyholder.

In Figure 10.2, you can see that the cash value component is not an apples-to-apples comparison in evaluating the premium of this type of life insurance based on that of a term life policy where 100 percent of the premium is an expense.

What happens with any cash value product is that in the early years (before age 60 in the example), you pay more into the policy than the actual cost from the insurance company. The extra amount of money you pay goes into a cash value account held by the insurance company. After age 60 in Figure 10.2 is when cost becomes greater than the paid premium, so the company subtracts the difference from the built-up cash value and adds that to your premium to pay for your cost of insurance. As long as money remains in the cash value account, your premium will remain level.

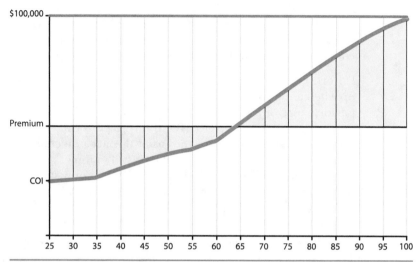

FIGURE 10.2: Cash value life insurance premium and benefit by age.

So although your premium may be much higher with a cash value policy than a term policy, it is unfair to say that the entire added premium is cost. A large portion of the higher premium may be going into the cash value account in the early years of the policy. This money can be withdrawn or borrowed against if you wish, so it really is your money. However, you have to be careful with withdrawals and loans. If money is not in your cash value account to supplement your premiums in the later years, you may need to increase your premium payments to match the increased cost of insurance.

The Three Main Types

Cash value life insurance can be divided into three main types of policies.

Whole Life (WL). With WL insurance your level premium is set so high that the insurance company guarantees from the outset that your premium will remain level for the life of the policy. The advantage of WL is that at some point, if the cash value earns more than the guaranteed rate, your policy may become *paid up*. This means that there is enough cash in your cash value account to pay your cost of insurance for the remainder of the policy owner's life.

The term **paid up** refers to a cash value life policy in which the owner no longer needs to pay future premiums. With any cash value policy, it is only truly paid up when the cash value plus the minimum guaranteed interest or dividend is sufficient to pay the maximum expenses that the company could charge for the remainder of the policy.

Unfortunately, some agents will claim that a policy is paid up when either the assumed interest or return, or the past performance or interest rate, is sufficient to pay the policy for the remainder of its term. But if future performance does not meet expectations, the cash value account could actually be depleted while the policy is still in force. If this happens, the policyholder may have to not only start paying premiums again, but pay a premium that is much higher than originally planned.

Universal Life. With a UL policy you can pick a premium from nearly anywhere between the term premium and the whole life premium. Your cash value account will equal the excess premium deposits that are being made and the interest the insurance company credits you for holding your money. Whether your premium remains level for life depends on what interest rate was assumed at the time of application and on the amount of premium you choose to pay. If rates are consistently lower than the assumed rate, your planned premium is set too low, or you skipped payments, you may need to pay higher premiums at a later date to match the rising COI. If rates are consistently higher, you may be able to suspend premium payments for a period of time.

Variable Universal Life. VUL is similar to UL, except that your excess premium, or cash value account, is invested in mutual fund-type accounts. With this product, you are taking the risk that the mutual fund-type accounts (actually called separate accounts) will outpace the interest-bearing accounts of a UL or WL policy. But again, beware if investment performance is poor. You may need to increase your premium payments down the road.

So Which One Do I Choose?

Now that you understand the two major types of life insurance, which is the best product for you? The first thing to remember is that term means temporary. If you feel that your need for insurance is also temporary, then term life insurance can be for you.

Term is a good choice if you really can't afford anything else. It may be that 100 percent of the death benefit you need now is much better than 25 percent of the death benefit you might have for the same premium if buying a cash value policy.

For temporary needs, make sure that you match the term of insurance with the need. For example, if you have children and the youngest is 5 years old, you may want a 20-year term policy that will last until all the kids are through college. If your spouse isn't working full-time, maybe he or she could consider returning to the job once the kids are raised. This will dramatically reduce your life insurance need from that point on.

> **Unsolicited Advice**
>
> When estimating your insurance needs, be careful about assuming that your spouse will return to work following your premature demise. Their estimated earnings may not be what they once were; the longer someone is out of the workforce, the lower the wages they may need to accept in order to re-enter.

If your only retirement is your 401(k) plan and other savings, then buy term, if you can get a term policy that will last until you plan on retiring. As your 401(k) grows, your need for insurance will reduce because you become self-insured. In other words, once your 401(k) can produce the income necessary for you to retire, it also will provide your spouse or family with enough money to "retire" without your income.

If none of these scenarios applies to your situation, consider purchasing cash value life insurance.

Look to the Future

No matter which type you've decided on, before making a life insurance purchase you should not only consider your current health, but also what your health needs may be down the road when you may have to replace or increase coverage.

Following is list of health conditions, provided by TermQuote.com, that may affect your ability to get life insurance, or the premiums you may pay.

- Family history of cardiovascular disease or cancer. ("Family" includes parents and siblings.)

- High cholesterol or high blood pressure levels. Both have been linked to hereditary causes, so it's a good idea to check your family history for these issues.

- Driving history, including reckless driving and DUI or DWI, as well as any history of alcohol or substance abuse or treatment.

- Nicotine use. Carriers will vary on this, so be sure to shop around if you are an occasional cigar smoker or smokeless tobacco user.

- Your parents' health conditions and medications. Although their ailments may not keep you from getting insurance now, you need to know whether they have hereditary conditions, such as diabetes, that may affect your future insurability.

If any of these health issues presents a concern, you should speak to a professional about designing a plan appropriate for you that may include both term and cash value insurance.

In addition, you may want to consider a cash value policy if you absolutely want life insurance until you die, no matter at what age, or you will be relying on a defined-benefit pension plan for most of your retirement income. If you don't need to save as much in your 401(k) plan, you may not self-insure until retirement or even later.

It's Okay to Just Say No!

A good rule to remember is this: if anyone ever tries to sell you life insurance for any reason other than the fact you need it, just say no! There are some circumstances in which life insurance is purchased as part of an investment plan. But this is only appropriate if you've maxed out contributions to all your tax-deductible retirement plans and are in one of the top tax brackets. The basic appeal revolves around two benefits of cash value life insurance. First is that your cash value account grows tax-deferred, similar to the money in an IRA or 401(k) plan. Second is that, unlike in those retirement plans, with life insurance you can borrow your own money as a tax-free withdrawal and pay yourself back the interest on your loan.

But the problem with these scenarios is that the analysis, or pitch, completely ignores the impact that the cost of insurance, fees, and commissions have on performance. Rarely can the tax deferral compensate for the expenses to make life insurance a good investment as an investment vehicle only. Unfortunately, there are all sorts of life insurance-selling scams out there that play on this tax deferral but don't hold up under a real analysis.

I've always felt that if the life insurance industry was regulated the way the mutual fund industry is regulated, people would buy more life insurance simply because they would understand what they are buying. Instead, companies and their agents rely on various schemes to try to make life insurance either appropriate when it's not, or more appealing than it is. So that said, here is what you need to watch out for—my list of Top 3 Sleazy Schemes used to sell life insurance to people who don't need it.

Sleazy Scheme Number 1: The tax-free retirement plan. This one should fall by the wayside because of the new Roth IRA and Roth 401(k). Simply put, the concept is to cash in your 401(k) and buy a variable life insurance (VUL) policy, or buy a VUL policy instead of contributing to a 401(k). The rationale is that you can pull money from a life insurance policy tax-free instead of being subject to taxation when you withdraw your money, as from a traditional 401(k). This supposedly means more income in retirement. The problem with this pitch is that it never properly accounts for the lack of a tax deduction that you would get from the 401(k) but not the life insurance—or the effect that insurance costs would have on your investment performance!

Sleazy Scheme Number 2: Be your own banker. The story on this one is that you should put 100 percent of all your cash flow for saving and investing into a whole life insurance policy. The idea is that as you build up cash value you can "borrow from yourself" instead of from the bank, and over your lifetime you will save enough money in interest payments to make the life policy a better investment than your 401(k) or any other investment plan. While this sounds good and has some merit, it misses out on a concept called "opportunity cost." In other words, what could your money be earning elsewhere, if invested in something other than a whole life insurance policy? The answer is, a whole lot more.

And finally ...

Sleazy Scheme Number 3: The tax deferral. Would you like your mutual funds taxable or tax-deferred? This was actually taught as a _close_ for VUL sales. After the agent presented a pitch for investing in mutual funds, they would ask this question. Since most would answer "tax-deferred," people who thought they were buying mutual funds often ended up with a life insurance policy instead! Again, the biggest problem with doing this is that it is very hard to demonstrate that the tax deferral of a life insurance policy actually offsets the added insurance company costs that come with the policy.

> A **close** refers to a sales technique, usually a phrase or question, that is designed to convince you to agree to purchase the product being sold.

Separating Financial Planning from Insurance

I once worked for a financial planning company and was their top producer for the year. Trouble was, I did almost all investment business because my clients were at or near retirement age, were self-insured with their accumulated assets, and just didn't need life insurance. At our annual conference they had a top producers' panel. I was originally a little miffed when I wasn't invited to speak, but afterward it wasn't hard to figure out why. During his presentation, one of the other top producers said, "I don't wait for the client to come in to determine if they need variable life insurance; I decide why they need it before they come through the door!" He received an ovation, and I was on my way to starting my own company within the year. You see, the financial planning company was owned by a life insurance company.

To many life insurance companies, financial planning is synonymous with buying an insurance policy. Insurance agents are taught how to sell you insurance, but not necessarily taught to assess your needs. That's not a reason to avoid buying life insurance, however; just a very good reason to be prepared with some knowledge so you can make a good, informed decision.

So How Do I Know If I'm Getting a Good Deal?

The best thing about term life insurance is that it is one of the few products for which shopping is truly black and white. Pick a term, or time frame, and an insurance amount and choose the lowest premium. That's it. The only thing to watch for is the "bait and switch." This really isn't an intentional type of switch, but what happens is this. Many advertisements will quote extremely low premiums that are accurate, but that you'd have to be Superman to qualify for. Once you've gone through the application process and are told that your premiums will be higher than quoted, you are less likely to go elsewhere and go through the whole process again. Don't assume that the company with the lowest rate for Superman also provides the lowest rate for someone with health issues.

To avoid this scenario, check out the questionnaire in Figure 10.3, which is provided by TermQuote.com. This questionnaire is used to pre-qualify applicants so that they can provide accurate life insurance quotes. My suggestion is to copy the questionnaire, complete it accurately, and use it with any company you choose to get a quote from. Remember, a quote is just that—it is not guaranteed until your application is underwritten and approved.

Cash value insurance is a completely different issue. I remember a period in the early 1990s when *Financial Planning* magazine ran a series of articles and follow-up commentary on the subject of how to determine the cost of a life insurance policy. At that time, *Financial Planning* was probably the top industry publication for real financial planners (as opposed to the pseudo-planners or product salespeople). For a group of experts to argue the issue, you can bet that the answer is far more complicated than it needs to be.

The problem is that insurance companies are not required to disclose certain information. Instead, you are given a "ledger" illustration similar to what you'll see in Table 10.1. The ledger includes two separate illustrations. The first is based on "projected" assumptions on cost of insurance, rates of return, mortality, and so on. In other words, it's a piece of fiction. The second illustration is a worst-case scenario, showing what will happen if the insurance company gives you the lowest interest allowable by contract and charges you the highest expenses allowable. Reality will likely fall somewhere in between—but that is a big gap.

Your name :

Mailing address/email address/fax information/phone:

Date of birth: / / / /

Sex: M F

What amount of coverage are you looking for? ($50,000 min.)

Duration: 10 15 20 25 30 years

Do you currently have any life insurance?   Y N

If yes, how much?

Are you looking to replace your current coverage?   Y N

Have you used any form of tobacco/nicotine in the past 5 yrs?   Y N

If yes type and amount:

Date of last use / / / /

Are you a US citizen?   Y N

If no, are you a permanent resident?   Y N

If a permanent resident, how long have you lived in the US?

Have you ever been diagnosed w/diabetes, cancer, heart disease?   Y N

Have you been diagnosed w/high bp, cholesterol or sleep apnea?   Y N

Are you currently taking any medication?   Y N

If so:

Name?	Name?
For what?	For what?
How much?	How much?
How long?	How long?

Any other medical information we should know?

May I get your :   Ht   Wt

Have you lost more than 15 lbs in the last year?   Y N   How much?

Do you have a parent/sibling diagnosed w/stroke, cancer, heart disease, or diabetes before age 70? Who, what, age, and age at death?

Have you traveled outside of the US in the last 3 years or plan to in the next 2 years? Where, how long, and why?

Your occupation? Are you a member of the armed forces/military?   Y N

Are you involved in any hazardous activities? For example: Piloting, Sky Diving, Racing, Scuba Diving. If yes, details

Have you ever been treated for anxiety, depression, alcohol or drug abuse? When, how long, any relapses for drugs or alcohol?

For anxiety/depression: any attempted suicides, hospitalizations, loss of time from work? Details

FIGURE 10.3: Health and lifestyle questionnaire for getting an accurate insurance quote.

Table 10.1: Example of a cash value life insurance ledger.

Year	Age	3.00% Interest Rate Guaranteed Basis				5.4% Interest Rate Nonguaranteed Basis			
		Total Annual Premium Outlay Paid Annually	Cash Value	Surrender Value	Death Benefit	Total Annual Premium Outlay Paid Annually	Cash Value	Surrender Value	Death Benefit
1	31	$813	$273	$0	$200,000	$813	$506	$0	$200,000
2	32	$813	$555	$0	$200,000	$813	$1,040	$0	$200,000
3	33	$813	$968	$0	$200,000	$813	$1,605	$0	$200,000
4	34	$813	$1,394	$0	$200,000	$813	$2,201	$0	$200,000
5	35	$813	$1,833	$0	$200,000	$813	$2,830	$464	$200,000
6	26	$813	$2,262	$330	$200,000	$813	$3,493	$1,561	$200,000
7	37	$813	$2,681	$1,203	$200,000	$813	$4,193	$2,715	$200,000
8	38	$813	$3,090	$2,086	$200,000	$813	$4,932	$3,928	$200,000
9	39	$813	$3,487	$2,975	$200,000	$813	$5,711	$5,199	$200,000
10	40	$813	$3,873	$3,873	$200,000	$813	$6,533	$6,533	$200,000
11	41	$813	$4,248	$4,248	$200,000	$813	$7,401	$7,401	$200,000
12	42	$813	$4,588	$4,588	$200,000	$813	$8,316	$8,316	$200,000
13	43	$813	$4,915	$4,915	$200,000	$813	$9,282	$9,282	$200,000
14	44	$813	$5,205	$5,205	$200,000	$813	$10,302	$10,302	$200,000
15	45	$813	$5,457	$5,457	$200,000	$813	$11,377	$11,377	$200,000

continues...

(Table 10.1 continued)

Example of a cash value life insurance ledger.

Year	Age	3.00% Interest Rate Guaranteed Basis				5.4% Interest Rate Nonguaranteed Basis		
		Total Annual Premium Outlay Paid Annually	Cash Value	Surrender Value	Death Benefit	Total Annual Premium Outlay Paid Annually	Cash Value	Surrender Value	Death Benefit
16	46	$813	$5,670	$5,670	$200,000	$813	$12,512	$12,502	$200,000
17	47	$813	$5,844	$5,844	$200,000	$813	$13,709	$13,709	$200,000
18	48	$813	$5,976	$5,976	$200,000	$813	$14,972	$14,972	$200,000
19	49	$813	$6,041	$6,041	$200,000	$813	$16,305	$16,305	$200,000
20	50	$813	$6,038	$6,038	$200,000	$813	$17,712	$17,712	$200,000
21	51	$813	$5,964	$5,964	$200,000	$813	$19,196	$19,196	$200,000
22	52	$813	$5,793	$5,793	$200,000	$813	$20,762	$20,762	$200,000
23	53	$813	$5,521	$5,521	$200,000	$813	$22,414	$22,414	$200,000
24	54	$813	$5,121	$5,121	$200,000	$813	$24,135	$24,135	$200,000
25	55	$813	$4,587	$4,587	$200,000	$813	$25,952	$25,952	$200,000

This leaves me with two choices: either spend about 10 pages to explain the ins and outs of cash value insurance (don't worry, I'm not really going to do that), or recommend that you need to find a really good financial planner. If you have health issues now or feel you could in the future, if you own your own business, or if you have a million-dollar-and-growing net worth, a good planner can walk you through these issues and help you shop for a product that caters to your specific needs. If you do decide this is the right decision, be sure to review the section in Chapter 7 on how to find the right advisor.

For everyone else, there is one thing I want you to look at in Table 10.1. Notice that there is the column for cash value that we have talked about. But next to it is a column for surrender value. Eventually, the balances in each column will be equal (in this example, it happens in Year 10). Until then, there is a difference for this reason: the insurance company paid a commission to an agent when the policy was issued, so the insurance company needs to keep your policy on its books for a period of time to recoup what it has paid out in commissions. To encourage you to keep the policy, they charge a pretty stiff penalty for cancellation. So a very good rule of thumb with any insurance product is that the longer the surrender period and the bigger the surrender charge, the larger the commission that was, or will be, paid. And more importantly, the bigger the commission, the less money available to be invested for your benefit.

I've found that companies that pay very large commissions are often less concerned with product performance as well. For a cash value life policy, a 10-year surrender is actually pretty short. More common is 15 years; avoid any policy that approaches a 20-year penalty period. So one way to check up on recommendations that you may receive is to ask for a ledger illustration and compare how long it takes for the surrender column to equal the cash value column for each policy.

So with all this knowledge, what will you do? Well, that's up to you, but no matter what type of insurance you choose, you can use the information in this chapter to shop for the best deal. The basic economic theory that competition among companies results in similar product pricing falls apart with life insurance. There are huge differences in premiums for identical products. Keep it simple. If term life insurance fits your needs, buy term. If you buy cash value insurance, buy it for the insurance benefit, and avoid pitches that are designed to get you to pay higher premiums. And above all, run away if you hear phrases such as "insured pension plan" or "tax-deferred mutual funds!"

The Bottom Line

- You probably need life insurance, and it's important to know how to calculate how much is right for you.

- There is a significant difference between term life insurance and cash value life insurance.

- It's a good idea to look at term life insurance first, but be sure to match the term of the policy to the time frame of your need.

- Don't forget to check into your family history to determine if you may develop health conditions that could affect your future insurability.

Understanding Your Taxes and Tax Withholding

What You Will Learn

- How our tax system works

- What you actually pay in taxes

- How taxes affect your investments

When it comes to taxes, I have just one opinion: our current system stinks. We pay way too much, productivity is punished, and we get way too little back for what we pay in. We have created a system where members of our legislatures enhance their chance of re-election by spending more and more government money, with little restrictions based on whether the money is really available or not.

My job is to make money for my clients. And one way to make more is to give less away to the taxman. Also, I would argue that my clients, and all of us in general, benefit from a strong economy, and you cannot separate tax policy from economic growth. We have massive government liabilities that will eventually have to be paid, and we can do that in one of two ways: raise taxes, or grow the economy so that the liabilities become a shrinking portion of the government's income. This is the same as your decision to take on debt when you're young, with the anticipation that you will be making payments from a larger income down the road. The difference is that the U.S. government doesn't have a life span, and assumes that income (tax revenue from a growing economy) will continue to grow.

One estimate is that to pay our current future obligations for Social Security and Medicare alone, based on the current size of the U.S. economy, taxes would need to be increased by 30 percent. It doesn't take a Ph.D. in economics to realize that that kind of tax increase would quickly grind economic growth to a halt.

It's Your Responsibility

The other problem I have with our tax system is that each individual has the responsibility to calculate how much we have to pay the government each year. And then, after we go through the time and expense of trying to figure out their rules, if we make a mistake, they have the audacity to charge us interest and possibly penalties for miscalculating our bill!

Let's say that you brought your car in to the garage for repairs and service. When the mechanic was done, he would give you a list of what services he performed and parts he replaced. He then told you to calculate the bill and send it in. And by the way, it is up to you to figure out the right price for parts and labor. And if you're wrong, he will then tell you what the right amount was supposed to be and charge you for the miscalculation. Oh, and by the way, he has up to three years to let you know that you made a mistake. Now, I'm thinking that no one would put up with this kind of system to pay for our auto repair bills. And yet we quietly go about paying the government in this manner every year.

Unfortunately, our system is also one that lends itself to cheating. From housekeepers, home repair people, those who are self-employed, wait staff, and others who rely on tips, there is a lot of income that never gets reported. And for every "cash" transaction, you and I end up paying their fair share as well as our own.

So my goal in this chapter is for you to come away with an understanding of what you pay in taxes now, and what you will pay in the future if you continue to grow your income. I also want you to understand the importance of minimizing your tax liability whenever practical. It is a real failure of our government that people hesitate to use tax deductions for fear that the IRS will penalize them in some way. This is an unfounded concern. As Judge Learned Hand, considered the most influential non-Supreme Court judge in U.S. history, said, "Anyone may so arrange his affairs that his taxes shall be as low as possible; he is not bound to choose that pattern which will best pay the Treasury; there is not even a patriotic duty to increase one's taxes."

I want to emphasize this last point—it is not your patriotic duty to pay more in taxes than you have to. Part of the function of taxes is to modify behavior, increase taxes to reduce bad behavior (cigarette taxes), or increase behavior through tax deductions (charitable giving). So if the government offers a tax deduction, it is because they want to encourage that behavior.

The confusion arises from all the stories about people being carted off to jail for participating in various illegal tax avoidance schemes. Part of the problem with our tax code is that either provisions are vague, or the authors were just not capable of foreseeing all the applications and ramifications of their legislation. Then lawyers get involved, and things get really confusing! But in fairness, for the individual the tax code is not that complicated, at least not early in your working life. Complications arise as finances become more complex.

Getting a Refund Does Not Mean You Don't Pay Taxes

Some people like to get a refund. I've even heard the comment, "I don't pay taxes; I get money back every year!" But if you get a refund, all you are doing is letting the IRS use your money for free over the course of the year. If that has been the case, and since you haven't been missing the money, you should consider taking that money and investing it to benefit you, instead of the IRS!

Return vs. Investment

Take a look at Table 11.1. Let's assume that you get a $780 tax refund each year. If you instead invested the $780 into your 401(k) plan, you would have an additional $38,550 accumulated in 20 years, assuming an 8 percent rate of return. Not bad for money that you didn't miss anyway!

Now look at the last two columns. Assuming a 25 percent tax rate, by contributing $780 a year in a pre-tax account such as a 401(k), you would reduce your tax liability by $195 a year. So by simply investing your money into your own account, instead of giving the IRS an interest-free loan, you could have an extra $195 a year. Maybe that's not a lot of money over the course of a year, but it's free. Wouldn't a couple hundred bucks help out at holiday time to buy gifts with cash instead of adding to your charge cards? If you hold on to it for five years, you could put the money toward a $1,200 vacation—again, paid for with cash instead of credit. All from the IRS, just by taking advantage of tax breaks.

Table 11.1: Table showing possibilities if investing the same amount of money ($780 per year) instead of taking it as a tax refund.

Year	Investment	Ending Balance	Tax Savings	Ending Balance
1	$780	$842	$195	$211
2	$780	$1,752	$195	$438
3	$780	$2,735	$195	$684
4	$780	$3,796	$195	$949
5	$780	$4,942	$195	$1,236
6	$780	$6,180	$195	$1,545
7	$780	$7,517	$195	$1,879

Year	Investment	Ending Balance	Tax Savings	Ending Balance
8	$780	$8,960	$195	$2,240
9	$780	$10,520	$195	$2,630
10	$780	$12,203	$195	$3,051
11	$780	$14,022	$195	$3,506
12	$780	$15,986	$195	$3,997
13	$780	$18,108	$195	$4,527
14	$780	$20,399	$195	$5,100
15	$780	$22,873	$195	$5,718
16	$780	$25,545	$195	$6,386
17	$780	$28,431	$195	$7,108
18	$780	$31,548	$195	$7,887
19	$780	$34,914	$195	$8,729
20	$780	$38,550	$195	$9,637

This is what I mean by moneynomics—using your money for you, and making it work for you, instead of against you. You never know when an opportunity may arise that will require money for you to take advantage of it. Remember, banks don't lend money to people who don't already have money.

What I'm showing you here is how to be in a position to take advantage of your own "butterfly effect"—a potentially life-changing opportunity. Don't be stuck at the retirement home bemoaning the "one that got away." Because I'm not talking about fish.

Ready to Do Your Taxes?

Before you read the next sentence, I want you to commit to reading the rest of the paragraph before deciding whether to skip this section. You should do your own tax return each year. And yes, you can do it. And after reading what you can do with your tax savings, you will probably want to do them on your own.

Single, Head of Household ... What Are You?

First, you need to determine what type of taxpayer you are. This is known as your filing status. Status is determined as of the last day of the calendar year. Single taxpaying status is pretty self-explanatory. If you are single (unmarried) with no dependants, you will file as a single taxpayer. Federal tax law does not recognize domestic partnerships or common-law marriage, so if you are in either of these situations, you will still file as single.

Head of household can be a little more complicated, and if you think you qualify you should look up Tax Topic 353, "What is Your Filing Status?", which can be found at www.irs.gov. Simply put, a head of household is someone who is unmarried, has a dependant, and has paid more than half the cost of maintaining a home for the year. Even if you're married, you may qualify as head of household if your spouse did not live in the home for the last six months of the year. If you think you may qualify as head of household, it is worth looking up all the rules because you will get higher deductions and lower tax rates than if you were to file as a single taxpayer.

For a questionnaire developed by the state of California to help determine whether you qualify as a head of household, go to www.ftb.ca.gov/individuals/hoh/selftest/Index.html.

Filing Joint or Separate Returns

If you're married, you can actually choose whether you prefer to file with your spouse or separately. With a joint return, all income is aggregated onto one return, as are all deductions and credits. Separate returns allow the flexibility of reporting incomes separately and allocating expenses to one return. For example, if you're an employee of a business you're only allowed to deduct business-related expenses if they exceed 2% of your adjusted gross income (AGI). If you file a joint return, your expenses may not exceed this limit, but they may if the income is split on the two returns. The same may apply for deducting large medical costs incurred in a year. Other things to consider may be to avoid or minimize the Alternative Minimum Tax (AMT), or to qualify for dependant or child care credits. Even if none of these apply, in Ohio we sometimes find that while filing separately has little affect on your federal return, it does result in lower state tax liability. However, remember that you cannot use itemized deductions on one return and take the standard deduction on the other.

Confused? And we've barely progressed past filling out your name on a tax form! Now you're beginning to see why I get on my soapbox over our tax system. The last thing a single parent (or anyone really) should need to do is spend money on a tax software package or a professional tax preparer; but unless you're sure that you only qualify as a single taxpayer, it might be a good idea. The tax software/preparer will walk you through all the steps to determine your best filing status. They can also prepare your returns both jointly and separately to determine the best result for your situation.

Deductions

If you're an employee of a business, have few (if any) investments, and no investment real estate, you will probably file a 1040EZ. The 1040EZ is exactly that: "easy." There is absolutely no excuse for anyone with a high school education to not complete a 1040EZ on their own. If you have dependants, then you will need to file a 1040A. And if you have *itemized deductions,* you will file a regular form 1040.

Before moving on, let's look at some itemized deductions so you can determine which tax form to use.

> **Itemized deductions** are certain expenses that you can use to lower your taxes.

Medical and dental expenses. These expenses are only deductible to the extent they exceed a certain percentage of your income. Remember from the insurance chapter that your premiums should be a before-tax deduction. If you also have a 125 plan, where you reimburse yourself with pre-tax dollars, you cannot count those expenses for a deduction either. If you have incurred unusually large medical costs, you are excused from preparing your own taxes. Instead, work with a professional tax preparer.

State and local income taxes. Taxes that you pay other than to the federal government are tax-deductible. Note that sales taxes are not deductible, although they were at one time. The rationale behind this is that you are not supposed to be double-taxed. Think of it this way, if you spend your income on, say, a pair of shoes, you are taxed on that income as it was spent. You are taxed again on that income, as income tax.

Real estate and/or personal property taxes and home mortgage and investment interest. The only interest expense that is deductible based on consumption is the interest paid on your mortgage. This could be on a primary or secondary mortgage (a home equity loan). There are limits, so view the IRS rules on this. But most of you should have no problem here. You can also deduct interest on mortgages for a second home. If you own a property that you collect rent on, you are again excused from preparing your own tax return. Go see a tax preparer. If possible, get a full-time CPA to do your taxes; if he or she has experience in real estate, you could wind up saving a good amount of money.

Charitable contributions. Charitable contributions are an obvious source of abuse in the tax code. They also play a controversial role in some tax reform proposals. First, the IRS has put restrictions on claims for "cash" contributions. You must have a receipt or acknowledgment letter from the recipient for cash donations, and a copy of your cancelled check if the donation was made by check. Read IRS Publication 526 at www.irs.gov for more information. But, simply put, you cannot claim that you donated a certain amount of cash and then just claim a deduction. But on the other hand, if you truly make donations, document and deduct!

Casualty and theft losses. These deductions are only allowed if they were not reimbursed by insurance.

Job expenses. Certain expenses related to your current job, or when seeking a new job, may be deductible. Again, however, they are subjected to certain limits.

And that is about it. For the average Joe or Jane, the bad news is that there are few opportunities to reduce taxes. The good news is that there's very little to report. So there's no reason not to be doing your own taxes. Even with itemized deductions, this is way too simple to pay someone to do it for you. And don't say that you're too busy to do it yourself. It will take you more time to gather your paperwork and travel to an appointment than it will take you to complete the form.

It's important to understand what share of your income goes to the government in the form of federal and local taxes, as well as taxes for Social Security, Medicare, and Medicaid. The latter programs are far too underfunded to be around when you need them, unless changes are made soon. And unless you and your friends get motivated to do something about it, you can be fairly certain that my friends won't. After all, *we're* the big beneficiaries of *your* tax contributions. (I'll at least take a moment here to say "Thanks!")

Forms

So let's jump right in and take a look at the forms I mentioned earlier. Table 11.2 is a list of the three tax forms you could use to file your tax return, and a description of who can use each one. You can also find this info online at www.irs.gov.

Table 11.2: IRS TAX TIP 2006-04.
The three forms used for filing individual federal income tax returns are Form 1040EZ, Form 1040A, and Form 1040. If you are filing a federal income tax return on paper, use the simplest form you can. Using the simplest allowable form will reduce the chance of an error that may cost you money or delay the processing of your return.

1040EZ You may qualify to use Form 1040EZ, the simplest form, if:

- Your taxable income is below $100,000
- Your filing status is Single or Married Filing Jointly
- You are under age 65
- You are not claiming any dependents
- Your interest income is $1,500 or less

1040A You may be able to use Form 1040A if:

- Your taxable income is below $100,000
- You have capital gain distributions
- You claim certain tax credits
- You claim deductions for IRA contributions, student loan interest, educator expenses, or higher education tuition and fees

1040 If you cannot use either a 1040EZ or 1040A, you probably need to use Form 1040. You must file form 1040 if:

- Your taxable income is $100,000 or more
- You claim itemized deductions
- You are reporting self-employment income
- You are reporting income from sale of property

List of tax forms and descriptions.

A section of the 1040EZ is highlighted in Figure 11.1. The only difference between the EZ and other forms are the deductions you can claim. You step up to the 1040A or 1040 with dependants and deductions. If you need one of the other forms, you can get a copy from the IRS website at www.irs.gov and follow along, making sure to add in info for your dependants and the amount of your deductions. I want you to go through this so we can determine whether your *tax withholding* at work is close to what you should expect your actual liability to be. If you withhold too much, you get a refund; if you withhold too little, you'll write the IRS a check at tax time. And we already know that you can use the money more than the IRS can.

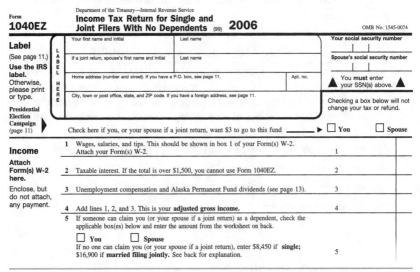

FIGURE 11.1: Section of 1040EZ form from 2006.

There are only a couple of things you need to know to complete your tax return aside from your own name, address, and Social Security number. On Line 1, enter your annual income. Use the gross wages number from your paycheck and multiply by 24 if you're paid twice a month, by 26 if you're paid every two weeks, or by 52 if you're paid weekly.

Go to Line 5 and follow the directions—enter $8,450 if you're single or $16,900 if you're married with no dependants. Subtract whichever number you entered from the income you entered on Line 1. Use Schedule X in Table 11.3 below to figure your tax if you're single, and Schedule Y if you're married.

Table 11.3: Schedule X—Single.

If Taxable Income Is Over—	But Not Over—	The Tax Is
$0	$7,550	10% of the amount over $0
$7,550	$30,650	$755 plus 15% of the amount over $7,550

If Taxable Income Is Over—	But Not Over—	The Tax Is
$30,650	$74,200	$4,220 plus 25% of the amount over $30,650
$74,200	$154,800	$5,107.50 plus 28% of the amount over $74,200
$154,800	$336,550	$37,675.50 plus 33% of the amount over $154,800
$336,550	no limit	$97,653 plus 35% of the amount over $336,550

Schedule Y—Married Filing Jointly or Qualifying Widow(er).

If Taxable Income Is Over—	But Not Over—	The Tax Is
$0	$15,100	10% of the amount over $0
$15,100	$61,300	$1,510 plus 15% of the amount over $15,100
$61,300	$123,700	$8,440 plus 25% of the amount over $61,300
$123,700	$188,450	$24,040 plus 28% of the amount over $123,700
$188,450	$336,550	$42,170 plus 33% of the amount over $188,450
$336,550	no limit	$91,043 plus 35% of the amount over $336,550

This is just an estimate of your actual tax liability. When actually filing your taxes, you will get a W-2 tax form from your employer, and you will use that number for your gross wages number on line 1.

Simple Tax Calculation

From Table 11.4 we can calculate that for a single individual making $30,000 a year without itemized deductions and with no other income, you will pay $2,892.50 in federal income taxes, or just under 10 percent of your gross income. With this information, you can go to your human resources representative at work and ask them to adjust your tax withholding to be closer to your actual liability. This is done on a W-4 form provided by the IRS.

Table 11.4: Simple tax calculation table.	
Tax Calculation	
Income:	(Monthly gross wages) $2,500 × 12 = $30,000
Deduction:	$8,450
Taxable income:	$21,550
Tax from Schedule C:	$755 + ($21,550 – $7,550) × 15% = $2,855.00

On more than one occasion I've heard comments from a client's spouse such as, "I used to work, but our taxes went up so much it wasn't worth it," or, "When I worked all my income went to taxes." I even once had someone tell me they didn't accept a promotion and a raise because after the increase in taxes it wasn't worth it. This doesn't make sense.

From the tax tables above, you can see that as your income moves up into another bracket, only your income above that level is taxed at the higher rate. Your taxes on previous income are not affected by making more money. So that kind of thinking is ridiculous. It never hurts to make more money. Ask Bill Gates. I often tell clients that my goal in life is to pay a million dollars in taxes! The more taxes you pay, the more money you made. We may have *repressive* tax rates, but they are not *regressive*, at least at the federal level.

> **Repressive tax** means that the rates are strict.
>
> **Regressive tax** means that the rates decrease proportionately as the amount taxed increases.

It's amazing to see people's reactions to how much they have to pay in taxes when they become self-employed. While working for someone else, it's easy to not really pay attention to your tax withholding; it's just a number on your pay stub. But when you're self-employed, you write a check once a quarter to the IRS for your estimated tax liability. That would be $4,000 per quarter on a $90,000 income (assuming some state and local taxes), plus over $3,000 for Social Security and Medicare!

So using the information in Table 11.5, let's look at how much an individual can pay in taxes.

Table 11.5: FICA Tax Table.

Tax	Tax Rate	Maximum Wage Base	Maximum Tax
Social Security	6.20%	$94,200	$5,840.40
Medicare	1.45%	No limit	No ceiling

In Table 11.6, I've looked at four different incomes in the Gross Income column. By using data for average itemized deductions for different income ranges, I inserted an estimated itemized deduction number to compute federal income taxes. I've also included *FICA* taxes, Ohio state income taxes (we are the twelfth-highest taxed state in the United States, so fortunately for most of you this number will be lower).

> **FICA** stands for the Federal Insurance Contributions Act. It is the law that requires employers to withhold a percentage of salary from employee paychecks and deposit that money instead into designated government accounts. These accounts provide benefits to U.S. citizens through Social Security. FICA withholding supports retirement income, disability insurance, and survivor benefits.

Most analyses of taxation stop at income taxes. But I've added two other taxes that are very common: property tax and sales tax. Property taxes will vary dramatically just among neighboring communities, let alone from state to state. So this may be an arbitrary number, but it's not unrealistic. Same for the sales tax number. I made a fairly random semi-educated guess that the average person spends 10 percent of their gross wages on items that would fall under sales tax rules. This percentage would actually tend to rise significantly with income. It would also vary year to year based on major purchases such as a car or home appliances.

Table 11.6: Estimated Total Tax Payments.

Gross Income	Estimated Deductions	Taxable Income	FICA	Federal	Ohio State	City	Property Taxes	Sales Tax	Taxes Total all Taxes	as % of Gross
$30,000	$13,198	$16,802	$2,340.00	$1,680.20	$1,337.10	$600	$1,818	$210	$7,985	26.62%
$75,000	$17,999	$57,001	$5,850.00	$7,795.15	$3,900.75	$1,500	$4,500	$525	$24,071	32.09%
$150,000	$26,194	$123,806	$7,697.49	$24,069.68	$8,914.50	$3,000	$9,360	$1,050	$54,092	36.06%
$250,000	$66,950	$183,050	$9,590.40	$40,658.00	$17,250.00	$5,000	$14,400	$1,750	$88,648	35.46%

Assumptions: Single rates applied, assumed home ownership and mortgage payment of 25% of gross income. 6.25% 30 yr mortgage (6.75% for highest income). 90% of mortgage payment is tax-deductible interest. City taxes fixed at 2%, sales tax of 7% based on applicable purchases equal to 10% of income. Property taxes assumed to be 1.5% of home value based on a mortgage being 80% of home value. Estimate of itemized deductions from www.ria.thomson.com/about/pressroom/pr042006. pdf.

Now I really want you to look at that last column. I fully understand the need for taxes, just not the need for the complexity that creates bureaucracy. That, in turn, absorbs a large chunk of those taxes before they ever get to their intended destination. Here's what I mean.

Look at the taxes a typical person making $75,000 a year pays. It's nearly a third of her gross income. But that's not all. That person's employer matches her FICA taxes dollar for dollar up to $92,000 a year, so that's another $5,850. Plus, the employer pays a couple percent of the total payroll cost into unemployment compensation and workmen's compensation insurance. Now, some people say that these are employer taxes, not part of the personal tax code (which technically they are), but they are paid as part of the employer's payroll. In other words, without employees, the employer would not pay the taxes.

My point in including unemployment and workmen's compensation is that they are taxes that go to pay toward the "social safety net" that we have for injured, unemployed, and retired workers. Which are government-provided social services, dependant on tax revenue. In the same vein, although not a tax, let me include health insurance cost, which in Chapter 7 we saw would be about $250 a month, or $3,000 a year, for a 29-year-old female. That all adds up to another 13.8 percent of her $75,000 gross salary—or a total of over 46 percent of her gross salary.

Including employer and employee taxes and health insurance premiums gives us a closer comparison to other countries that have socialized health care. So right now, on just $30,000 a year of income, nearly $15,000 is being paid to the government, or health insurance company, to maintain our government spending and social welfare programs. Well, not really. Because even this is not enough; the U.S. government currently owes $8.5 trillion for loans that they have had to take out to keep the government running. In 2006, $406 billion was collected from you, and is being put toward only the interest on the debt that past generations have accumulated. And it is just getting worse.

Earlier I said that based on the current size of the U.S. economy, it will take a 30 percent rise in taxes to pay future obligations for Social Security and Medicare/Medicaid. That would put total taxes based on personal income and payroll taxes up to nearly 65 percent for most wage earners! My point is we can no longer afford boondoggle politics. We are going to have to decide what we really need to support and what we don't, or hope that this country can grow its economy at a pace we've never seen, which is highly unlikely when 45 percent of the average worker's wages are going to taxes and insurance. Oh, by the way, that isn't all the taxes you pay. I didn't include alcohol taxes, gasoline taxes, cigarette taxes, hotel taxes, airfare and airport taxes, and a whole bunch of other special taxes that I can't keep up with. For more information, one site to check out is www. federalbudget.com.

Remember that we are now paying $400 billion a year just in interest on past overspending. Think of how much less we could pay in taxes, or how many more federal social programs we could fund, if we weren't paying $400 billion in interest. The government budget is just like your personal budget—if we borrow today, it has to be repaid tomorrow. This prevents you, and future generations, from fully benefiting from your own future income. For more information, and some interesting info, check out the website of Citizens Against Government Waste's website at www.cagw.org.

Tax Strategies

This will be a very short section. It used to be that financial planning had a lot to do with tax planning. Today, there is very little an individual on a payroll can do to minimize his or her taxes. Most tax incentives and planning are implemented at the business level. If you are self-employed, a good CPA and financial planner can be very important in minimizing your taxes. And I do mean "and." You need both. Many times after I recommend a tax strategy to a business owner, he or she will say "Why didn't my CPA tell me this before?" The answer is that a CPA is trained to look at the past and report it accurately. Financial planners are trained to plan for the future. These are two different mind-sets that are more often than not mutually exclusive talents.

For individuals, there are a couple of strategies to employ. One revolves around the use of tax deductions. If you have no tax-deductible items to report, you can still use the standard deduction. In 2006 the standard deductions were $5,150 for single taxpayers, $7,550 for head of household, and $10,300 for married taxpayers filing jointly. These are the minimum amounts you can deduct from your income even if you have no itemized deductions or if the ones you have do not add up to more than the appropriate standard deductions.

Let's say you are single, own a condo with tax-deductible interest on your mortgage, pay property taxes, and give to a few charities every year. But the total of all of these allowable deductions adds up to $4,500, which is less than the standard deduction. In effect, you "waste" your deductions each year. What you can do is "bunch" your deductions in one year to increase your itemized deductions in that year. Then, take the standard deduction the following year.

Time Your Deductions Right

Here's how it works. Without a change in the standard deduction, over two years you would have total deductions of $10,300. Instead, you could make two years of charitable contributions in one year and prepay your property taxes for the next year, as well. So you would have your total deductions of $4,500 for the year, including your mortgage interest.

Of that amount, let's say that $1,000 is for charitable contributions and $1,200 is for property taxes. In December, you could make your charitable contributions for the following year, and prepay your property taxes. So your total itemized deductions would be $4,500 for the tax year plus $1,000 of charitable contributions for the following year plus $1,200 in property taxes due for the following year, for a total of $6,700. The following year, you would then just use the standard deduction of $5,150, for a two-year total of $11,850. This gives you $1,550 of extra deduction over two years. If you're in the 25 percent tax bracket, that would be an extra $387.50 in your pocket. Not bad for just changing the timing of expenses that you planned to make anyway.

> Deductions are subject to a limitation. Once your income reaches $72,250 for single filers or $150,000 for joint returns, you start to lose a portion of your tax deductions.

Other Techniques

Most other things you can do have been covered in other chapters, but are well worth reviewing. I feel that your tax situation will get worse before it gets better, so it's best to learn now, even if you can't implement until later what steps can be taken.

Borrow using tax-deductible interest. A tax deduction is an expense that reduces your taxable income. One of the most common deductions is for interest paid on most mortgages. As a homeowner, you will have purchased your most expensive asset and your best tax deduction. Maximize your deduction by borrowing the maximum amount for as long as possible with your primary mortgage. Don't make yourself "house poor," but if you expect your income to rise, it doesn't hurt to stretch your budget on a house purchase. Just understand that the longer you finance for and the less you put down, the longer it may be for you to have enough gain in the home's value to make a future move possible. Although there are some restrictions (check them out at www.bankrate.com), once you have equity in your home, the interest on a home equity loan is also tax-deductible—no matter what it is used for—up to $100,000. So whenever you borrow, especially for major items, compare interest rates to the after-tax interest rate you could receive on a home equity loan. To calculate your after-tax interest rate, use the following formula:

Interest Rate × (1 – Top Marginal Tax Bracket) = After-Tax Interest Rate

For example, if you are married and have a combined taxable income of $75,000, you would be in the 25 percent tax bracket. If you can get a home equity loan at a 7 percent interest rate, your after-tax interest rate would be calculated as follows:

7 percent × (1 – .25) = 5.25 percent

Just be prudent when using your home as collateral for a loan. In a worst-case scenario, even in a bankruptcy, you will have to continue making mortgage and home equity payments or lose your home.

Use a before-tax account (Section 125 or Cafeteria Plan) for your employee benefits. If you have health insurance, disability insurance, life insurance, or a handful of other optional employee benefits, make sure that you sign up to have the premiums deducted from your account on a pre-tax basis.

College Tuition Deductions and Credits

If a member of your family is currently enrolled in a higher education institution, then you may qualify for a tax deduction or tax credit. Deductions and credits can only be taken by the person who is responsible for the payment of tuition and fees. Each has different rules (deductions and credits are different) and you can't use both, so let me explain.

The tuition and fees deduction allows you to deduct up to $4,000 per year of qualifying expenses. The deduction is taken right on your 1040 tax return on line 34 (for 2006 tax returns). Qualifying expenses include the cost of books, software, room and board, and tuition. You may qualify for the deduction as long as you are not claimed as a dependant on another return, and if you do not file separately if married. Income limits are $65,000 to $80,000 for singles and $130,000 to $160,000 if married.

The Hope Credit allows you to offset up to $1,500 your first year of school and up to $2,000 your second year of tuition and fees with a tax credit. A tax credit is a dollar-for-dollar reduction in your actual tax liability. You must be enrolled at least part-time to use this credit.

The Lifetime Learning Credit provides up to a $2,000 credit for expenses paid for tuition and fees. There is no minimum amount of enrollment necessary to use this credit, but it does not apply to room and board. This is a great credit for when you're taking a class or two while also pursuing your career. As with all tax incentives, there are income phase-outs. For the Lifetime Learning Credit and the Hope Credit, they are between $43,000 and $53,000 for individual filers and $87,000 and $107,000 if married and filing jointly.

> Generally, the tax code provides two types of incentives: deductions or credits. In most instances, a credit is more beneficial.

In Table 11.7 you can see the difference between deductions and credits. If you assume that your tax liability is $6,000 before applying a $2,000 tax deduction, then after your deduction your tax liability would be $5,500. With the tax credit, a $2,000 credit reduces your tax liability by the full $2,000.

Table 11.7: Deductions vs. Credits.
Tax Deduction:
Deduction × highest marginal tax rate = value of your deduction
Example: $2,000 deduction × 25% tax bracket = $500 tax savings
Tax Credit:
Tax liability without credit – tax credit = new tax liability
Example: Owe $6,000 in federal taxes – $2,000 tax credit = $4,000 tax liability

You may need to do a little work if you think that you may be eligible for one of the education tax breaks, because you can only use one of the three. Since income limits are different, that may be your answer. But if you're eligible for more than one, be sure to do the math to determine which is the most valuable for you.

Tax-Advantaged Investing

Our economy is based on capitalism. Businesses are privately held (as opposed to government ownership), and in order to grow they create capital (meaning money) by selling stocks and bonds to the public. There are several tax laws that encourage investing. But beware—just because an investment has tax advantages doesn't mean that it is appropriate for your situation. Let's look at a couple and discuss the pros and cons. First we'll see how investments are ordinarily taxed. Then we'll see the difference between short- and long-term capital gains, and between dividends and interest.

If an investment is bought and sold for a gain, you will pay taxes based on how long the asset was held. For stocks and nonresidential real estate the gain is taxed at your top tax rate unless the investment was held for more than a year. Qualified dividends are taxed at a maximum of 15 percent, while interest is taxed at your maximum tax rate. Details are in Table 11.8.

Table 11.8: Investment Tax Rate Table.		
Type of Capital Asset	**Holding Period**	**Tax Rate**
Short-term capital gains (STCG)	One year or less	Ordinary income tax rates up to 35%

Type of Capital Asset	Holding Period	Tax Rate
Long-term capital gains (LTCG)	More than one year	5% for taxpayers in the 10% and 15% tax brackets; 15% for taxpayers in the 25%, 28%, 33%, and 35% tax brackets
Dividends	N/A	5% for taxpayers in the 15% tax bracket and 15% for all others
Interest	N/A	Ordinary income tax rates up to 35%

With an understanding of normal taxation we can now look at some investments, and how we can use tax rules to our advantage. And in the next chapter I'll talk more about some specific uses for various investments.

College 529 Plans

Think of a College 529 Plan as a 401(k) plan for college savings. Instead of employer sponsors, each state sponsors its own 529 plan. Like a 401(k), you will have a selection of mutual funds, usually from one or two fund families, from which to choose.

Advantages. Accounts are set up in the parent's name with the child as a beneficiary. This way, the parent retains control of the funds after the child turns 18. The money also counts as a parental asset instead of one of the child's assets for financial aid purposes. While accumulating money for college, the account grows tax-free. And as long as funds are used to pay for a qualified education expense, funds from the account are withdrawn tax-free, as well. Rules will vary by state, but if you have a state income tax, contributions into a 529 plan may qualify for a deduction when calculating state taxes.

Disadvantages. To avoid abuse of the tax-free status, the IRS limits changes in investments to one change per year. This inflexibility requires the investor to adopt a buy-and hold-strategy, so it is very important to use the same investment strategy that I laid out in Chapter 8 for your 401(k) plan. Be conservative. Buy high-dividend-producing funds, or large- or mid-cap value funds. Don't let a broker talk you into being more aggressive because you may have a long time (10 or more years) until you use the funds. Also, remember that funds withdrawn for a non-qualifying education expense will be subject to taxes and a 10 percent penalty.

Qualified Dividends

I've already talked about the advantages of dividends as an investment strategy. But stocks that pay dividends have an advantage in taxable accounts as well.

Advantages. When investing for income, dividends are taxed at the lower dividend rates you saw in Table 11.7. But even when looking for growth, dividends can be a great strategy. Many companies offer dividend re-investment programs (DRIPs). If you buy shares directly from a company's DRIP plan, not only will you pay little or no commission, but they will also hold your shares for you and buy new shares automatically at no com-mission with your dividends. Also, instead of never quite knowing what the future holds for interest from a bank, once a company begins paying dividends they are extremely reluctant to reduce payments or stop them altogether. In fact, many companies have consistent histories of raising their dividends.

Disadvantages. Dividends come from stocks, and even stocks of the biggest, most stable companies are, well, stocks. That means they are not an alternative, in terms of risk, to alternative higher-taxed interest-paying investments. More information can be found at www.DRIPcentral.com.

Insurance Company Products

Cash value life insurance and annuities both offer tax-deferred growth, but withdrawals are treated differently.

Advantages. Tax-deferred growth for both annuities and life insurance cash value. Life insurance cash values can be withdrawn based on first-in, first-out (FIFO) tax treatment. Withdrawals are assumed to be a return of your investment first, and as such are tax-free. Once cumulative deposits have been withdrawn, the balance is taxed as ordinary income. However, tax-free loans can be made against cash value.

Disadvantages. Withdrawals from annuities are taxed as ordinary income. Withdrawals are also subjected to a 10 percent penalty if withdrawn prior to age 59 ½. The cost of a cash value policy makes it nearly impossible for any life insurance to be termed "a good investment."

Individual Retirement Accounts (IRAs)

The IRA was created in 1974 and was fairly simple. You could save $2,000 a year for yourself, and another $250 for a nonworking spouse, in an IRA. Your contribution was tax-deductible and it grew tax-deferred until it was withdrawn. Past the age of 59 ½, you paid income tax on withdrawals; prior to that age, you paid an additional 10 percent penalty on withdrawals. Today, this simple plan designed to encourage savings has been changed into one of the most moronic, albeit useful, sections of our current tax code. So instead of having one simple savings plan that nearly everyone used, we now have four … which almost no one uses. That's our government for you. And now, the players are:

Traditional IRA

The descendant of the original IRA, this is the personal retirement account that is most like a 401(k) plan at work. Although there is no company match, your contributions may be tax-deductible, and your earnings grow tax-deferred until withdrawal. Unfortunately, Congress decided that too much money was being put away in IRAs, depriving the federal government of much-needed revenue, so they came up with a new set of rules.

If you do not participate in any other qualified plan, such as a retirement plan at work, you can deduct your IRA contribution from your taxable income at any income level. The limit is $4,000 if you're under age 50 and $5,000 if you're over that age.

However, you may still be able to deduct an IRA if you have a qualified plan at work on a phase-out schedule based on your income, as follows.

Income limits for IRA deductibility:	
Joint	$75,000 to $85,000
Single or head of household	$50,000 to $60,000
Spousal IRA	$150,000 to $160,000

The way the phase-out works is if your income falls between the ranges above, then the deductible portion of your contribution is reduced by $1/10$ for $1,000 of income. For example, if you are married and filing jointly, have a joint income of $80,000, and are under 50 years of age, you would be limited to a $2,000 deductible IRA for the year.

If you're single, you might assume that your limits would be more than those for a married couple, but no—you get your own income schedule to determine deductibility. Which is a good thing, since your income limits are much higher than half those for a couple. And if you're married, with a nonworking spouse, you can make up to $150,000 and make a full contribution for your spouse.

Understand that the only reason to put limits on who can deduct an IRA fully is to limit the loss of tax revenue to the government by those who could otherwise take advantage of this saving incentive. So Congress decided that at a certain point, you are too rich to be allowed to take advantage of a tax-deductible IRA. If you're single, you're "too rich" at $50,000; if married with two incomes, you're "too rich" at $75,000; and if married with a nonworking spouse, you're "too rich" at $150,000. Remember these amounts for future reference.

Also note that these contribution limits only apply to new contributions. If you retire or change jobs, there is no limit as to how much money can be rolled over into an IRA from an existing retirement plan. If you can afford to put in an additional $2,000 above the deductible limits in my example, it would grow tax-deferred but you would not get a tax deduction for that amount. I don't recommend that you do this. When it comes to withdrawing your funds at retirement, you cannot simply withdraw your taxed portion at one time and pay taxes. Instead, you must track your after-tax deposits and divide the total by your total deductible deposits to form a ratio of nondeductible to deductible deposits. Then every time you make a withdrawal, you use this ratio to determine the portion that is not taxed. If you don't keep track of this ratio, you will pay taxes again on your after-tax money. The burden of proof in any IRA withdrawal is on you, the taxpayer. Got it? If not, don't worry about it—just don't do it!

Roth IRAs

Roth IRAs are fairly new to the scene, having been created in 1998 by Congress. They are somewhat the opposite of a traditional IRA in that the benefits are "back-loaded." With a traditional IRA you receive an immediate benefit from the tax deduction you receive when you make your contribution and pay taxes on the withdrawals. With a Roth, you do not receive an immediate deduction, but when you withdraw money after age 59½, the withdrawals are completely tax-free. Mathematically they are absolutely identical choices, assuming that your tax rate when you make withdrawals is identical to your tax rate at the time you contribute. Since this takes a little crystal ball gazing, it is not surprising that opinions are all over the place when comparing the traditional versus the Roth IRAs. Depending on who you ask, Roths will fall somewhere between the best thing since sliced bread and the biggest tax boondoggle in U.S. history.

While reality will fall somewhere in between, here is what you need to think about if faced with the Roth or regular IRA decision. The bottom line is where are your taxes headed? If you think you will pay more in taxes when you retire then you should use a Roth IRA, and if you think your tax rate will decline you should use a deductible IRA. Since income limits are much higher for a Roth IRA, this could be the deciding factor. But you could also choose to contribute to a Roth IRA instead of making tax-deductible contributions to your 401(k) plan that are not matched by an employer. So this discussion can really apply to a large number of potential investors.

When I give talks and I'm asked how much a person needs in retirement, my answer usually is "For everyone it's different and it depends on what your vision of retirement is. Personally, I won't retire until I know I can have more income than I have now." My explanation is that when I'm not at work now, I'm out spending money. I can't just sit around the house, and I hate yard work. So for me, a Roth IRA may be a good choice. But honestly, if you look at the numbers as far as how much the "average" worker has saved, the reality is that very few people will have as much income when they retire as they have while working. And with less debt (hopefully), kids out of the house, college paid for, maybe downsizing the residence, most people don't really need as much income in their retirement as they did during the bulk of their working years. Those that tend to have more money in retirement are typically those with high incomes, and don't qualify for either IRA anyway.

So far we've assumed that tax rates stay the same as today, and you just need to make a reasonable guess about your personal income levels. However, another consideration is tax policy. If you think income tax rates will rise dramatically, then a Roth IRA will offer you a hedge against higher personal tax rates in your retirement. As skeptical as I am of our elected officials being able to keep a lid on spending and taxes, I really believe that the overall taxes we pay now are about as high as they can go. At some point, the benefit of higher taxes is offset by a slower economy, and that doesn't benefit anyone. One caveat to this, however, is health care. If health care shifts from the private sector to a government program, then health-care premiums will be replaced by a tax increase to pay the government's cost.

A second consideration is an idea that is bantered around a bit, and that is the idea of a "flat tax," consumption tax, or what they call in Europe a value added tax. No discussion is necessary, other than to understand that under these scenarios, all income is tax-free! Instead of an income tax, you pay extra tax when you buy stuff, similar to a national sales tax. While the head winds are strong against such a change, it does make a great deal of sense, and may provide a means of increasing tax revenue without crimping the economy. In this case a contributor to a deductible IRA would receive the benefits of both a current tax deduction and tax-free income in retirement.

And the last thought: there is nothing written in stone that says a Roth IRA's distributions will forever be tax-free. If we truly have the deficit problems that some predict over Social Security, Medicare, and Medicaid, an easy tax to pass will be on the "rich" that are receiving tax-free income from Roth IRAs.

The bottom line to me is that "a bird in the hand is worth two in the bush." In other words, take the sure-thing tax deduction now, and do not worry about what happens in the future.

However, Roth IRAs do have some short-term advantages over tax-deferred or traditional IRAs. First, to be able to fully contribute, your income can be as high as $95,000, with a phase-out up to $110,000. For joint filers the phase-out begins at $150,000 of annual income and ends at $160,000. These are much higher income limits than for a traditional IRA.

The biggest advantage that a Roth IRA has over a traditional IRA, or even your 401(k) plan, is that you have limited access to your funds prior to retirement or age 59 ½, which you don't have with tax-deductible investments. Since you have already paid taxes on your contribution, you do not have to pay tax again when the money is withdrawn.

Your earnings, which grow tax-free, will be taxed and a 10 percent penalty will be paid if withdrawn prior to age 59 ½. Well that's the general rule, and of course there are exceptions to every rule. So just like a traditional IRA, you can make earnings withdrawals from a Roth and avoid the 10 percent penalty, but you will be taxed on the withdrawal, for the following events:

- College expenses for yourself or an immediate family member

- In the event of permanent disability

◻ Use of funds to purchase your first home

◻ To pay certain medical expenses

So the biggest difference that a Roth IRA brings to the table is the ability to withdraw your own contributions, tax-free and penalty-free, any time. This can be a useful feature.

In Chapter 8, I mentioned the interviews on the morning show where different people, representing different age groups, expressed their biggest financial concern. The 30-something couple said that saving for their children's education and their own retirement were their concerns. Now, if it comes down to one or the other, I always recommend saving for retirement since there are no co-op programs, work-study programs, loans, or scholarships for retirement. However, from the inflation data in the Prologue I'll be the first to say that paying for college is not what it used to be. And with colleges willing to lend as much as necessary to "help," some parental assistance would certainly benefit most future college students.

But part of the problem with actually saving money is that by saving, any balance you have may be counted against you when determining your potential financial aid. One way around this, as we've seen, is the College 529 Plan. The other is the Roth IRA. Here's how it works.

Let's look at what happens if you start at age 34 and invest $4,000 a year into a Roth IRA. Remember that you do not receive a tax deduction for your investment, but within certain rules your investment does grow tax-free. In Table 11.9, I'm assuming a 10 percent growth rate. If you're really good at planning and start a Roth IRA when your son is born, you'll have a balance of just over $200,000 when he's ready to go off to college. But more importantly, you've made $72,000 of contributions that can be withdrawn penalty-free and tax-free to help with his tuition. Plus, you still have $128,636 of tax-free earnings that can stay in your account and continue to grow for retirement.

Table 11.9: Roth IRA Growth.

Age	Investment Year	Beginning Balance	Annual Contribution	10% Investment Return	Ending Balance
34	1	$0	$4,000	$400	$4,400
35	2	$4,400	$4,000	$840	$9,240
36	3	$9,240	$4,000	$1,324	$14,564

continues...

(Table 11.9 continued)

Age	Investment Year	Beginning Balance	Annual Contribution	10% Investment Return	Ending Balance
37	4	$14,564	$4,000	$1,856	$20,420
38	5	$20,420	$4,000	$2,442	$26,862
39	6	$26,862	$4,000	$3,086	$33,949
40	7	$33,949	$4,000	$3,795	$41,744
41	8	$41,744	$4,000	$4,574	$50,318
42	9	$50,318	$4,000	$5,432	$59,750
43	10	$59,750	$4,000	$6,375	$70,125
44	11	$70,125	$4,000	$7,412	$81,537
45	12	$81,537	$4,000	$8,554	$94,091
46	13	$94,091	$4,000	$9,809	$107,900
47	14	$107,900	$4,000	$11,190	$123,090
48	15	$123,090	$4,000	$12,709	$139,799
49	16	$139,799	$4,000	$14,380	$158,179
50	17	$158,179	$4,000	$16,218	$178,397
51	18	$178,397	$4,000	$18,240	$200,636

Total Contributions: $72,000   After Withdrawals: $128,636

Two advantages of this strategy are that you are not penalized for either saving for college or keeping the entire balance for retirement. Under current financial aid rules, money in a retirement account is not counted as an asset that is available for tuition. And if Junior gets a full-ride scholarship, the money can still be withdrawn tax-free and penalty-free for your retirement.

Education Investment Choices

While we're on the subject of education, let's take a look at how the government has given us tax incentives to save and help pay for college.

Coverdale Education Account. The Coverdale, or Education IRA, allows for a $2,000 contribution annually. The contribution is not pre-tax; however, the earnings are tax-free if used for qualified education expenses. So this is similar to a Roth IRA or a College 529 Plan. A nice feature of the Coverdale is that it can be used for education expenses at all levels, from kindergarten through high school, as well as for college. Although it's certainly limited at only $2,000 a year, it can be quite beneficial when planning well ahead.

As with all IRAs, there is a phase-out income range where the Coverdale becomes unavailable. For singles, the income phase-out is between $95,000 and $110,000 of income. For joint filers, the phase-out is between $190,000 and $220,000. The main advantage of a Coverdale is that you can invest in anything that you can invest in for a regular or Roth IRA. This provides a great deal more flexibility than the limited choices in a College 529 Plan. It also allows you to change your investments more than once per year, whereas a College 529 Plan only allows investment changes annually.

Savings Bonds

Savings bonds were extremely popular at one time. They evolved from what were called "war bonds." Back during World War II, the government encouraged the purchase of savings bonds, or war bonds, as a way to finance the war effort. It was considered your patriotic duty to help out by buying bonds. Employers did their part by allowing employees to buy bonds through their payroll, the way we invest in 401(k)s today. So many times I'll see large numbers of bonds when helping to settle a client's estate, but since fewer companies allow for payroll deduction for bonds today, they have become less familiar to succeeding generations. That's a shame, because they really aren't a bad savings alternative. Here's how they work.

There are two kinds of savings bonds: EE Bonds and I Bonds. EE Bonds accrue a fixed interest rate for the life of the bond, which is typically 30 years. This means that the interest isn't actually paid the way it is with a typical savings account. Instead, the "interest" is added to the initial purchase price each year. A big advantage is that, like an IRA, you do not pay taxes on your earnings until you cash in your bond. From November 2006 to April 2007 that rate was 3.60 percent. Now, that isn't too exciting, but remember two things. First, take the term "savings" literally, and remember the purpose of saving. It simply means to put your money somewhere and to get it back in real terms, or in after-inflation dollars. So if inflation is running 3.5 percent and you cash in your bonds, you are still a little behind in real terms after you pay taxes on your gains. There is one exception to this, and that is if you use your proceeds to pay for higher education. Current tax laws allow you to cash in savings bonds, and pay no taxes on your earnings if you use the proceeds to pay education expenses.

To do better you could buy an I Bond, but with an I Bond your interest will vary each year. Currently, they pay 1.45 percent interest, which is fixed. But in addition they pay a bonus interest rate that is allegedly equal to the inflation rate. Thus the name "I" Bond, or Inflation Bond. In the fourth quarter of 2006 that bonus rate is 3.17 percent, for a total interest rate of 4.52 percent. Currently that is the better deal. But always compare, and remember that the EE Bond interest rate is fixed, while the I Bond's rate will very annually.

The trouble with both is that in real terms you still lose purchasing power since college costs have risen at nearly twice the rate as prices for the overall economy. But with the savings bonds your money is safe. A good strategy would be to invest money earmarked for college in savings bonds when the student is in the last couple of years of high school, and invest money that is earmarked for the last year or two of college after your student has enrolled in college. At this point, you want your money in savings, not investments. A modest return is much better than any kind of loss when tuition bills are only months away.

But again, you have to look at the income limits to see whether your savings will be tax-free. For a single taxpayer, the tax exemption phases out from $63,100 to $78,100 of income. For married filers it's between $94,700 and $124,700. Now, this presents a little bit of a problem. For IRAs the income limits come into play at the time of investment. You pretty much know your income at that time. And if you're close the IRS gives you up to the time you file your tax return to either make your contribution or re-characterize a contribution made earlier in the year that you don't qualify for. But in this case, the tax advantage takes place when you cash in the bonds, maybe 20 years after purchase. A lot of assumptions need to be made on whether bonds would make a prudent long-term savings or investment.

But don't just look at savings bonds as a college savings investment. If you look at the yield on the I Bond, by definition your return will be 1.45 percent more than the inflation rate, and your "interest" is tax-deferred until you cash in your bond. A rule of thumb in financial planning is that you should have three to six months of your net income in savings for emergencies. Now, that may seem extreme, but consider that three months is also a typical time frame for finding a new job if suddenly unemployed, and three months of expenses is really not that much.

For more information, a great Web page to check out is http://invest-faq.com/articles/bonds-us-savings.html.

Tax-Saving Summary

There are different income limits for being able to use tax deductions, personal exemptions, and contribution limits to retirement savings and college savings plans. And so, what we end up with is inconsistency. If a taxpayer is "too rich" for one, then shouldn't they be "too rich" for the others as well? In an attempt to limit tax advantages to the rich, the government has just created a confusing mess. So what was a really good idea—the original IRA—has become a set of convoluted rules that hinder usage instead of encouraging it by those who do need to use it the most. As always, the rich can afford advisors to help with their tax planning, and will find ways to save on taxes. But too many in the middle class end up confused by all the various rules and qualifications, and end up missing out on deductions that they could be eligible for.

One of President Bush's initiatives was a lifetime savings account. Unfortunately, the momentum for the plan lost its initiative somewhere between Iraq and North Korea. But this was a proposal that truly deserves bipartisan support. The lifetime savings accounts would eliminate all the tax-advantaged savings accounts now, and replace them with a single account, with a single new set of rules. Contributions would not qualify for a tax deduction, but could be withdrawn at any time, for any purpose, completely tax-free. What a novel idea: a plan that would encourage everyone to save, and not tell you what to do with your money after you've saved it! It would be a big boost for those trying to improve their financial circumstances, but who are currently frozen by confusion. No wonder it never got off the ground.

The following table is a summary of beginning income phase-out levels for several tax deductions, credits, and investments. The table assumes an individual filer.

Table 11.10: Tax Deduction Phase-Out Summary.

FICA Taxes	Taxation ends at $92,000 gross income
Tax Deductions	Phase out at $72,250
Tuition Deduction	Phase out at $65,000
Hope Credit	Phase out at $43,000
Lifetime Credit	Phase out at $43,000

IRA Deductibility	Phase out at $50,000 (assumes eligibility for a company-sponsored pension plan; without a company plan there is no income limit)
Roth IRA	Phase out at $95,000
Coverdale IRA	Phase out at $95,000
EE Savings Bond	Phase out at $63,100
	Only if used for education expenses

Getting Tax Preparation Help

Remember that the 2006 tax code is over 16,000 pages long, and growing every year. So once you get past the 1040EZ it may not be a bad idea to get some guidance in completing your return.

The first step for many of you will be to use a computer program to help with tax preparation. Both Intuit and H&R Block offer tax preparation software. The biggest advantage of using these products is that they should be kept up-to-date. But remember, you are responsible for your tax return, not the software company. I have had clients who have either missed tax deductions or claimed inappropriate deductions, or both, when using software packages. Software is best used when you have some familiarity with the tax code and tax rules and regulations. The IRS has come a long way on the Internet. It is always advisable to double-check IRS rules at www.irs.gov and then search for the publication(s) that apply to your situation.

Despite my advice, many of you will end up going to a tax preparer for your return. Here's the problem. At the affordable level, you're likely to get a preparer who knows little more than you do and is armed with one of those same off-the-shelf tax software packages. I remember one argument with a tax preparer over a client's deduction where I kept citing the tax code, and all he kept saying was "But my software won't let me (fill in the deduction)!"

Your best bet is to look for qualifications, which would lead you to a CPA. Problem there is that a CPA will be expensive, and won't guarantee accuracy. I think it's *Money* magazine that either asks, or used to ask, for volunteers to prepare a tax return each year based on information provided by the magazine. Each year, no one would accurately calculate the proper tax liability; rarely did two preparers even come up with the same answer! And these were professionals who volunteered, not seedy fly-by-nights caught by an undercover crew. This just goes back to my initial premise: there is a major problem with our tax code. If 16,000 pages of rules and regulations aren't enough evidence, then isn't the fact that "professionals" many times can't even figure it out? Tax reform shouldn't be a party-line issue—it's a consumer issue.

The Bottom Line

- Completing a tax return is not that difficult for most of us and is essential to understanding how you are taxed.

- If you add in all sources of taxation based on your pay, nearly 50 percent goes to some government entity somewhere to pay for all the government services and programs that they provide.

- We are facing a potentially devastating economic crisis. We owe for our past debts, and have future obligations that we can't now pay. Simply raising taxes above today's onerous rates is not a viable solution.

- Use tax-advantaged programs to save and invest now; it will never get any easier.

Glossary

A-share mutual fund   A mutual fund that charges you a sales fee at time of purchase to pay the mutual fund salesperson a commission.

accredited investor   Some investments limit investors to those with a million dollar net worth, or who have had annual earnings of over $200,000 for the prior two years. These are accredited investors.

adjustable rate mortgage (ARM)   A mortgage whose interest rate changes over time based on an index.

after tax   What you're left with after your investment gains are taxed. Saving taxes can be the safest way to increase your investment returns.

amortization   The gradual repayment of a mortgage by regular scheduled payments. An amortization schedule will show the remaining balance to be paid after each payment.

annual percentage rate (APR)   The total yearly cost of a mortgage stated as a percentage of the loan amount; it includes the base interest rate, primary mortgage insurance (PMI), and loan origination fee or points.

average annual return   A way of measuring an investment's performance as an annual figure.

B-share mutual fund   A mutual fund that is sold by a MFS that has no up-front fee, but annual service fees of up to 1% and a surrender charge if sold within the first (typically) five or six years of ownership.

bank money market account   Basically a savings account with a minimum balance requirement and/or some restrictions on withdrawals. In return, the bank will pay a higher interest rate than on a regular savings account.

bear market   A term used to describe a stock market where prices are falling. Historically refers to a 20% drop or more.

bond   A form of loan issued by corporations and governments.

bounced check   A slang term used when a check is written for more money than is available in the account to draw on.

budget   A written statement showing all income sources and expenses.

bull market   Refers to the stock market when prices are rising.

cafeteria plan An employee benefit where an employee is given a dollar amount to use toward benefits and a "menu" of benefits from which to choose.

cash value life insurance A form of insurance in which a portion of your premiums in the early years is used to fund a cash value account. In the later years the cash value account may be used to subsidize your premium payments to cover the cost of insurance. Never to be confused with an investment product.

checking account A savings-type account at a bank or credit union. It has the additional feature of allowing for withdrawals with checks and/or an ATM card. Since balances are typically low, and bank expense high (to clear the checks), the interest paid is typically much lower than on savings accounts.

closing costs Expenses incurred by buyers and sellers in transferring ownership of a property. Sometimes referred to as settlement costs.

co-pay A portion of an expense that is covered by insurance, but must be paid by the policyholder.

co-signer A secondary signer on a credit application, usually required because the primary borrower would not qualify for the loan on their own merits. The co-signer assumes full responsibility for repayment of the loan.

collateral Property that is used to secure a loan. If payments are not made, the lender has the right to the property.

commission A fee paid to a salesperson by a company for selling their product.

company match Refers to the amount of money that an employer will contribute to your 401(k) plan, based on a match to your contributions. This is also known as "free money," and you should maximize your receipt of it.

consumer price index (CPI) An index created by the government to show you how much less the money in your pocket is worth compared to years prior.

credit report A report of an individual's credit history prepared by a credit bureau and used by a lender in determining a loan applicant's score.

credit union A not-for-profit bank that is owned by the depositors instead of shareholders. In theory, much more consumer-friendly than a bank; however, regulators have forced this service gap to narrow. Still the best place to start when looking for "banking" services.

debit card A card that looks like a credit card, but is used to withdraw your own money from a checking account.

debt Borrowing money from someone with a commitment to repay.

debt-to-income ratio The ratio of monthly debt payments to monthly income. This is used by lenders to determine whether they should extend additional credit to a potential borrower.

deductible The amount that you must pay when filing an insurance claim before the insurance company begins to pay their share.

defined-benefit plan A form of retirement plan in which retirement benefits are determined by a formula that usually involves your salary, age, and years of service. Many times referred to as pension plans.

defined-contribution plan A form of retirement plan in which retirement benefits are determined by the amount of contributions and earnings made during a working career.

depreciation   The loss in value of an asset over time.

discretionary expense   An expense that is not required to be made.

diversification   A basic tenet of investing, easily interpreted as "don't put all your eggs in one basket." While simple in theory, proper implementation is much harder as it is designed to offset investment risks of one security by holding different securities that do not share the same risk. For example, holding several mutual funds does not necessarily diversify the risk of losing money in a stock market decline.

dollar cost averaging   An investment method in mutual funds and is way to benefit from stock market volatility. By investing the same dollar amount periodically you automatically buy more shares when the market is low and fewer when prices are high.

dumpster diving   Rummaging through trash cans and bins for discarded personal documents that contain account numbers, passwords, and/or social security numbers. Buy a shredder and shred all financial documents, including junk credit card offers, to discourage dumpster divers from accessing your personal information.

early withdrawal penalty   Typically refers to investments that are granted tax- advantaged status by the IRS, but have penalties if withdrawn prior to age 59 ½.

efficient market theory   A stock market theory that is mostly popular among academics, it states that stock prices always reflect a "fair" price since the current price reflects the sum of all known information about that stock. And since all information is readily available to the public today, there is little to gain by "stock picking" to beat the market. Efficient market theory is quoted by advocates of using index mutual funds for investing.

FDIC   The Federal Deposit Insurance Corp. insures deposits made at covered banking institutions. Only covers bank deposits, not other investments such as mutual funds or annuities, sold at a bank.

FHA loan   A mortgage that is insured by the Federal Housing Administration (FHA).

FICO score   Your credit score expressed as a number between 300 and 850; the higher it is, the better.

flipping   A real estate term used to describe the process of buying a home with the intent of selling it in a very short time at a profit. Usually involves buying distressed properties and making quick, low-cost improvements.

403(b)   Similar to (but not exactly like) a 401(k) plan, used by nonprofit organizations.

foreclosure   The process by which a lender takes back a piece of property due to lack of mortgage repayment.

fridge list   Used to track household income and expenses. It is suggested to keep it on your refrigerator as a reminder to keep it up-to-date and accurate.

fundamental investing   Describes a process for picking stock investments that relies on company financial data and economic data.

gross income   Your pay before any deductions or expenses are subtracted.

growth investing   A style of investing where the investor is looking for fast-growing companies that can continue to grow their earnings. Since such companies tend to have high-priced stock, this style is referred to as "buy high and sell higher."

hacking   The act of breaking into computer networks, databases, or personal PCs to obtain sensitive or confidential data. While commonly thought of as a problem for large corporate and government networks, private individual networks are becoming more frequent targets as security is many times too lax.

health maintenance organization (HMO)   A type of health insurance plan in which the insurance carrier negotiates rates directly with specific health-care providers for lower rates. Insureds are generally allowed to use providers outside of the HMO, but at a higher cost.

hedge fund   An unregulated investment company, similar to a mutual fund, but only available to "accredited investors." A hedge fund has no limits on the types of investments it can make.

index fund   A mutual fund that tracks the performance of a specific index. While cheap to the investor, an investor's goal should be better performance, particularly protection on the downside.

interest-only mortgage   A mortgage in which in the early years payments go toward paying off interest instead of interest and principal. After the initial period the loan will "reset" and begin to amortize, with the associated higher payment. These loans are not for the novice. If you're a first-time home buyer, save your money for a larger down payment and finance on a conventional 30-year mortgage.

introductory rate   An initial teaser (low) interest rate designed to sucker you into applying for a loan or credit card.

investment debt   Any debt where the proceeds are used to acquire an investment.

IRA rollover   The IRS allows you to "roll over" an IRA or pension plan into a new IRA or pension plan without paying taxes or penalties. The amount rolled over is not subject to the annual contribution limits.

joint tenancy   A form of co-ownership giving each owner (or tenant), equal interest and equal rights in the property, including the right of survivorship.

junk fees   Fees that are added to a transaction to boost profits, but that don't represent true expenses of the seller. Common in both car sales and in mortgage lending.

lease   Typically refers to a way to purchase a new car with a lower monthly payment, but popular for the purchase of many larger items by businesses. In a lease the borrower's, or lessee's, payment is only based on a portion of the value of the property and on the interest for the entire value. At the end of a lease the lessee has paid down the value of the property and can typically purchase the property at that reduced value, known as residual value.

lien   A legal claim against a property that must be paid when the property is sold.

lifestyle debt   Financing items that are consumed well before the debt is paid.

liquidity   A term that refers to how available your money is after you make an investment. For example, a checking account is 100% liquid. Investments may be illiquid because of surrender charges or penalties for withdrawals over a certain time period, or because you want to be able to count on withdrawing your money at any time.

load mutual fund   A generic term for any mutual fund that pays some type of commission to an MFS. Only purchase when the MFS is offering a more skilled service than you can provide for yourself.

loan-to-value ratio (LTV)   The amount of a mortgage divided by the value of the property.

market capitalization   A way to determine a company's value. It is the current selling price of a company's stock times the number of shares of stock the company has issued.

moneynomics   Taking advantage of economic fundamentals like taxes and inflation to make seemingly small financial decisions today that may have a large financial impact on our future.

mortgage broker   A mortgage salesperson who represents several mortgage companies. Many brokers will specialize in non-traditional mortgages that target niche markets that might include non-prime, first-time home buyers, self-employeds, and high-value homes.

mutual fund   An investment company that typically invests in stocks or bonds of domestic and foreign companies.

mutual fund salesperson (MSF)   A person who is licensed and employed to sell mutual funds, but probably has little more knowledge to do so than you do.

National Credit Union Administration (NCUA)   A government agency that regulates credit unions and insures deposits.

negative compounding   Refers to the fact that an investment loss takes a larger percentage gain for the investment to increase back to its original value.

net income   Gross income less all payroll deductions and personal non-discretionary expenses.

no-load mutual fund   The cheap way to buy mutual funds; you won't pay a commission but you won't get any help,

either. If you're ready and willing to do a little bit of homework and pay attention to your account, this can be the way to go. No-load funds are also used by many RIAs who manage client accounts without commissions, but instead charge a management fee.

non-discretionary expenses   Expenses that must be paid for personal welfare (food, housing) or due to personal commitment (loans, rent, utility bills).

opportunity cost   What you could be earning with your money should you be doing something different with it.

pension portability   The ability to take the balance in your pension plan with you should you change employers.

phishing   Sending e-mails that appear to come from a legitimate financial institution, with a link back to a fraudulent e-mail address or website in the name of that institution. Phishers will ask for account information that will be "required" due to some change. Never respond to an unsolicited e-mail with any personal information. If uncertain, call the financial institution and ask if the e-mail was legitimate.

points   A one-time charge by a lender that can be used to reduce the interest rate over the life of the loan.

preferred provider organization (PPO)   A health insurance plan in which services are provided by a pre-determined group of health-care providers. While providing cost savings, a PPO may severely restrict the ability to use health-care providers outside of the pre-approved organization.

progressive taxes   A tax system in which the marginal tax rate increases at stages with rising incomes. Only income above predetermined levels are taxed at the higher rate.

prudent debt Debt that is generally accepted as necessary. The amortization period of the loan is less than the life of that which is acquired with the debt.

rate lock When applying for a mortgage, the borrower can choose the interest rate at the time of application, or wait and choose, or lock-in, an interest rate between time of application and time of closing the loan.

real vs. nominal "Real" refers to how much money it takes to buy the same amount of stuff today as in some point in the past. "Nominal" is the face value of the money in your pocket.

refinance Paying off one debt with the proceeds of a new loan. Usually done to lower interest rates and/or payments.

residual value The projected value of an auto, or other property, at the end of a lease. This is used in determining the initial lease payment.

roll down A systematic way to accelerate debt payoff by making minimum payments on all debts except either the highest interest rate debt, or the largest balance debt. This system maximizes the impact of your monthly payments and can dramatically decrease the amortization period for a group of debts.

rollover Refers to the transfer of a 401(k) account, or other retirement account, into an IRA without paying taxes or penalties on the transfer.

Roth IRA An individual account that allows an individual to contribute to a retirement account where the earnings grow tax-free until withdrawal. There are limits to who can contribute based on income, and limits on withdrawals without paying a 10% penalty.

Section 125 plan A tax provision that allows expenses for certain employee benefits to be deducted from an employee's paycheck on a before-tax basis.

Standard & Poor's 500 (S&P 500) An index made up of 500 blue-chip stocks. The index is commonly used to measure stock market performance. Although you can't directly invest in the index, several investment products are available that are meant to duplicate the S&P 500's return.

spyware Software applications that invade a PC and track activities or change settings.

take-home pay Gross pay less payroll deductions that include taxes and employee-paid benefits.

tax credit A tax preference item that allows for a dollar-for-dollar reduction in tax liability.

tax deduction A tax preference item that reduces the amount of income that is subjected to tax.

tech-wreck A reference to the bear market in U.S. stocks from 2000 to 2002. Technology stocks were hit the hardest with many companies going out of business entirely, and many others saw their stock values dropping by 80 to 90 percent.

technical analysis A way to analyze investments that relies on the stocks' prior market movements and daily volume of shares traded. Ignores any fundamental knowledge of the company or general economic outlook.

tenant's insurance policy An insurance policy for renters to compensate for loss to their own property and for that of the landlord, should the tenant be responsible. Also known as renter's insurance.

term life insurance   A form of life insurance that is purchased for a specific period of time, or term. Since on most policies the term expires while the policyholder is relatively young, premiums can be very low. Before purchasing, look into your family health history. If insurability may be an issue later in life, you may need to bite the bullet and purchase a permanent or cash-value policy while you can.

title insurance   Insurance to protect the lender (lender's policy) or the buyer (owner's policy) against loss arising from disputes over ownership of a property.

underwriting   The process by which an insurance company determines whether to make an offer of insurance and if so, what premium to charge.

upside-down   A lending term that refers to being in a position where a borrower owes more on a loan than what the item purchased with the loan is worth. A common position in the first year or two when financing a car with little or no money down, or when leasing.

utilization ratio   Used as a factor in calculating your credit score and refers to the amount of your outstanding credit as a percentage of available credit.

value investing   An investment strategy that relies on buying stocks at companies at prices that are determined to be below market value. Commonly termed as a "buy low and sell high" strategy.

variable annuity (VA)   A combination of a mutual fund-type investment with a nominal life insurance benefit that allows the investment to be tax-deferred. Optional insurance, investment, and income guarantees can be purchased at added costs. They also pay a much higher commission than do mutual

funds, so you should be wary of the purchase if recommended. Although VAs may have a function in a portfolio later in life, if you're under 40 they would be an investment of last resort if you have already maxed out contributions to all other retirement vehicle options. They make no sense for a "buy and hold" investor since they are taxed at a higher ordinary income rate rather than the reduced capital gain rate.

vesting schedule   The period of time where an employee must work for a company before the company's contributions to the employee's pension plan actually belongs to the employee.

yield curve   A graphical depiction that shows the relationship between short-term interest rates and long-term interest rates.

zero-down mortgage   A mortgage that finances 100 percent of the purchase price of a property. If you are unable to save even 5 percent of the purchase price of a house, you should avoid purchasing and rent until you can save for a down payment. The exception is for investment property—always put as little down as possible on an investment property.

Useful Websites

Personal Finance

www.bankrate.com
A good unbiased resource for everything financial.

www.CFP.net
Financial planning information, plus a link to find a CFP® in your area.

www.consumeraffairs.com/finance
"Knowledge is power!" Consumer news, reviews, complaints, and product information.

www.dinkytown.net
This site provides great, easy-to-use investment calculators.

www.financialplan.about.com
Financial planning on about.com, a great source for all the basics.

www.naaim.org
The National Association of Active Investment Managers. This is an independent group that promotes active investment management. If you're looking for an investment advisor, they have a "find an advisor" link.

www.interest.com
Not only will you find information on all types of borrowing here, but this site also features a debt roll-down calculator.

www.kbb.com
Website of Kelley Blue Book. Contains comprehensive auto information and pricing.

www.savingsecrets.com
A fantastic website that provides tips on saving, eliminating debt, borrowing, and all things related to personal finance.

www.termquote.com
Term life insurance quotes are available on this easy-to-understand website.

www.twentysomething.com
Demographic info ... all about you!

Investing

www.401Advisor.com
This website provides 401(k) investing (and general financial) advice.

www.AAII.com
The single best site for any individual investor.

www.my401kAdvisor.com
The Pension Reform Act of 2006 encourages employers to offer specific 401(k) investment advice for their employees. This is one site that does that for companies and individuals.

401kadvicesite.com
Specific steps for 401(k) investors to take to maximize investment returns.

www.dripcentral.com
A listing of stocks available for direct purchase and free reinvestment of dividends.

www.etrade.com
One of the most popular discount brokers.

www.fool.com
Website of The Motley Fool, a respected multimedia financial education company.

www.msiebert.com
Low cost, no minimums, and dividend reinvestment on select stocks make this online broker tough to beat.

www.smartmoney.com
Named the Best Overall Personal Finance Site two years in a row from Yahoo! Internet Life, this site has consistently been named "Best of the Web" from Forbes magazine.

www.tdameritrade.com
A great website for online brokerage services.

Tax Information

www.fairtax.com
Resources and information on taxes and the Fair Tax Act.

www.IRS.gov
Official website of the Internal Revenue Service. Important tax forms can be found here.

ria.thompson.com/about/pressroom/pr042006.pdf
A website that provides estimated itemized deductions by income level.

www.taxcut.com
Provided by H&R Block, this website provides several different options for affordable tax return software.

www.turbotax.intuit.com
Tax return software that's downloadable, inexpensive, and easy to use.

Federal Budget Information

These sites provide information on where your tax dollars go:

www.cagw.org
www.federalbudget.com
www.feedthepig.org

Real Estate

www.bankrate.com
Great information on mortgages with plenty of beginner resources.

www.zillow.com
This site allows you to look up the value of a property by address.

Health Insurance

www.dol.gov/ebsa/faqs/faq_consumer_cobra.html
The rules on keeping your health insurance if you change (or lose) your job.

Identity Theft

www.consumer.gov/idtheft
The Federal Trade Commission's official site for combating identity theft. Includes instructions on filing a complaint.

www.privacyrights.org/identity.htm
A nonprofit site founded by Linda Foley, an identity theft victim herself.

www.fightidentitytheft.com
One of the best identity theft blogs on the net, this site was started by Dave Nielson to distribute information.

www.opcva.com/watchdog
Site created by "Virginia Watchdog" Betty Ostergren, who has garnered attention for publishing sensitive personal data belonging to leading politicians. She doesn't disclose information, but publishes links to where information can be found. Her goal is to encourage redaction laws that allow individuals the right to blur personal data found on the web.

How Long Do I Keep It?: Financial Record Retention

Many financial records are now maintained on the Internet as many financial institutions suggest that account owners "turn off" paper statements and instead opt for online record keeping. I'm not a big conspiracy theory buff, but the very fact that "cyber-terrorism" is a word compels me to suggest that you keep plain, old-fashioned paper copies of your most important financial records. You could choose to audit your statements online, but I would strongly suggest printing year-end statements for your permanent records.

Type of Record	Years to Keep	Explanation
Tax returns, cancelled checks, receipts, contributions to charities, retirement plan contributions, mortgage interest, records for all deductions	Seven years for individuals; permanently for business owners	The IRS has three years to audit your return, and you have three years to file an amendment, if you find an error on a past return. The IRS also has six years to audit your return if they feel that you under-reported your income. There is no limit if the IRS feels that you committed fraud.
IRA contributions	Permanently	For nondeductible IRA contributions, you may have to prove that you already paid taxes when you make withdrawals.
Retirement plans	One year	Always keep your most recent annual statement (making sure to shred the prior year's statement). Keep until the account is closed.

Bank records	One year/ indefinitely	Keep your most recent statement, and shred the old one when the new one arrives. Keep as long as necessary if needed to document purchases or payments.
Brokerage accounts	Indefinitely	You must document price paid and sale proceeds for your taxes. Match "buy" and "sell" confirmations and file with your tax returns. Keep year-end statements that summarize all the activity for the year.
Bills	One year	Keep until receipt of payment is documented.
Credit card receipts and statements	Indefinitely	Check statement monthly with receipts. If they match up, shred the receipts. Keep statements to validate warranty purchases. Keep statements for seven years if they contain tax information.
Pay Stubs	Calendar year	Shred stubs as each new one is received to check that information is accurate. At year end, check your W-2 statement to make sure it matches your year-to-date (YTD) information on the last stub. If so, shred the stub.
Home records	Until home sells	Currently, the sale price of a personal residence is tax-free. However, laws change. If residential real estate is taxed, you will want to have all home improvement expenses recorded to reduce your taxable gain.

Information from Marquette National Bank and Catherine Williams, President of Consumer Credit Counseling Services of Greater Chicago. Published at www.bankrate.com.

Index

I